Spirited Medicine:
Shamanism in Contemporary Healthcare

Cecile Carson, MD
Editor

with

Tom Cowan, PhD, Bonnie Horrigan, José Stevens, PhD
and the Society for Shamanic Practitioners

BALTIMORE, MD 2015

Copyright © 2013 by
Society for Shamanic Practitioners
All rights reserved.

Permission to reproduce in any form
must be secured from the Society.

First printing, 2013, Baltimore
Second printing, 2015, Baltimore

Please direct all correspondence and book orders to:
Society for Shamanic Practitioners
www.shamansociety.org
PO Box 100007
Denver, CO 80250-0007

Library of Congress Control Number 2012954455
ISBN 978-0-615-73248-0

Published for the Society by
Otter Bay Books, LLC
3507 Newland Road
Baltimore, MD 21218-2513

www.otter-bay-books.com

Printed in the United States of America

Table of Contents

Preface: Why Shamanism?
    Bonnie Horrigan... *v*

Acknowledgments...*xiii*

Introduction
    Cecile Carson, MD...*xv*

Expanding the Clinical Mind

    I.   Mastery and Mystery: Models for Today's Healthcare
           Cecile Carson, MD... *1*

    II.   Indigenous Shamanism and the Western Mind
           Ann Drake, PsyD *17*

    III.   Indigenous Roots of Psychotherapy
           Farrell Silverberg, PhD *29*

    IV.   Medicine Stories: Shamanism and Personal Narratives
           Carin Roberge, PsyD.. *43*

    V.   Shamanism and Psychiatry: Initiation to Integration
           Stephen Proskauer, MD *55*

Shamanism in Conventional Healthcare Settings

    VI.   Reverent Participatory Relationship in Integrative Medicine
           Evelyn Rysdyk *69*

    VII.   Shamanism in the Surgical Suite
           Carol Tunney, MD *85*

VIII.	Hospital-Based Shamanic Practice	
	Alan Davis, MD, PhD	107
IX.	Tending the Spirit of a Medical Clinic	
	Krista Farey, MD, MS	123
X.	Parallels in Healing: Shamanism and Osteopathic Medicine	
	Michael Verrilli, DO, MS	135
XI.	Shamanic Naturopathy: An Integrative Approach	
	Melissa Dawahare, NMD	149
XII.	Shamanic Intervention in a Cardiac Rehabilitation Program	
	Sandra Ingerman, MA	159
XIII.	Shamanic and Psychotherapeutic Healing of Trauma	
	Daniel Foor, PhD	169
XIV.	A Shamanic Presence in Hospice Care	
	Leslie Bryan, MA	181

Traditional Forms of Shamanic Care

XV.	South African Indigenous Healing: How It Works	
	David Cumes, MD	197
XVI.	Soul Retrieval in Central and South America	
	Alberto Villoldo, PhD	217
XVII.	Reviving the Tradition of Faery Doctoring	
	Tom Cowan, PhD	227

Coming Home

XVIII.	Shamanism and War-Induced Post-Traumatic Stress Disorder	
	Edward Tick, PhD	245
XIX.	Conclusion	
	Cecile Carson, MD	261

Preface

Why Shamanism?

In some respects, healthcare has never enjoyed such sophisticated and effective interventions as it does today. We send cancerous tumors into remission with powerful, targeted pharmaceuticals; we remove hearts from the dead and transplant them into the living; we replace hips with mechanical devices; we watch what is happening inside our brains with imaging machines; we reshape corneas with lasers; and we drill tiny holes in the wall of a woman's egg to inject a single sperm, enabling fertilization in couples who were heretofore barren. Current stem cell and human genome research promise even greater feats. But with all these scientific wonders at our fingertips, why study shamanism? Is there any value in understanding how ancient peoples—who had little or no technology—healed what ailed them? Did our distant ancestors know something important about health, healing and the vast universe we call home that we have perhaps forgotten?

The professionals who contributed to this book think the answers to those questions are yes.

To be clear, no author herein disparages modern medicine. Quite the contrary, the shamanic community embraces it and is ever thankful for its capacities to keep humans healthy and alive. At the same time, despite medical science's progress, we also know that the quest for dominion over illness and disease is far from over. We only have to look at life's larger patterns to be confronted with the irony of our ways.

The truth is, as soon as we cure one disease, we are immediately faced with another. Polio diminishes and AIDS flourishes, and when we find medicines to stave off the ravages of AIDS, along comes SARS and Avian flu. 'Killing' off one cause of death just seems to give 'birth' to another. There is also the matter of unintended consequences. One problem solved always gives rise to a new problem because nothing exists in isolation, and the multitudinous, often hidden connections are too often only revealed after the fact. In trying to lessen starvation, we use antibiotics to grow more food more quickly but the resulting bacterial mutations threaten the potency of one of our most useful medicines. We create pharmaceutical drugs to treat a host of ills but many of them produce side effects worse than the original ailment they were meant to cure. Our treatment for infertility results in not one child born but three or four or seven, and the 'good life' we worked so hard to attain has helped create an epidemic of obesity in our children. Even more ironic, the use of tobacco, once part of sacred ceremonies to evoke communion with God, is now a leading cause of death.

I think we all see Coyote—the archetypal trickster who teaches us the secrets of spiritual and physical laws—laughing in the shadows. In fact, sometimes it feels as if humanity is engaged in a comical tug of war, except that we do not know who or what is on the other end of the rope.

For these and other reasons, an ever-growing number of people sense that something is missing from our explanations of how the world is ordered.

Twenty-first century medicine operates in the visible, biochemical and molecular dimension of that which can be measured using technology. It seeks to discover the physical laws that govern all life, the constants that do not change. Although this approach has yielded a plethora of knowledge, the system could be likened to auto mechanics wherein there's a blueprint for the manufacturing process, a manual of fixes, a spare part for everything involved, and it all works the same way all the time. But in spite of our desire for order and control, human beings never behave with the same consistency as machines and not a single medical intervention currently available is effective 100 percent of the time. In fact, it's not even close.

But why not? If life is truly governed by biological and chemical laws, why do different people taking the same pharmaceutical drug manifest different side effects or different rates of healing while some don't experience any effect—good or bad—at all? When two people are exposed to the same germs, why does one get sick but not the other? When two cancer patients with the exact same symptoms are given the same treatment, what is it that makes the difference between remission for one and death for another? And when three people with the same degree of cardiac disease each follow a different therapeutic regime, how can they all be healed?

One could argue that genetic differences account for the variations or that immune system strength plays a part, both of which are probably part of the answer, but the gathering wisdom is that in confining our investigations to material aspects alone, we have only engaged part of the human equation. In the past fifty years, medical studies in mind-body medicine, placebo effect, energy medicine, psychoneuroimmunology, biopsychosocial medicine and spirituality have taught us that the invisible aspects of who we are play a defining role. We have learned that our thoughts and beliefs, our web of relationships, our attitudes and emotions, and our spiritual or religious connectedness have a very real and often large effect on our health and wellbeing.

Just as quantum physics revealed that extremely small elements and exceptionally large bodies of matter have different patterns of behavior governed by differing rules, human inquiry long ago illuminated the fact that our spiritual side—our consciousness, our soul, and our *élan vital*—is subject to a completely different set of laws than those affecting our physical selves. A simple case in point is that gravity has no effect on the mind although it has a very real effect on the body. Conversely, Jungian analysis wouldn't affect the chemical reaction between baking soda and water although it can help bring someone out of a deep despair. Indeed, we bury our dead bodies in the ground while believing our souls ascend to heaven.

This is, of course, what made it so easy for scholars to declare that religion and science addressed different realms, that psychology addressed the mind and medicine dealt with the body and 'never the twain shall meet.' But what the ancients knew and what modern researchers are now proving is that the two systems in human beings—biological and spiritual—are so deeply intertwined with each other that a positive idea like hope can affect how certain physiological systems, such as our immune system, function, and changing brain chemistry can alter one's mood. Even more interesting is the new research, suggesting that positive emotions such as compassion and love in one person can actually produce a physical healing effect in other people.

If we really want to bring to bear all possible healing powers, we need to transform our concept of self from one confined to our body alone to one that addresses the whole of who we are. Our medicine must fully acknowledge that we are more than just physical beings; we are also spiritual beings. Just as scientists have come to realize that the quantum states of two or more objects must be described with reference to each other even though the individual objects may be separated in space (quantum entanglement), we must come to terms with the fact that we are also entangled beings. As Einstein so brilliantly declared, "A human being is part of a whole, called by us Universe, a part limited in time and space. He experiences himself, his thoughts and feelings, as something separated from the rest—a kind of optical delusion of his consciousness. This delusion is a kind of prison for us, restricting us to our personal desires and to affection for a few persons nearest us. Our task must be to free ourselves from this prison by widening our circles of compassion to embrace all living creatures and the whole of nature in its beauty."

Fortunately, to learn about this 'whole' we do not have to start from a baseline of zero. Much knowledge about this subject has already been accumulated. We simply need to revisit what the ancient religions and medical systems codified about the spirit, and then consciously and deliberately, using modern techniques of inquiry, investigate and document anew how the fundamental laws and concepts that govern the unseen realms actually work. And this, of course, brings us to the subject of shamanism.

First let me clarify that the word shamanism originally referred to a religious practice in Siberia and Central Asia, but it has come to be associated with indigenous healing practices all over the world and throughout time as anthropological and ethnomedical research revealed similarities in ancient worldviews and approaches to healing. This umbrella definition is how we are using the word shamanism in this book. The practice has been with us for at least 40,000 years; it was humankind's first religion and first medicine. From ancient times into the present, no matter which continent they lived on, or in which age they existed, or to which social structure they found themselves immersed, shamans engaged with the spiritual realms and learned ways to help their communities heal from disease and trauma, stay in balance with the environment, and live in right relationship with each other and the spiritual domains.

Of course, there is a vast array of methods, artifacts and rituals, and a multitude of cosmologies associated with the subject—humans are like that. We are diverse. But there are also common core principles that underlie all the cultural trappings. I would be remiss not to point out, however, that these same core concepts have been explored, articulated and embraced by many other philosophies and religions that have made humankind's spiritual nature the subject of earnest inquiry. There are many roads up the mountain, as it were. But it is the gifts of shamanic knowledge that are we are concerned with here.

First and foremost, all forms of shamanism recognize that reality has many dimensions. That which we can see, hear, touch, feel and taste with our physical bodies or measure with machines does not represent the totality of what is; it simply comprises one grouping of aspects. Scholars throughout time have attempted to describe these other realms—Jung coined the concept of the 'collective unconscious;' the aboriginals in Australia articulate it as the Dreamtime; Christian mystics describe heaven not only as a place but also a state of mind; Buddhists talk of four different Bardos, which are transitions between states of being; and shamanic cultures know the different dimensions as the Lower, Middle, and Upper Worlds, among other names.

A corollary to this idea is that our normal, walk-around-and-think state of mind is but one level of awareness available to us and that there are other states of consciousness through which we can interact with the different dimensions of reality. In *The Tibetan Book of Living and Dying*, Sogyal Rinpoche writes about "mastering the different dimensions of mind." Christian mystics reach ecstatic states through prayer in which they have visions and come to know God. Sufis dance and Hindus meditate to change their awareness, and as Shirley Nicholson writes in her book, *Shamanism*, "One of the outstanding characteristics of shamans is their familiarity with realities other than those of three-dimensional space and linear time known to our usual waking consciousness."

The next shamanic principle of interest is that not only are there other realms and not only can we access them, but this interaction can be beneficial should we choose to engage correctly. Despite the difference in nomenclature, shamanic healers from a wide variety of traditions tell us that healing can be aided or even manifested completely when power or information flows from these 'non-ordinary' realms into the ordinary world in which we live. Again, you can find similar views in other traditions, such as the healing miracles performed by Christian saints.

The last fundamental principle is one that Michael Harner, PhD, founder of the Foundation for Shamanic Studies, so aptly told me one evening in the middle of a huge thunderstorm, and that is: "We are not alone." Shamanism fully acknowledges the existence of other types of beings, most importantly God or the Great Spirit or Num. But shamanic people also talk about this same divine energy manifesting as lesser gods and goddesses, angels, spirits, or dead ancestors, and it is this 'One' and these 'Others' who will help us, should we know how to ask.

But this book is not about what our ancestors did. This book is about what we are doing today. In the following pages, case studies presented by physicians, psychologists, naturopaths, ethnographers, and others show how ancient shamanic techniques such as soul retrieval, power animal retrieval, extraction, divination, song, medicine stories, and ritual offerings have helped modern patients reclaim health in a variety of ways. Further, they reveal that shamanic techniques are currently being used quite successfully in rehabilitation centers, county health clinics, hospital operating rooms, and in the private offices of physicians and psychologists in metropolitan areas.

Let me reiterate that no one is advocating that we throw away the imaging machines, the pharmaceuticals, the lasers, the nanotechnology or the vaccines. Instead, because we have borne witness repeatedly, we are simply suggesting that asking spirit (in any of its many forms) to be present in the healing process is helpful and should be part of normal care.

The power that comes from spirit is a different kind of power than we humans have and it does not follow physical 'laws.' This sometimes scares us because without a doubt, it is a power that we do not control. In these matters, we are never the decision makers, only the facilitators. But why not engage this healing power every chance we can?

Before closing, there is another important gift to be found in shamanic cultures that I would like to talk about because of its relevance to health—the idea of correct perspective. Much of Western culture operates on the premise that human beings are the most important species on the planet (and perhaps the entire universe) and that the earth and all other life are here for our use and pleasure. Shamanism teaches that humanity is but part of a grand whole, that all life is sacred and that instead of being users, our true charge is that of caretakers. In this same vein, Western science teaches evolution as the survival of the fittest, and seeks to understand the biological and chemical mechanisms that underlie its unfolding so that we can enhance our own survival. In many ways, it's a race of sorts. Shamanism also teaches evolution, but in this case it is co-evolution and it holds that when we live by right action and in right relationship to the entire universe, then we place ourselves in a state of grace through which we can receive more of creation's gifts. This is true not only on an individual level, but as more and more people do this, a very different future—indeed, a better future— unfolds for all forms of life.

Thus, an important aspect of shamanic healing lies in helping people restore balance to their minds and lives so that they can partake of the goodness of the world. This is one of the underlying principles in such things as the Brazilian pilgrimages to Caninde to pay their part of the contract when St. Francis has helped them; in forgiveness ceremonies such as the Hawaiian *Ho'o pono pona* where transgressions are acknowledged and forgiven so that freedom from the past is achieved; in the concept of "respectful reciprocity" of the Andeans that is celebrated by *Pukllay*, an eight-day renewal ceremony, and in the Hopi's work through prayer, fasting and ceremonies which were given to them by Massau'u, the Great Spirit, to bring balance back to the world.

That's why the question on the table is this: Can shamanic wisdom aid healing, reduce healthcare costs, and improve lives? Can we help people achieve physical and psychological health and even call further blessings into being by using some of these ancient principles that promote connection with spirit and restore balance within the whole?

Tens of thousands of years of shamanism suggests that we can.

This book does not represent the end of the journey to re-integrate shamanic wisdom into the modern world but rather a beginning. We have a host of techniques to evaluate, a wide river of philosophies to explore, many experiments to engage in, and a thousand prayers to say as we sort wheat from the chaff, real from imaginary, and effective from non-effective. And in the end, the results of our efforts will stand for themselves. Did we bring a better world into being?

It is my belief that the answer will be yes.

Bonnie J. Horrigan
Co-Founder, Society for Shamanic Practitioners

Acknowledgments

What a delight and privilege it has been to assemble this group of essays by groundbreaking clinicians who have bravely taken shamanism into new territory! My great thanks to each of the authors for their efforts to assemble what they do in a way that inspires and enriches.

My gratitude extends also to the clients and patients represented in the case examples in these pages. In our striving to serve them, they have also taught us and moved us by their courage, their questions, and their openness to expanded healing modalities.

This book would not have achieved lift-off without strong wings and an able body. Bonnie Horrigan built the plane, handed me the joystick, and has flown co-pilot the entire trip. Ed Kinney provided fuel for the journey through a most generous donation. José Stevens and Tom Cowan maneuvered the ailerons with their fine editing to keep things aloft and moving well. Edith Jaffe jumped on board to organize necessary details in the interior compartments, and Sandra Ingerman offered her wisdom and experience to help launch the publishing process for our landing spot. What fine companions!

Of course we know who is behind it all. The spirits are laughing and nudging each other, providing the wind. They know what is needed, and I suspect that in the times when we drifted off course, they brewed up a storm to blow us back on track. Words fail in expressing thanks for that!

Introduction

Spirited Medicine:

Shamanism in Contemporary Healthcare

This book is a collection of voices recording shamanism's inroads into contemporary Western healthcare. As more and more conventional practitioners study the ancient healing techniques of indigenous cultures around the world, they are recovering aspects of the art of healing that were lost during the rise of technology. The discipline is in re-discovering and understanding what our ancestors knew; the creativity is in incorporating these lost arts into modern practice in ways that work for 21st century cultures.

The most ancient form of healing known, shamanism has 40,000 years of an unbroken presence in most continents of the world to the present day. Thus it is both 'old news' and radical 'new news.' Interestingly, as it re-emerges, shamanism is both shaping and being shaped by American culture, a process that may guide us back to the very essentials of what makes us healthy and keeps us alive.

When I began my medical training 40 years ago, I kept looking for ways to attend to the whole person. My training showed me parts: bones, cells, neurons, metabolic fluid balances, normal and abnormal emotional states, surgical techniques, diagnostic procedures. I learned to lift up every metaphoric scab and peer underneath to label the thing gone wrong, then to develop a plan of attack to correct it. Yet something in me knew a much larger piece was missing, but I had no way to name it, to understand it, nor to make a healing response to it.

Over these past few decades, the pendulum has begun a slow swing away from a highly biomechanical approach to illness. As a profession and a people, we have recognized the power of emotions and stress to impact the healing process. In trying to understand the why and when of illness onset, we have learned to see beyond just the individual person to the myriad of interpersonal and social systems in which this individual is imbedded. And we have come to understand

and document the power of the mind to impact bodily processes. And yet there has still been something missing.

We have been incorporating and sanitizing cross-cultural healing forms by calling them 'holistic,' or 'alternative,' or 'complementary,' often plucking them out of their rich cultural, historical, and philosophical contexts. These forms have broadened our therapeutic options, but we are still left with a hunger for something more to offer to the 'worried well' and to those who suffer deeply beyond their physical pain.

We stumble with words in trying to name this missing piece: 'meaning,' 'vitality,' 'soul,' 'spirit.' The scientist and the healer inside each clinician struggle with each other – the scientist wanting empirical data, the healer informed by a source beyond the proof. We recognize at some deep level that illness often requires us to do soul-level work, but the medical training of most Western clinicians puts constraints on this role.

The authors in this book speak about the return of the soul to our Western healthcare system, about a larger framework in which to hold our work. Many clinicians, trained to be autocratic and control the medical care, have already expanded the framework and learned to be a good 'listening ear' and collaborator with the patient, looking at what is right with a person rather than just what is wrong. But the practice of shamanism requires a much bolder step. It requires that the clinician move his personal 'self' out of the way and become a conduit for the spirits to bring their power and inspiration through to address a fuller dimension of healing: the re-ordering of the self from the impact of illness, the re-membering of the broken and forgotten relationship to the larger web of life, and the recognition that we are more than our physical bodies.

Expanding the Clinical Mind

Since the model we carry in our minds directs our behavior, the first section of this book explores new ways of thinking about our role in supporting health and deeper levels of healing. It begins with comparing the levels of healthcare that can guide a therapeutic response and the importance of leading with the most logical one that fits the circumstance: biomedical, biopsychosocial, and transpersonal. The transpersonal model includes the spiritual or soul level, and shamanism is its most ancient form.

This section also highlights the importance of language in selecting words that not only expand and enrich our concepts of the healing process, but also in naming this process in a way that reduces resistance or objection, as many people equate 'soul' or 'spirituality' with religion or dogma.

Following her initiation with a Malaysian shamanic healer, Ann Drake offers a detailed comparison of indigenous shamanism and the Western mind as Western medical care arrived in the remote village in northern Borneo where her teacher lives. We also learn about the power of stories both in healing and in illness, especially the unexamined stories, and how awareness can change the story and its effect on lives.

As one becomes increasingly able to view ordinary reality and medical process through a shamanic lens, more parallels become visible, and we see shamanism alive in Western culture in ways that are not necessarily bound to indigenous ritual and paraphernalia. Farrell Silverberg powerfully illustrates the parallels between the psychotherapeutic principles of transference and countertransference of the unconscious mind and the shamanic role of shapeshifting into a patient's world to take on and transmute an illness. He also speaks to the ethics of handling information from the non-ordinary domain, as shamanic practitioners bridge between ordinary reality and non-ordinary reality information and guidance.

In shamanism the spirits speak primarily through symbol and metaphor, these two being the 'DNA' of our individual life stories of health and illness. These stories organize and direct us in a fundamental way through the process of deep self-identification. Such stories are beyond 'data;' we become the stories that we and others tell about ourselves. Carin Roberge takes us step by step through the development of a healing story through 'word doctoring,' a process fundamental to shamanic cultures. Medicine stories highlight the requirement of 'right speech,' especially with those who are ill and vulnerable as their stories become disrupted by the illness. Healing stories become templates for re-ordering one's return into right relationship with all aspects of our lives through proper naming.

The last chapter in this section takes us into an intimate journey of a clinician's transformation that goes beyond just the conceptualization of a larger model of healing. In healthcare we tend to focus on the 'other,' forgetting that the transpersonal dimension requires transformation of both clinician and patient. Steve Proskauer shares five developmental stages of integration he experienced incorporating the domain of spirit into his life and his work.

To summarize, this section highlights the first steps in a transpersonal stance toward healthcare: (1) expand our conceptual models of relating to those who are ill, (2) become aware of shamanic parallels to already existing clinical care, (3) be mindful of words in naming and shaping stories that heal, and (4) allow ourselves to break open into our own Larger Selves to 'become the medicine.'

Shamanism in Conventional Healthcare Settings

In this next section the authors collectively illustrate a variety of forms shamanism can take in particular medical contexts through extensive case examples. All are shamanic practitioners in Western medical settings, and their work sites are richly varied: hospital, clinic, private practice. They run the gamut from birth (Tunney in obstetrics) to death (Bryan in hospice care) – shamanism from alpha to omega.

There are many other types of healthcare settings and creative adaptations of shamanism that exist in Western medical care, too. For example, I know of a birth doula in the northeastern U.S. who welcomes the spirit of the baby to be born and orients it to its path down the birth canal. I also know of a coroner in the Midwest who does psychopomp (guiding the souls of the dead to the Light) for his patients after the autopsy, escorting their souls to the Light after tending to their bodies.

Many of the shamanic practitioners in these two sections have been trained in 'core shamanism,' a process developed by anthropologist Michael Harner who studied shamanic cultures throughout the world for decades and delineated a basic or 'core' process in all of them that was not culture-bound.[1] As he began to teach this spiritual methodology of contacting spirit helpers in non-ordinary reality to thousands of Westerners, it became a primary means for shamanism to begin to integrate into Western culture. There are some who make distinctions between 'shamanism' and 'neo-shamanism' – the former relating to one's training through indigenous teachers and the latter through non-indigenous teachers – but both have the same heart and soul, and both get results.

Another important aspect of shamanism is that it is inherently innovative: rather than following a prescribed protocol, the spirits guide the process of healing. Through such guidance, shamanism is mutating its outer form in response to specific patient needs and clinical settings, and these settings, in turn, are being transformed by these new forms.

The shamanic interventions throughout the book illustrate core concepts of shamanic illness and shamanic interventions. Basically, from a shamanic viewpoint there are three primary causes of illness: loss of spiritual protection, loss of one's vitality or soul essence in surviving physical and emotional challenges of life, and the presence of spiritual intrusions.[2] In treating these spiritual causes of illness, the shamanic worker will intervene with a return of a lost power animal, a soul retrieval, and/or shamanic extraction. These interventions may or may not result in physical benefit, but there will be a change in overall wellbeing.

There are other important shamanic functions for healing as well: divination, ritual and ceremony, psychopomp depossession of wandering spirits who have intruded and are impacting the life of an embodied person, tending to the spirits of land and animals, and teaching patients themselves how to connect to their own spiritual helpers for guidance, support, and healing.

Evelyn Rysdyk brings the ancient call of the circle and 'reverent participatory relationship' to her work as a shamanic practitioner in a multidisciplinary healthcare clinic. She outlines the form this group of providers uses by which the connection between and among providers and clients is well-tended, despite differences in roles and expectations.

In her work as an obstetrician/gynecologist, Carol Tunney examines surgery as a sacred ceremony; the risks of acquiring a shamanic illness while under the influence of anesthesia; the benefits of shamanic healing before, during, and after surgery; and the healing benefits of supporting the patient's mind and spirit.

Alan Davis describes his process of naturally integrating a shamanic perspective and treatment into an inpatient rehabilitative medicine setting with hospitalized patients recovering from stroke, heart attack, orthopedic problems, or brain and spinal cord trauma. He highlights the constraints of his own Western medical training as he deals with issues of screening for spiritual resources, informed consent for shamanic healing, and the need to minimize the use of shamanic paraphernalia.

Everything has a 'spirit,' including the spirit of a place or an institution. Krista Farey's work underscores the spirit of a place as the 'patient,' taking on the healing of an entire family medicine clinic in a large multicultural urban setting. In this process, she utilizes art, song, group healing, and indigenous shamans who are also medical patients of the clinic.

Michael Verrilli maps the similarities between osteopathic medicine principles and those of shamanism, which are a shared belief in the unity of the body and the unity of life. Osteopathy as a science is informed by spirit and has both scientific as well as spiritual foundations, and Verrilli gives rich examples of this unity.

Another Western healthcare discipline that has 'soul' and relationship to the natural world as one of its tenets is naturopathy. Melissa Dawahare offers a number of examples of the integration of shamanism into naturopathic medicine as both a naturopath and a registered nurse.

One of the leading edges of shamanism in Western medicine is the opportunity to do research on whether spiritual intervention can improve health outcomes. Sandra Ingerman, Sara Warber, and Kate Durda compare results of a control and test group of patients in a cardiac rehabilitation program using a shamanically-based intervention, and Ingerman offers caveats about future research in shamanism.

The diagnosis of Post Traumatic Stress Disorder (PTSD) has been gaining in prominence in the medical field as the impact of unprocessed emotional and physical traumas becomes increasingly recognized in military veterans and survivors of domestic violence and natural disasters. Daniel Foor outlines an approach to healing PTSD that utilizes both shamanic healing methods and psychotherapy, and the necessary and parallel contributions they both make.

Perhaps in no other aspect of Western medicine is a shamanic framework so obviously needed as in end-of-life-care. Dying often engenders great fear and suffering in medical settings. In her work on the hospice unit of a large metropolitan hospital, Leslie Bryan supports and escorts patients' souls to move on to the spirit world. She outlines the step by step process she uses that includes how to make initial contact, the importance of flexibility and variety with each person, recognizing and moving through the transition point into active dying, and aftercare.

Traditional Forms of Shamanic Care

Some Western-trained clinicians are also initiated shamans of indigenous cultures. In this section we see the importance of the particular cultural form the initiate was given while working with the spirits in adapting it into modern healthcare settings.

David Cumes is an initiated African sangoma and conventionally-trained urologist who uses standard urological training for 'curing,' sangoma medicine for psychospiritual aspects of a health problem, and divination by 'throwing the bones' for both.

The curandero tradition of Central and South America works on a paradigm complementary to biomedicine. In his Peruvian Inkan shamanic training, medical anthropologist Alberto Villoldo works with healing the chambers of the soul, much like working with the chambers of the physical heart and explains the cultural mindset that sees these two approaches as a seamless therapy.

Historian Tom Cowan has brought forward the faery doctoring tradition of Celtic countries into contemporary shamanic practice to explain and treat many illnesses and conditions today that exhibit symptoms associated with traditional faery illness. Some of these illnesses Western medicine has been unable to diagnose or address effectively, such as chronic fatigue syndrome, unexplained lethargy, tiredness and unexplained aches and pains. He opens a door into the realm of faery not only for healing but also for extending our relationship to the natural world.

Coming Home

No book on shamanism and healthcare would be complete without addressing the sacred and profane dimensions of healthcare settings and healthcare providers. For example, at the end of medical school, physicians swear a Hippocratic Oath to do no harm, creating a covenant relationship with their patients. This is not a business relationship nor a customer relationship. But in the time pressures of everyday Western medical care and the need to limit the overabundance of high-priced, high-tech interventions, the 'bottom line' of healthcare dollars has come more and more to guide clinical decision-making. This has created a 'profane' dimension in medicine in which every diagnosis is coded and a unified 'standard of care' treatment plan generated. As the pendulum swings back toward a more balanced approach to healing, we must remember the 'profane' does not preclude a 'sacred' dimension in which the highly unique needs of the soul are addressed. For this, shamanism is a resource beyond measure.

Ed Tick's work with returned veterans of Vietnam and Middle East wars suffering from PTSD is a powerful template for this kind of healing. In his work with forgiveness, initiation, and identity, we can see parallels for non-veteran patients who are transformed by their illness and never return to the 'normalcy' they once knew.

Perhaps those of us in healthcare can learn to find a different metaphor from the 'war' metaphor we use to 'battle' illness and disease in contemporary medicine. Perhaps a different metaphor can help us find our way home to the deep healing that awaits both patient and provider alike through soulful practice.

Cecile A. Carson, MD
SSP Founding Board Member

---

[1] Harner M. *The Way of the Shaman.* HarperSanFrancisco, 1990.

[2] Ingerman S. *Shamanic Journeying: A Beginner's Guide.* Boulder, CO: Sounds True, 2004.

Expanding the Clinical Mind

I
Mastery and Mystery:
Models for Today's Healthcare

Cecile Carson, MD

We are dreaming the wrong dream of health in Western medicine. Our overfocus on mastery and control of illness turns us away from the mystery of falling ill. Like Nasrudin in one of Idries Shah's Sufi teaching tales, we are busy looking under a street lamp for an important key we have lost, and when asked where we lost it we point to a dark alleyway nearby. In the story, Nasrudin is asked why then is he searching for this important key under the lamplight, to which he replies, "Because this is where the light is!"

The models we learn in today's healthcare training put constraints on where we search for healing for ourselves and for others. We are taught to tolerate uncertainty as if it were an affliction rather than an invitation to turn toward the dark alleyway. We need bigger models, deeper models, to begin to navigate our way into the 'fruitful darkness.'[1]

Tending souls is an important aspect of any healing work, yet the models we are trained in address only the biomedical and emotional aspects of a patient, and suggest that those two realms constitute complete care. Soul-level care beckons us further into a model called 'transpersonal medicine,' a term coined decades ago in psychology that recognizes the role of mind, consciousness, and spirituality in healing – powers that transcend those of the limited body or personality of the individual person.[2,3] The potency of the oldest known form of soul healing, shamanism, is demonstrated by its persistence through the millennia.

When I began to introduce the transpersonal dimensions of the healing process to medical students, residents, and faculty by simply offering protected time and sanction to the topic, the floodgates of their experiences opened and allowed them to share in a way that had not previously been possible. The stories and wonder came pouring out. It is not that uncanny events do not occur in clinical care, but the reporting of them is discouraged or disallowed as a valid source of medical conversation.

I also found that introducing a chart comparing and contrasting predominant models of health care to a transpersonal framework (see appendix 'Models of Health Care') [4] was quite helpful in encouraging clinicians to explore their own experience of the healing process. The chart lays the groundwork for a clinician to build on his current medical and interpersonal skills, rather than feeling these skills should be abandoned when addressing the transpersonal dimension.

Evolution of the models of healthcare

Biomedical model

The first model in the Models of Healthcare chart is biomedicine. This is the empirical domain of healthcare, where technology reigns supreme and where great advances in medication, surgery, and biomedical tools have transformed outcomes for many diseases. Biomedicine's dominance began in the 1940's with the introduction of penicillin. It is a vital and necessary part of healthcare, yet the model is incomplete. Its focus is rational thought, objective data, and coming to the right answer. It asks "What's wrong?" and "Where does it hurt?" and works from there. A clinician caught up in the power of technology to identify the diagnosis and work toward a cure as his primary goal often, inadvertently, abandons the patient to address all the other aspects of the illness on his or her own. In fact, so significant are the achievements in this realm of medical care that most people believe the future of medicine lies in this direction.

Larry Dossey, MD, writes: "[Biomedicine's] emphasis is on the material body, which is viewed largely as a complex machine. . . guided by the laws of energy and matter laid down by Newton 300 years ago. According to this perspective the universe and all in it – including the body – is a vast clockwork that functions according to deterministic principles. The effects of the mind and consciousness are absent, and all forms of therapy must be physical in nature – drugs, surgery, irradiation, and all others."[5]

Biopsychosocial model

The biopsychosocial model was first articulated by George Engel,[6] an internist and psychoanalyst. In this model, the patient is seen as embedded in multiple interacting systems: an ascending hierarchy from subatomic particles, to molecules and tissues, to organs, to the person and beyond, to the two-person dyadic relationship, and extending to larger systems of family, community, culture, society/nation, and biosphere. Illness is viewed as originating in a perturbation in one of the levels in the systems that ripples through the other levels to create symptoms at the 'person' level. An important conceptual expansion for healthcare, this model broadens the base of therapeutic options as it asks different questions, moving beyond "What's wrong?" to "Why is this disease in this person now?" and "How has this illness affected you?" It brings both rational and emotional resources to bear as it sanctions a collaborative approach of both clinician *and* patient as the source of guidance in care. It also searches for the key disturbance in the cascading systems encompassing the patient as a central issue to be addressed.

For example, when I was a medical resident, I worked with a teenager with very unstable insulin-dependent diabetes, who had a series of hospitalizations for diabetic coma as her blood sugars went wildly out of control. During each hospitalization, her blood sugars were stabilized within 24 hours, but no specific physical cause such as infection was identified, and she was discharged home in a matter of days. The cycle continued for several months until the medical team noticed that at the time the hospitalizations started, she had developed a major conflict with her father around independence/dependence issues, both medically and developmentally. When this was addressed, the hospitalizations stopped.

Transpersonal model

The transpersonal model requires a vital conceptual shift: the clinician moves beyond being a 'listening ear' and dyadic collaborator to becoming also a 'hollow bone' for the Larger Order of Things to work through. This contrasts with the more familiar ordinary state of consciousness in which we conduct most medical care. In the shamanic form of transpersonal care the spirits, rather than the clinician, are in charge and guide the process of treatment. The questions this framework asks are different as well: "What's trying to happen?" and "What's *right* with this person?" and "If this symptom had a voice, what might it be saying?" This model views health and illness as a dynamic process, a trajectory of growth for the person at all levels; it addresses the soul or spiritual dimension more than just the personality or personal embodiment; and it works to re-order the deeper Self and recover meaning. It requires a deep exchange between clinician and patient beyond role boundaries, and a willingness for the clinician to be changed as well as the patient. Clinician and patient stand in each other's presence, soul to soul, without judgment. In this dimension, the clinician does not know what is best for the patient but agrees to be in service and enter the dark alleyway to experience the mystery of falling ill on the soul's progress in this life.

At the transpersonal level of care, the language shifts from subject-object (I will tend you) to inter-subjective (I-Thou): two subjects and not a subject-object. Often the form of language that is the truer expression of this level is symbol and metaphor, story, poetry, and song.[7] Not the stuff of usual medical conversation!

My own training in healthcare mirrors this evolution in trying to integrate the three healthcare frameworks: I completed an internal medicine residency in 1977, did a mind-body fellowship in medicine and psychiatry with Engel to learn the biopsychosocial model, worked 10 years in a primary care practice while teaching at a medical school and doing counseling for 26 years, and have had over 25 years of shamanic training and work. The shamanic training, coupled with my own personal psychotherapy, loosened much of the constraints of the traditional Western medical training I received.

One does not have to incorporate the transpersonal dimension on faith alone. Everywhere, basic bio-beliefs are being called into question.[8] Scientific studies over the past several decades have been steadily building up data that verify a reality beyond the five senses that impacts health and illness. Daniel Benor made a survey of studies of spiritual healing published in the English language before 1990 and found 131 controlled experiments dealing with the healing effects on enzymes, red blood cells, cancer cells, yeasts, plants, animals, and human beings. Fifty-six of the studies showed statistically significant results at a probability level of <.01, and twenty-one at a probability level of .02 - .05.[9] Other studies document the transpersonal impact of intention[10] and prayer[11] on effecting healing.

It is extremely important to remember that all three models are vital to healthcare and are in no way exclusive of each other; in fact, they are nested models, and the clinician's task is to engage at the logical level that the patient's circumstance requires while bearing in mind the other levels that are operative as well. For example, I would not ask "How is this for you?" or "Tell me more about your family" to a patient in the ER who needed urgent cardio-version for a lethal cardiac arrhythmia. Nor would I overemphasize pills, procedures, and tests for someone who had a stable chronic illness and was struggling to make sense of their life. Regardless of the model I begin with, however, I would never lose sight of the dark alleyway waiting for its proper time to be explored.

Allopathic dismemberment

Even before I began any shamanic training, my understanding of medical care began to shift. I saw profound emotional and spiritual healing taking place in patients at the same time their physical bodies were deteriorating and dying. I began to personally experience the physical symptoms of new patients I was about to see in the office exam room before I picked up their chart to read what their presenting health concern was. Synchronicities abounded: walking past a dying patient's room on an unexpected break just in time to hold her for her last breath; being called awake by something in the middle of the night:

At 3:00 a.m. I am awakened suddenly from deep sleep by an image of my patient M. drifting out into the cosmos. Inexplicably, I go downstairs and sit in meditation for a few minutes, finding myself saying, "M. come back; come on back," over and over again. I then go back upstairs to bed and to sleep. I find out a week later from an angry M. that she had once again tried to kill herself, this time with an amount of medication she carefully calculated to be twice the minimum lethal dose listed in a toxicology text. She was shocked to find herself alive the following morning. She reported taking the pills around 11:00 p.m. the night I had been awakened. She carried the diagnosis of borderline personality disorder, had been quite unstable, and had been working both with her psychiatrist and with me as her internist. There had been no inkling of her plan at our last visit two weeks previously, nor any contact between us by phone or message.

Although these experiences defied usual explanations, I instinctively felt they should not be dismissed as 'epiphenomena' or curiosities – that they represented true phenomena that are about our relationship to a Larger Order of Things. I discovered these phenomena take many forms, and may seem confusing as they are articulated through the particular lens the observer is using. A Jungian analyst might report the phenomena as 'synchronicity' or as an aspect of the 'collective unconscious;' a religious person as 'angelic or divine intervention;' a parapsychologist as 'out of body' or 'psychic' experiences; a shaman as working with 'helping spirits.' It seemed to me that it was not so important what we called this larger relationship, but that we recognized its powerful potential in our lives, and particularly in our work with patients.

Shamanic strategies in ordinary medical settings

Some years ago I surveyed Western-trained clinicians who had also been trained by the Foundation for Shamanic Studies and who were willing to talk about how they were using their shamanic training in medical settings. I was surprised to find that many of the respondents, especially those in primary care settings, reported they did not use their shamanic training at all. They cited a number of reasons for this, in particular, medico-legal and ethical concerns and the lack of a sense of how the form in which shamanism had been taught to them could apply to the clinical encounter.

Yet I have discovered that looking through the transpersonal lens to extend it into a shamanic framework is actually a small step. It does not necessarily require drums or rattles, and it does not have to take extra time. There are shamanic strategies that use many subtle processes that can provide a more meaningful interaction between clinician and patient, as well as facilitate the possibility of a deeper level of healing.

Shamanic strategies that I have found useful in ordinary medical settings sort themselves out into roughly three categories: intrapersonal, interpersonal, and use of ritual and ceremony. Obviously these categories overlap as well.

Intrapersonal strategies

Intrapersonal strategies help us deepen our awareness of the connectedness of all things and of our appropriate place and proportion to the healing process. They help us include the spiritual dimension as a regular and essential part of our work. This is perhaps the most essential part of shamanic influence: our attitudes, beliefs, words, and gestures all create or limit healing possibilities by the stance we take.

The first intrapersonal step is to open to a Larger Order of Things. As we move into a transpersonal or shamanic framework, the challenge of clinicians is being able to tolerate the unknown, as so much of medical care already deals with great amounts of uncertainty. I think we cleave to biomedicine as much as we do in healthcare because it can give definitive answers, albeit in a limited way, in addressing the whole illness. Rachel Remen, MD, shares that her own Western medical training taught that the unknown was to be converted to the known as quickly and cost-effectively as possible. Yet she learned over the years that the unknown is a very important part of life; it is the mystery in life that sustains and strengthens us. A colleague taught her to relate to the unknown as an artist does, as a blank canvas and a place of revelation.[12]

I have a medical colleague who stands just outside the door of the exam room of his patients and pauses for a few seconds, allowing an in-breath to sweep his mind clear of any preconceived notions of how the encounter is supposed to go, then letting an out-breath blow them away. Only then does he put his hand on the doorknob to enter.

The second intrapersonal step is setting the intention. In my own practice, my intention is to remember the soul of every person who crosses the threshold of my office and to get out of the way of what needs to happen. It helps me hold a stance of creative not-knowing, as well as to open to a greater web of connection for the purpose the patient and myself have for being together. I ask spirit allies for help, and often intentionally merge with them in a difficult situation.

A third intrapersonal strategy is setting up the workspace. I know a number of clinicians who use images and sacred objects in their space to help remind them of their larger purpose. Routine use of an energetic clearing process such as decree or the burning of incense can be quite invigorating, especially when we are having a difficult day or in a state of burnout. We can also work with the spirit of our institution or healthcare organization, invoking assistance.

An image I keep with me in the office is a picture of a broken, bare, isolated pine tree next to a pool of water. Reflected in that pool is the pine tree's image: full, whole, covered in beautiful needles, and surrounded by other trees. I know one of my roles as clinician is to hold a similar image of wholeness of the patient, especially at times when he or she cannot hold it on their own.

A fourth intrapersonal step is clearing the clinician's limiting beliefs about what is possible. Opportunities abound in a medical setting for becoming aware of the 'medical trance' that we have been trained to stay in; that is, the assumptions about how a disease process should progress. Statistics are a two-edged sword, both helping to guide an appropriate biomedical response to the illness at hand, and at the same time, limiting us in considering the exceptions, the miracles, the energetic options that are not bound by three-dimensional reality. Patients often feel that their clinician has no hope for them, yet a transpersonal perspective always generates hope through a positive expectancy about what is possible.

I experienced this first hand when a beloved relative was diagnosed with pancreatic cancer that was already beyond the physical boundaries necessary for surgical resection. He was in a significant amount of pain, and had just been prescribed narcotics for relief. He lived a long distance away from me, and wanted me to review his CT scan reports as he considered alterative therapies for his treatment. I knew it was important to him that I see the reports, yet I knew that they would stimulate in me a kind of historical despair from all the cases I had seen through the years and the grim probability of only a few more months of survival. I didn't want the reports to overshadow all the beautiful, joyful, and playful aspects of our relationship. Nor did I want to withdraw my affection and connection to protect myself from his impending loss. When the reports arrived, I lit a candle and bathed the papers with the smoke from burning sage, setting the intention to release any unnecessary negativity about his prognosis. I merged with my helping spirit and read the report while filled with deep connection and possibility. Then I lit a fire in my fireplace, and set each page afire, releasing any fixed ideas about how things could be for him. He ultimately used both alternative therapies and experimental medical trials for his treatment, and lived for almost a year, pain-free. During that period, we could laugh and enjoy each other and speak expectantly about what might be possible.

Other intrapersonal steps use synchronicity, dreams, divination, and journeywork to explore patient concerns from a deeper perspective.

I remember driving through a busy interstate interchange while trying to decide about whether to bring up the spiritual dimension to a support group of patients I was starting that evening. At that very moment, a large hawk flew right to my windshield, spread its huge wings at me, and veered off into the middle of dense traffic. I took it as a sign to 'pay attention,' and connected the two – I had learned that for many cultures eagles and hawks represent spirit messengers as they fly between the worlds. "I'll talk about it!" I said to its disappearing back. It turned out to be the most successful and inspiring group experience I had ever had up to that point in my work. Over time, I have come to assume that everything that happens to me may have an important message, particularly things that seem to be negative. So if multiple roadblocks keep coming up as I try to push my will through on some project or process, I am learning to stay open to what this might be telling me – which paradoxically keeps me more connected to the Larger Order of Things rather than pushing me away.

One of the most familiar transpersonal experiences to all of us is monitoring our dreams for important messages. In many cultures the dream state is considered an active part of one's life. A shaman would consider dreaming one way to enter non-ordinary reality, though not necessarily with the same intent and control as entering it from a conscious, waking state. Robert Moss offers an excellent set of tools for working with this interface, particularly in journeying back into a previous dream one might have had, to explore its message further.[13]

A nurse colleague of mine trained in anthropology and ministry believes that all things are a journey when viewed through a transpersonal lens: a dream, a shamanic flight, ordinary reality experiences, or bodily symptoms.[14] The language of symbol and metaphor speaks deeply to us all through each of these forms, and we can use them for ourselves, as well as for our clients and patients. To help others open to the messages and meanings, for example, we can assist them in starting a reflection or visualization from their reverie or dream images – because they've already been there.

Interpersonal strategies

Interpersonal strategies allow us to hold the sacred dimension in thought, speech, and presence with another person. So much is possible for the healing process by using just these, without necessarily including formal shamanic techniques of soul retrieval, extraction, or depossession. While the latter are important forms of shamanic work, they do not lend themselves easily to a medical setting.[15]

In the interpersonal encounter there is great power in being an un-anxious presence to whatever difficulty the patient brings. This creates a supportive and sacred container through which all of the healthcare frameworks can be held and addressed.

Shamans use 'word doctoring' or naming as a method for spirits to give the energy of a name to heal. We can use our words in clinical care with the same mindfulness, recognizing that words are shamanic in their ability to shape energy and create reality. When a person feels his suffering is properly named, he often feels relieved and can then turn his attention to what resources need to be accessed. Much like a patient sitting in a Navajo sand painting whose symbols help re-name and re-order his place in the universe, our stories, symbols, and metaphors are the tools in naming.

For example, a woman in my office felt like she was falling apart, and I was able to agree with her, saying: "Yes, I think you *are* having a nervous breakthrough." She began to laugh and relax, as color flooded back into her face – a dramatic shift from her pale, withdrawn body and voice of a few moments before. "So what do I have to do now?" she asked.

Whatever we name we reinforce. Most clinicians do not understand that, and use terms like "Don't worry" and "It won't hurt," unaware that a negative in front of the word does not change its impact on our deeper levels of consciousness.

Words are hypnotic as well. When the naming is properly done, words can be used to access deep inner resources through suggesting a beneficial resolution.

A patient with metastatic breast cancer once told me she was the black sheep in her family, and if anyone in the family deserved to have cancer, it was she. She said there were some things she had done in her life that she hadn't been able to tell anyone. There was a man in her life who wanted to marry her, even knowing the extent of her disease, and she had been refusing. I asked, "What would it mean to make a clean breast of things?" With these words, she spontaneously went into a deeply altered state for several minutes, her eyes darting back and forth as she tried to integrate the message. When she again focused on me, her eyes were bright and shining. "Thank you very much," she said simply. I learned a few weeks later that she had become engaged, and that the quality of her life had significantly improved.

Remen reflects, "When someone is given a diagnosis, it is a true confrontation with the unknown. This is often very difficult for people, and yet therein lies the great opportunity. We might actually say to people, 'Your diagnosis is cancer. What that will mean remains to be seen.'. . . . What I do with people is to accompany them in their meeting with the unknown, and help them open up to it rather than close it down."[16]

Subtle shamanic interventions

There are medico-legal and ethical constraints that clinicians feel in bringing shamanic work into the healthcare encounter, and I think each person needs to find their own moral compass in the work. Certainly, journeying to helping spirits for their perspectives on how to integrate shamanism in one's own healthcare setting can help, as well as conversations with other shamanically-trained clinicians for ideas. Because I see so much of the shamanic at work in the ordinary, I do not feel shut off from this resource as I do my daily work. How we language the transpersonal dimension to patients is key. For example, when patients ask me to "Pray for me, please," I ask if they would be open to the form that I do it in: that is, sending healing energy to them. I have never had a refusal.

For others, the strength of our relationship allows me to introduce shamanic elements of my work more directly. Michael Harner has adapted shamanic techniques to Western medical and psychotherapeutic settings by developing 'shamanic counseling,' a method in which a counselor/shamanic practitioner teaches the patient how to journey to non-ordinary reality and facilitates the process, so that the patient gets his own answers directly from spirit. I have found this method particularly helpful with my patients, and I use taped or live drumming, or music with embedded binaural beat frequencies, to alter brain waves into the alpha and theta ranges. After several sessions, most people can continue to do it on their own.

A woman whose daughter had been killed in an accident three months before had been hospitalized for depression and attempted suicide after her death, and had been unable to go back to work. At an initial consultation meeting with me, she reported feeling her daughter around her at times, and longing to open to her, but afraid "I wouldn't want to come back." I assured her I could get her back if she wanted to experience the contact more deeply. At our next meeting, I used music with embedded binaural beat frequencies and suggested she relax, open, and allow herself to experience any energies or wisdom that wished to make contact for her healing or learning. Shortly after she relaxed into the music in a recliner, her body gave a small jolt, her face flushed, and tears began coursing down from under her blindfold. After a few minutes I invited her to return to ordinary reality. She was radiant as she took off the blindfold off and exclaimed, "She's changed so much! She's fine, and so much wiser!" She went back to work the next week, and then asked me how she could learn to do this for herself, saying "I know there must be some reason why I'm still here, and I want to find out."

It is also possible to do more formal shamanic techniques 'at a distance' while not physically present with the patient. However, this still requires the patient's permission.

A primary care colleague of mine was working with a woman who was dealing with depression and who had a non-healing spider bite that had already necessitated seventeen surgeries. She agreed to her shamanic help while still hospitalized, which my colleague did at a distance while at home. Spirit helpers guided her in a dismemberment and power animal retrieval for the patient, as well as giving her a message to deliver: Spider bit her patient to remind her of her creativity and to be true to herself. It said a big part of her had been lost, and she needed to dedicate herself to bringing that back to life again. She also needed to take back her power in her marriage. The physician then told her about the journey. Although the patient did not notice a dramatic shift afterward, her depression improved so that she was no longer suicidal (with no change in medication), and she was able to have two successful skin grafts for the first time over the bite area.

Part of a shamanic worker's task is to utilize spiritual resources already available to the patient. For example, while an attending internist in a chronic care facility, I had a new patient transferred from the hospital with a hip fracture and advanced breast cancer widely metastatic to bone and skin. She was a devout Catholic and had never before been separated from her family. She was in tremendous physical and emotional pain, and her loud wails began disrupting the entire floor. We used a great deal of narcotics and pain medication combinations, but the wailing continued. The head nurse and I noticed that her rosary was taped to her bedrail and, surprisingly, that her pain level and cries seemed worse after she said the rosary. I asked her what she was saying as she went from bead to bead. She responded, "Oh, my God, it hurts so much – I'm going to die!" I imagined that by the time she completed all the beads, that message had been profoundly reinforced. I then asked her if it were possible for her to imagine, at each bead, that God or Jesus or Mary was reaching out a healing hand and placing it on all the parts of her body – and her heart – that were having pain. She said she'd try. Within 24 hours her cries had ceased, and we were able to help her control the physical pain with half the level of narcotics we had been using.

We can also assist ourselves and others in the healing process by the use of ritual and ceremony – major tools in shamanic work. These are powerful in creating conditions necessary for transformation.[17] It can be as simple as joining an intention with a daily routine, or with a process or impending procedure – or it can be as complex as a carefully planned ceremony with group participation and witness.

Relationship to the spirit of things

In the world of the shaman, everything is inspired. We can extend our transpersonal relationships to include not only the animate, but the inanimate as well. Often the energy of medical settings has been negatively impacted by historical events, and shamanic work in healing the spirit of place can alter the experience of everyone connected to it.[18,19] Working with the spirit of place can also provide important guidance to individuals working there.

A nurse practitioner I know who was about to leave his job journeyed to the spirit of the hospital where he worked. Although he was working very hard, he was feeling a lack of support there at many levels. The spirit of the place showed him in a powerful metaphoric way that he was a key figure in the healing the institution needed, that he held the 'heart' of the institution, and then showed him his role. From this message, he chose to not leave but to stay and embrace the role as fully as he could.

Clinical roles in shamanic care

Shamanically trained clinicians often experience a dilemma in how to utilize shamanic techniques on behalf of their patients. Clinical settings and time pressures are one constraint; another is the ethics of offering it at all if it is not designated as a 'standard of care' for the patient's diagnosis or for the health care system.

There are a variety of roles the clinician can play in providing shamanic care. Although the roles are not exclusive, one may be more appropriate in a particular setting or circumstance, or more appropriate with a particular patient.

Clinical 'Shamanist'

The term 'shamanist' is attributed to Sarangerel, a contemporary Mongolian shaman.[20] She uses the term to mean those who know how to communicate with tutelary spirits, to work with dreams, and to perform personal divinations and journeys. Shamanists live out their days in profound orientation to the shamanic forces, and their devotional practices are a way to participate in the dynamism of the spirit within the place they live. Treating soul loss and other more formal shamanic techniques are not part of their practice. This is a role that any shamanically trained clinician can embrace.

Clinical Shamanic Practitioner

This role is seen less often in primary care or surgical settings. Many of the clinicians who take on this role of formally offering shamanic techniques such as psychopomp, extraction, soul retrieval, and power animal retrieval are those who can schedule protected time for this work with patients. Psychotherapists, for example, are often able to set up a framework and language for these procedures and to schedule it in the needed longer blocks of time. I have also seen clinicians who divide their work life, doing traditional Western medicine techniques on particular days and scheduling formal shamanic interventions on other days and/or other sites.

Clinician Referral to a Shamanic Worker

Another important role a clinician can take on is preparing the patient, through naming and reframing, for a referral to a capable shamanic worker in the area. For some clinicians, this can mean referral within the system when shamanic workers are already on staff and sanctioned by the institution as health care providers.[21,22]

Implications for the future

The implications for utilizing a shamanic perspective and interventions in clinical care are profound. If shamanic and other transpersonal care were routinely available, what would the outcome be in patient satisfaction, healing, and utilization of healthcare services? Would clinician satisfaction and burnout change? What if every organ transplant had an organ-specific soul retrieval? What if every surgical procedure were linked with a healing ritual, and what if arrangements were made for psychopomp after the death of each patient? What could happen to transform the healthcare field if we collectively shifted our beliefs about what is possible?

As shamanically-trained clinicians, we have endless possibilities in alliance with the spirits to become whole and then to be more available to serve our patients.

References

[1] Halifax J. *The Fruitful Darkness: Reconnecting with the Body of the Earth.* HarperSanFrancisco; 1993.

[2] Lawlis F. *Transpersonal Medicine: A New Approach to Healing Body-Mind-Spirit.* Boston: Shambhala; 1996.

[3] Dossey L. *Re-Inventing Medicine: Beyond Mind-Body to a New Era of Healing.* HarperSanFrancisco; 1999.

[4] adapted from Suchman A. Personal communication.

[5] Dossey L. *Recovering the Soul: A Scientific and Spiritual Search.* New York: Bantam Books; 1989; 263-269.

[6] Engel G. "The Clinical Application of the Biopsychosocial Model." in Frankel R. and Quill T., et al. *The Biopsychosocial Approach: Past Present, Future.* Rochester, NY: U. of Rochester Press; 2003, 1-20.

[7] Cowan T. "Twisted Language." *J. of Shamanic Practice* 2009; 2:2, 11-16.

[8] Lipton B. *The Biology of Belief.* Santa Rosa, CA: Mountain of Love/Elite Books; 2005.

[9] Benor D. "Spiritual Healing: Scientific Validation of a Healing Revolution." *Healing Research: Volume I.* Southfield, MI: Vision Publications; 2001.

[10] McTaggert L. *The Intention Experiment.* New York: Free Press; 2007.

[11] Dossey L. *Healing Words: The Power of Prayer and the Practice of Medicine.* HarperSanFrancisco; 1993.

[12] Remen R. *Choices.* 2009; 2:3, 27.

[13] Moss R. *Conscious Dreaming: A Spiritual Path for Everyday Life.* New York: Crown Publishing; 1996.

[14] Dombeck M. Personal communication.

[15] Harner M. "Core Practices in the Shamanic Treatment of Illness." *Shamanism* 2005; 18:1&2, 122-132.

[16] Remen R. *Choices.* 2002; 2:3, 28.

[17] Lawlis F. "Rituals." *Transpersonal Medicine*; 16-41.

[18] Eshowsky M. "The Spirit of Place and the Healing of History." *Shamanism* 2005; 18:1 & 2, 140-144.

[19] Farey K. see chapter 9, *Spirited Medicine: Shamanism in Contemporary Healthcare.*

[20] Sarangerel. *Riding Windhorses: A Journey into the Heart of Mongolian Shamanism.* Destiny Books; 2000.

[21] Hiatt J. "Transpersonal Care Program in an Institutional Setting." *Psychiatric Annals* 1999; 29:8, 480-483.

[22] Rysdyk E. see chapter 6, *Spirited Medicine: Shamanism in Contemporary Healthcare.*

About the author

Cecile Carson, MD, is an internist and counselor who has focused her work over the past several decades on the mind-body-spirit interface in teaching and clinical care, and in particular with people who are facing life-threatening illnesses. She was Clinical Associate Professor of Medicine and Psychiatry at the University of Rochester Medical Center from 1986-2006. Her great fascination is the endless variety of forms the healing process can take and she has explored and integrated shamanism, Reiki, hypnosis, neurolinguistic programming, therapeutic recreation, psychodrama, and dreamwork.

Appendix

Models of Healthcare

	Biomedicine	**Biopsychosocial Medicine**	**Transpersonal Medicine**
Focus of Attention	diseases, rational thought, objective data	patient in context of multiple interacting systems; subjective + objective; rational + emotional	meaning; deep connection with the patient without expectations or judgment
Foundation Question	"What's wrong?" "Where does it hurt?"	"Why this illness in this person now?" "How has this affected you?"	"What's happening in this moment?" "What's unfolding?" "If this symptom had a voice, what might it be saying?"
Clinician Task	diagnose and fix the disorder of the body; restore normalcy	identify the key disturbance in the system; support the psychological and social; create a partnership; negotiate; help	witness the suffering; be present to the patient's wholeness; be present to what is unfolding – for the patient, for you, and the relationship; accept what is; serve
Clinician Attitude With Patient	detached observer	participant observer	deep exchange beyond role boundaries; shared humanness; a willingness to be changed by the patient
Source of Guidance	professional expertise and mastery	patient and clinician in collaboration	symbols & metaphor, intuition, hunches, dreams, synchronicity (meaningful coincidences), consciousness beyond a 3-dimensional framework

II

Indigenous Shamanism and the Western Mind

Ann Drake, PsyD

Wisdom from an indigenous culture

Since the early 90's, I have studied with Ismail Daim, a gifted shaman who lives in the remote village of Matu near the South China Sea in Malaysian Borneo. I was a Peace Corp volunteer in Matu from 1967-1970, and during this time became intimately familiar with the life and customs of the Melanau people.

For the Melanau, shamanism has been the primary form of health care for centuries. They both respect and fear the spirits and make regular offerings to them for protection, guidance, and healing. They trust their shamans whether they need help finding a lost object, deciding when to plant, or in the removal of an evil spirit or cancerous tumor. The Melanau would not dream of building a house or traveling to a distant locale without consulting the spirits through a Bomoh or Dukun, the title given to a male or a female shaman.

In the early 1990's, as the country raced toward modernization, allopathic medicine was introduced to Malaysian Borneo only to be met by many with skepticism and distrust. The Malaysian government sent Ismail Daim a doctor's white coat and certified him as a bona fide healer. In this way they both honored his healing gifts and acknowledged shamanic healing as a cornerstone of the national health care system. Doctors in Western hospitals in the larger cities now invite my teacher to work with patients for whom biomedicine has been ineffective.

When Ismail Daim initiated me, I received a series of transmissions from the Bomoh that aligned my energetic field with the people of Matu. This allowed me to intuitively communicate with my Melanau clients through a spiritual and energetic fluency that transcended language, time, and space. As I began to practice shamanism in the United States, though, I quickly learned I needed to make modifications in my healing work to address the rational aspects of the Western mind, with its layered beliefs and emotional attachment to life stories.

In many indigenous cultures, a sense of community and trust in the spiritual realms is deeply embedded on a collective cognitive and energetic level. This trust creates an energy field that holds the shamanic work. Often in Western countries a sense of isolation and lack of community, coupled with a cultural disconnection from the mysteries of the shamanic process, results in an inadequate 'holding' for the shamanic work to deeply integrate.

Many of my clients struggle with the strong cultural imprints of Western society in which the notion of healing the soul to return the body to health is met with fear and ridicule. Some clients are open and receptive to shamanic work and are able to make life-altering changes; some experience benefit for a few weeks and then the healing gradually dissipates; for others, little or no progress is made. All who come want the work to make a difference, but some have difficulty grasping the energetic basis of shamanism and letting go of a mechanistic view of how to heal.

The Western mind, or mindset, describes a dualistic and linear thinking process that values rational thought over intuitive knowledge, while intuitive, non-linear thought predominates in most indigenous cultures. As the world becomes one via the vastness of telecommunication systems and Internet, we now see more blending of these styles of thinking. The interest in and practice of shamanism in Europe and the United States is an example of a shift away from a purely rational mindset. One of the responsibilities of shamanic practitioners in the West is to help with this shift to different types of knowing, while remaining mindful of the challenges in traversing these radically different systems of thought.

For example, Ismail Daim does not use drums or rattles; he calls in his spirits by lighting incense and turning a white bowl imbued with spiritual energy upside down to release his guides and teachers into himself and the room. Next, he places the bowl over his sacred healing objects and holds a knife on the client's pulses and other areas of the body that are of concern. When he places his knife, it is as if he were using a stethoscope to listen to his client's internal body processes. The knife is the instrument through which spiritual wisdom flows. He also places written prayers that alter the vibrational field of his clients into a bucket of water he then pours over them. Herbs are also part of his healing practice, and they are administered in a variety of ways—most of which would be unappealing or distasteful to Western clients.

Given the vast cultural differences between Malaysian Borneo and the United States, I have adapted the outer forms of my teacher's shamanic rituals, while holding the same inner intent and purpose. I work with the white bowl in the same way he does, but I also use drums and rattles to honor the traditions of the land on which I work. I have substituted crystals for knives as diagnostic and healing tools, since crystals are much less threatening to Westerners. And I sprinkle my clients lightly with water rather than pouring entire buckets of water over them.

Over the years of working with Western clients, my spirit helpers have taught me how to work with specific aspects of the energetic field that the Western mindset creates that differ from those of the Melanau culture into which I was initiated. These energetic aspects include thoughts, beliefs, emotions, and energy webs that occur both in the environment and through ancestral lines and that have direct impact on physical healing.

Releasing attachments to limiting stories

One of the difficulties of healing work in the Western world is attachment to stories that define our view of ourselves and what we believe is possible. Here in America, my shamanic guides have taught me to trace an energetic pathway within a person, following it to where blocked energy created by physical or emotional trauma resides in his body or energy field. They teach me that it is not enough to only remove this blocked energy; there is often a 'hook' buried deep inside created by the unconscious attachment to the stories that one makes from these life experiences. While the extraction of the blocked energy is essential, without the removal of the 'hook,' the soul essence lost at the time of the trauma cannot fully return.

For example, an eighty-year-old woman attended a workshop of mine that focused on the creation of a totem of guides and protectors for each of the seven major chakras.[1,2] As part of the exercise, we journeyed to discover if there were any blocks that needed to be removed so the chakras could flow freely. In the beginning we spent considerable time working with fear, which often resides in the first (root) chakra. When we arrived at the fifth chakra, which governs the expression of what is most deeply held in our heart, she began to weep. At the age of eighteen months she had fallen out of a second story window and barely survived. She spent months in the hospital and, by her own account, her life became defined and limited by this singular event. For years afterward she visited doctors, psychotherapists, and healers, but no one was able to help her heal fully from this psychic and physical trauma of the experience.

In her shamanic journey, she saw a healthy vibrant child in her pre-trauma state and realized that at one point she had been happy and free. She asked that I stop the workshop and do a soul retrieval for her. My guides instructed me to ask the group to support her for a few minutes while she invited this soul part fully into her heart and her being. They told me that the psychic imprint that resulted from her accident was that she be passive and have others take care of her. The soul part lost in the accident was now unburied and ready for integration. The spirit guides said it was essential that she do this part of the work herself to reclaim her power and vibrancy, and although she initially protested, the group held a strong energy field for her as she did so. For the first time in years, she felt strength and vitality flow through her, and she actually looked twenty years younger.

In an indigenous culture, a soul retrieval ritual would have been performed for her immediately after the fall, and she would likely have been spared many years of misery. Instead, she absorbed the energy of her mother's terror who helplessly watched her daughter fall out of the window. The child grew up very fearful, believing that she was defective and would never live a full and meaningful life. Western healing paradigms do not include work with the energetic tenacity of fear and other emotions, and it would probably have been ineffective for me to bring back the soul of the one-and-a-half-year-old without first working through the energetic power of the deeply embedded imprint of this experience.

Another example is Jane, with whom I worked for a number of years. She had experienced physical, ritual, and sexual abuse within her family and community. Whenever I did shamanic work with her it was quite powerful, and the symptoms she was experiencing disappeared. Later when she was home, she would once again become upset and begin to harm herself. There was one part of her that did not believe that she had the right to be well and another part that was attached to the story of her suffering and would call it back through self-abuse. These parts contained the energy of those who had harmed her. Even after I performed both extractions and depossessions, her mind held onto the beliefs that kept these alien energies in place. We were ultimately successful in shifting these beliefs through forming an alliance between her spirit guides and mine to provide adequate support in removing these deep hooks.

Ancestral energetic imprints

Through shamanic practice, I have learned that we each are born into a family that has a distinct energetic imprint. Not only are we taught the beliefs and customs of our family and culture, but we also absorb the specific energy pattern of our families and community. We tend to be drawn to people who feel familiar energetically, even if they are negative or destructive. These imprints are an aspect of our ancestral lineage and may be passed on for generations. When we address these energy patterns shamanically, healing can take place for all who came before and all who will come after the client.

I did some healing work in the United States for Bill, who had suffered with depression his entire life. Bill was sexually abused as a child, and as a result he suffered significant soul loss and absorbed negative energy from the perpetrator. A major focus of the healing work for him became the removal of this negative energy and the healing of generations of abuse, as well as the return of lost parts of his soul.

Bill's daughter had been molested and raped, and he felt guilty for not having been able to protect her from the horror of what he had also experienced. Initially when I told him about the healing of generations of abuse, he interpreted my remarks to mean that his 'bad energy' had caused his daughter to be abused, and he blamed himself. At first, nothing that I said could convince him that he was not responsible for his daughter's abuse. Only later was he able to understand this concept, and subsequently brought in other family members for healing. At that point he recognized that he was giving his ancestors and progeny a great gift by allowing the spirits to heal and transmute the intergenerational wounds.

In the West, it is difficult to grasp the concept of an 'energetic web' that is transferred from generation to generation. Interestingly, though, Western psychotherapy has a concept of behavioral states being passed from one family member to the next generation through an addiction gene,[3] and the shamans of the Melanau people believe that there is an addiction spirit that flows from one person to the next. Many indigenous cultures recognize that spirit intrusions such as this can also alter the physiology of the recipient and create an observable physical condition.

Often children experience soul loss from living with an addicted parent and are an open field for the addiction spirit to enter the body of the child. My teacher gave me a written prayer, placed in water and then given to the person to drink that removes this spirit from the field of the addicted person. When I have given the prayer in this manner, I have seen its power in removing both addictive behaviors and energetic imprints.

At first I was puzzled as to how written prayers, in a language that I cannot read, then scanned into a computer and copied, could have such power until I discovered the work of Masaru Emoto, a Japanese scientist.[4] Dr Emoto discovered that positive thoughts and words put into water create strong elaborate crystalline structures of the water molecules when frozen, whereas negative thoughts and words placed in it and frozen produce deformed and sludge-like crystalline material. I do not know what these Melanau prayers say, but the intent behind them is capable of significantly altering the vibrational field, which in turn alters aspects of the physical body.

The power of the mind to heal

Bruce Lipton[5] and Len Wisneski[6] have conducted research that radically challenges our understanding of life. They have shown that DNA is controlled by signals from outside of the cell that include messages from positive and negative thoughts. Lipton asserts that while our DNA may be our human blueprint, it is environmental and cultural factors that determine which aspects of this blueprint come into being. He has been able to document alterations in cellular structure by cognitive and environmental influences such as a family's ethnic background and religious orientation, the class and psychological stability of the family, and how race and gender are viewed within the culture. Thus it is not DNA alone that dictates who we are, but rather the multitude of environmental and cognitive factors that interface with our DNA to cause certain traits, strengths, and vulnerabilities to come forward. Through detailed placebo studies, Lipton builds a strong case for the power of the mind to heal conditions that previously required surgery or other forms of medical intervention. These researchers are rediscovering and documenting what generations of indigenous healers have known and practiced for centuries: that our minds and other outside influences greatly impact our health and wellbeing. These pioneers within the community of allopathic medicine may cause an alteration in the health and genetic makeup of us all as we collectively begin to understand the implications of their research!

One way I recognized the power of the mind to heal was when I was asked to offer healing for my teacher's wife. Ismail Daim is well known for his ability to cure cancerous tumors using herbs, prayers, and spirit guidance. His wife, Hwa Jung, had a tumor in her breast the size of a walnut. Initially she did not want to worry her husband and asked me to remove it. First I worked with my spiritual healing team from the divine frequency realm to energetically radiate the tumor and the area around it. This loosened the tumor's bond to the physical body, which paved the way for my spiritual extraction guide to remove it.

Although I did healing work for her, I must admit that I doubted my own ability to dissolve the tumor. I had great confidence to intervene and heal emotional and spiritual distress, but was less confident of my ability to dissolve cancerous tumors. I now realize that they too arise from the same source, but at the time I was still under the influence of a Western belief system that a physical healing of this nature was outside of my area of expertise. Nor did I fully comprehend at that time the power of Hwa Jung's belief in me and in this form of healing to successfully remove the tumor.

I was finally able to convince Hwa Jung to let the Bomoh know of the tumor, and he also gave her a healing after I had returned to the U.S. Through our combined efforts the tumor dissolved, and Hwa Jung has been free of cancer now for twelve years. Their belief in the spirits and in our ability to heal her was an important aspect of her healing and a powerful teaching for me.

Understanding attachment to negative emotional states

Many people are able to experience positive emotional states through spiritual practice and positive interactions with others, but they can also take on negative emotional states from one another. In extremely negative circumstances such as rape, the victim is likely to dissociate and leave her body. The negative energy of the rapist is discharged into the body and energy field of the raped person and remains there as a vile energy or possessing spirit. The person feels bad, dirty, spoiled, and shameful, but is usually unaware that she is carrying the negative energetic state of her perpetrator. Often the victim goes on to be abused again as the dark energy in her field attracts more abusive energy toward her. Sometimes a raped person becomes the rapist as she tries to purge this violent energy from her field. When the rape victim attaches to the feeling state of being bad and shameful, the perpetrating or 'evil energy' becomes part of the psychic structure. It is often difficult to successfully perform an extraction and soul retrieval if the mind has attached to the negative energy states to such a degree that it has become part of the personality.

I developed a deeper understanding of powerful attachments to negative energy by working with Rose, an herbalist born into a cult in South America. Her parents and siblings were cult members, and her attachment to her family was broken through a series of torturous and abusive experiences. Thus her main allegiance became to the cult rather than to her family unit. As I was preparing to do a depossession for her to remove the negative energy of the cult from her physical and energetic body, I asked Rose if there was any reason that she might want to keep this energy. A look of horror came over her face, and she struggled to catch her breath. It was a few moments before she was able to speak. When she did, she cried out, "No, no you can't take it away. If you do there will be nothing there and I will dissolve."

We did a journey to better understand her reaction and learned that as a baby, in the absence of a positive attachment figure, she attached to the negative energy of the cult. My guides instructed us to build an energetic bridge to a positive figure or container before removing the negative one. The guides also suggested that Rose build an energetic attachment to the plant spirits who had already been instrumental in her herbalist healing work. We created a ritual for inviting these spirits to be present for the depossession and to become the energetic container in which she would live. Her face and body relaxed as she slipped into their loving energy, and it became possible to remove the negative cult energy.

Emotions and evil spirits

During my last field trip to Sarawak, I looked on as Ismail Daim worked with a woman from a neighboring village. As I watched him, I saw that there was a dark energy around her neck and shoulders and realized it was the angry energy of a jealous person in her village. After the healing, I asked my teacher if evil spirits could be the energy of negative emotions. He smiled and said, "of course, it was the angry energy of another that was the evil spirit."

In the Bomoh's worldview, all strongly negative emotional states are referred to as evil spirits. People hire those who practice black magic to cast 'evil spells' on someone that they wish to harm. The harmful intent is the foundation of the negative energy that creates the 'evil spirit.' This phenomenon is known by many names in other cultures. In Tibetan Buddhism strong negative emotional states are referred to as 'demons,' and Buddhists are taught to pray to loving and wrathful deities for protection from the demons of anger, jealousy, envy, fear, and greed. In Jungian psychotherapy these negative emotional states are referred to as the 'unintegrated shadow,' [7] and in psychoanalytic thought they are conceived of as negative 'introjects.'[8]

Just as one gains information from one's guides to do healing work, one must also listen for the language and metaphor that will assist the client in releasing the negative energy. In Matu, naming the energy of an angry neighbor as an 'evil spirit' facilitates the release of this energy through the Bomoh or Dukun. By contrast, in the West the terminology of 'evil spirit' would likely be frightening. But a Westerner might easily relate to the concept of a neighbor's 'angry energy' being attached to him and readily choose to let it go.

Negative emotional states are just one aspect of what indigenous people refer to as evil spirits. There are also disembodied beings called evil spirits that attach to and inhabit wounded souls. When these beings are malevolent, they act as vampires to suck the life force out of their victims in order to grow in power as negative forces. However, in a majority of instances, shamanic healers are dealing with negative emotional states that appear to have a life of their own.

We all experience the negative energies of rage, hate, jealousy, greed, and fear as they flow over and through us, and at times render us impotent to their force. Why do some of us fly into a rage when we have a difficult encounter, while others go mute, dissociate, or disengage? Although there are many factors to our response, it is my belief that not only do we learn these responses from our direct experiences with others, but we also absorb energetic or vibrational patterns from our environment. If someone rages at us when we are small, that vibration enters our energy field. When we experience anger coming our way as adults, this vibration is activated and we either act out that rage ourselves or draw rageful energy to us. If one continues to absorb these negative or destructive patterns over time, there is a wearing down of the soul during the life span.

Healing with spirit guides and power animals

All of us carry negative energies that we have inherited, created, or received and that act as magnets for similar energetic states that others carry. Fortunately my spirit guides have instructed me in how to work with these negative energies or 'demons' through spirit protectors, given to both hold and assuage our negative responses to triggers from within and without.

I received six protective spirits as part of the initiatory transmissions from my teacher. Now when I teach shamanic practices, the first series of journeys we do are to find protectors in the six directions and to learn what particular vulnerability or 'demon' each one will help with.

We all have wounded parts to our personalities. Even if we have spent years healing these wounds, there are still vibrational threads that can be activated when we are tired, stressed, or triggered. When this occurs, we can take in a breath and feel the guide come to calm our mind and remind us that the response stems from a negative aspect of the past and does not need to be fed energy that could reactivate the pattern. It takes time and practice to lessen the negative response, but the idea that there is a loving protective presence to support and enfold us is enormously helpful.

In the West we tend to deny negative emotional states and feel that we are weak if we admit our wounds and vulnerabilities. We do not accept that they are a normal part of existence and that the goal is to work with them rather than deny their existence. As a result of our denial, we become attached to the stories that excuse our negative behaviors. By compassionately working with our demons through the help of spirit protectors, we can begin to heal and release these negative beliefs and energetic states.

The power of negative beliefs to block healing

Whenever I journey to discover why there are such different results from similar healing processes, my guides tell me that the beliefs and intentions that the client brings to the healing has impact on the results. Many people have opinions of themselves based on what others have told them. Children are told that they are bad, selfish, inconsiderate or a host of other negative adjectives, when in reality they are just being kids. Yet the negative words stick tenaciously and become part of the psychic structure.

Jill, a client with major depression, had been hospitalized on numerous occasions and came to me for a soul retrieval. She felt worthless and at times suicidal. After I blew the soul parts back into her and told her what I had seen and been told by our guides, she burst into tears saying, "I do not deserve to have these parts back or to have helping guides. I'm so bad and undeserving." Although I encouraged her to understand that she felt badly about herself as a result of how she has been treated and spoken to from childhood to the present, she could not believe that the guides and soul parts would want to be with her. She believed that her parents would never have treated her the way they did if she did not deserve it.

In our interview prior to this soul retrieval, it appeared that she might be unable to fully take in the energy of her guides and soul parts but she was too depressed to understand the complexities of the work. My guides recommended that I go forward despite this, in hopes that some aspect of the work might stay in her energy field and provide the ground for a shift in her despair. In fact, as she received the love of her guides and soul parts, the soul retrieval actually brought an awareness to her of these deeply held beliefs that had been major blocks to her healing. This, in turn, allowed her to give voice to how undeserving she felt. For true healing to occur, she first needed to understand and detach from the belief she was inherently bad and undeserving.

Conversely, it is impressive what a person can accomplish when she believes that she can break old patterns that have been destructive. Greta spent years in psychotherapy working through childhood abuse that led her to marry an abusive partner. Finally she had the courage to separate from her husband, but she spent each day locked in anger and fear as she struggled through the dissolution of the marriage and a painful divorce. She sincerely believed that something would shift inside her so that she could let go of the hurt and anger and get on with her life, but she did not know how to make this happen. Through an extraction and soul retrieval, we found that the husband held a large portion of her soul and that his angry controlling energy was embedded in her field. Upon the removal of the husband's energy and the return of her soul part from him, she felt free and whole. The obstacles that had kept them locked in conflict and unable to finalize the divorce fell away. She felt hope and optimism for the future and began to date again.

Cross-cultural potential

For the Melanau and other indigenous cultures, the community is often perceived as more important than the individual, and these cultures are ripe with rituals that define, celebrate, and bind the community together. In the intellectual and cultural dictates of the West, the individual is celebrated as primary, and shamanic practitioners in Western cultures often work against both cognitive and energetic imprints that may block the full reception and integration of spiritual healing. For this reason, rituals to integrate shamanic work are important. A daily ritual that honors, welcomes, and connects with spirit guides is essential for bringing their energies into one's vibrational field. Additionally, participating in shamanic circles that come together to journey and practice shamanism creates a community that collectively holds the power of the shamanic healing, embedding it within both the individual and group field.

The Western mindset is steadily being expanded by scientific data that show the power of the mind to transmute energy to bring about health and balance. The data being uncovered are consistent with the teachings from Ismail Daim, whose lineage is tied to the Islamic Unani tradition and other centuries-old indigenous practices, and which understands the mind as a powerful instrument that enacts change by focusing the combined energy of clear thinking with the wisdom of spirit guides.

How important it is for us to understand that the mind can also be used inadvertently to block healing and transformation when we attach to stories, energetic states and beliefs that keep us stuck in negative patterns! As we recognize the ways in which our thoughts hold energy in place, we can harness the power of the mind to change the vibrational field in a positive manner. Doing so opens us to deeper acceptance of the teachings of our spirit guides and of ancient healing traditions in our contemporary Western culture.

References

[1] Anodea J. and Vega S. *The Sevenfold Journey: Reclaiming Mind, Body & Spirit Through the Chakras.* Freedom, CA: The Crossing Press; 1993.

[2] Sharamom S. and Baginshi BJ. *The Chakra-Handbook.* Wilmot, WI: Lotus Light Publications–Shangri-La; 1988.

[3] Drake A. *Healing of the Soul: Shamanism and Psyche.* Ithaca, NY: Busca; 2003.

[4] Emoto M. *The Hidden Messages in Water.* New York: Atria Books; 2004.

[5] Lipton B. *The Biology of Belief: Unleashing the Power of Consciousness, Matter, and Miracles.* Santa Rosa, CA: Mountain of Love/Elite Books; 2005.

[6] Wisneski L. and Anderson L. *The Scientific Basis of Integrative Medicine.* Boca Raton, FL: CRC Press; 2005.

[7] Jung CG. *Modern Man in Search of a Soul.* New York: Harcourt, Bruce & World; 1933.

[8] Winnicott DW. *The Maturational Process and the Facilitating Environment.* New York: International Press, 1965.

About the author

Ann Drake received a doctorate in clinical psychology at the Antioch/New England School of Professional Psychology in 1989 and joined the faculty there. In addition to teaching, she has been a psychotherapist since 1972 and a shamanic practitioner since 1992. She went to Malaysian Borneo in 1992 and was initiated into the Unani tradition of healing. Since then she has developed a clinical and theoretical synthesis of psychology and shamanism and authored *Healing of the Soul: Shamanism and Psyche* (2003).

III
Indigenous Roots of Psychotherapy

Farrell R. Silverberg, PhD

In the cave of the *Trois Frères* in southwestern France, there is a painting of a shamanic healer that dates back to approximately 13,000 B.C. (about 15,000 years before Sigmund Freud and Josef Breuer published their 1895 *Studies in Hysteria*). Psychodynamic psychotherapists are accustomed to dating their legacy back to Freud, or to the important psychoanalysts who followed in the ensuing century. But this may be a bit shortsighted since psychotherapists hold much in common with prehistoric medicine men and women, and subscribe to theories and methods that are consistent with that ancient wisdom. Rather than being a relatively recent arrival on the healing scene, psychodynamic psychotherapy may have roots that stretch back tens of thousand years.

In 1939 Freud's ashes were placed in an urn at Golders Green Crematorium in London. Around 12,000 years earlier, at a burial site in Israel, an elderly woman thought to be a shaman had been laid to rest on her side, her legs folded at the knee with ten large stones placed on her body. This grave in Galilee contained 50 tortoise shells, a human foot, and body parts from various animals, indicating that the woman was seen as being in a close relationship with the animal spirits.[1]

Upon first glance, indigenous healers and psychotherapists may seem as far apart as the 12,000-year interval between the two graves. However, psychoanalysts and indigenous healers share the very important common belief that forces beyond our control, and phenomena that are not generally observed or observable in our ordinary daily awareness, affect our health. These forces have been identified by a variety of names depending upon the metaphor that one employs: the unconscious mind, the Tao, transpersonal fields, the effects of our core energies, the life force, our chakras, God's will, grace, Buddha-nature, the interconnectedness-of-all-things, synchronicity, the collective unconscious, fate, the remnants of past lives, or the spirit world. Whatever label is put on these unseen phenomena, most practitioners of a healing art acknowledge that matters of sickness and healing always involve more than meets the eye.

A key contribution of indigenous medicine is the conviction that not only is the source of a patient's illness from happenings in non-ordinary reality, but the practitioner must gain access to that dimension of reality to help free the patient of its adverse effects.

This treatment philosophy may sound familiar to the many psychotherapists who hold that emotional and relational health is indeed mediated in another dimension: the non-ordinary reality of the unconscious mind and its psychodynamics. This extremely important similarity with indigenous medicine is often missed in the psychotherapy profession, as it tends to be overshadowed by the metaphors that are used by traditional shamans – seemingly strange metaphors of animal spirits and possessions that distract us from noticing the shamanic roots of psychotherapy work.

Roots of illness in another dimension

Indigenous medicine and psychodynamic psychotherapy share a key perspective: in order to obtain a cure for certain maladies, something within non-ordinary reality (a realm of experience inaccessible in daily life) needs to be adjusted. Since non-ordinary reality is not readily available for direct observation and medical manipulation, such elements must be understood through metaphor. And in each of these metaphors for non-ordinary reality are theories about how things operate and systems of rules for this other dimension.

In the Piman culture of Northern Mexico, for instance, trespassing against the 'way' (or rules) of a powerful object in the spirit world will lead the lingering 'strengths' of that object to cause problems within the patient. The object is usually an animal spirit, and each class of animal spirit has rules. For instance, according to Bahr, violating the 'jackrabbit way' might make a patient suffer impulsive and out-of-control behavior, while violating the 'owl way' might make the patient become lethargic.[2] Such afflictions cannot be reversed without taking the world of spirits and strengths into account.

Likewise, in the culture of psychoanalytic psychotherapy, afflictions that have their roots in the unconscious mind cannot be understood or remedied without taking into account the theories or rules of that realm. In the psychoanalytic metaphor, powerful objects and forces in the unconscious mind of a person are created through psychically constructing an internal, mental representation of the energies of certain people, emotions, and beliefs into this non-ordinary realm. This process of creating inner representations is called 'introjection.' Once relocated in the non-ordinary realm of the unconscious, these introjected objects and energies create an internal, parallel universe in that invisible realm— a rather mystical sounding process that shares much with indigenous philosophy.

Of course psychoanalysts have their own rationales for the development of the non-ordinary world of the unconscious mind, such as the motive for introjection being based on the fantasy that: "If I have it inside me, I can control it effectively; it will not be on the outside where it can threaten me and destroy me."[3] It is a false fantasy, however, because these powerful internalized objects could, when trespassed against, cause toxic effects in the unconscious, thereby sickening the patient with emotional illness—and even cause such extreme effects as suicide.

In both shamanic and psychoanalytic metaphors, it is thought that the patient's transgression or the patient's parents' transgression (both usually unwitting and accidental) have effects in non-ordinary reality that lead to the patient's illness. In both the explanatory stories told by shamans and in the case of historical stories told by psychoanalysts, the interactions responsible for the current symptoms are thought to have occurred long before the patient developed the illness. Among the Pima, such interactions took place, "so long before, that the patient has forgotten what he [or she] did and, therefore, he [or she] required the services of a shaman to diagnose the sickness."[4] Bahr also points out that in the shaman's system of medicine, "Sickness comes from failure to follow the commandments of the way: failure to be careful, to remember, to believe, or to defer to things."[5]

The shamans of the Numic culture, which include North American Shoshone, Comanche and Ute tribes, are called in when an unremembered dream is thought to be causing an illness in the patient. "In the curing ceremony, the shaman discovers the dream and the person who dreamed it. The dreamer must confess the dream and relate its content publicly. Not until the dreamer confesses the content of the dream to the shaman can a cure be made."[6]

Sharing the indigenous medicine idea, psychoanalysts also believe that the source of an illness often occurred so far in the past that the patient has forgotten, and that this source may reveal itself to people through their access to the unconscious realm in dreams. Therefore in both psychoanalytic psychology and indigenous medicine, dreams are a 'royal road'[7] to non-ordinary knowledge. In the indigenous medicine practiced in Borneo, "Dreams are believed to be what the soul sees when it travels outside the body during sleep. Dreams are the only way in which normal people ... have contact with the spirit world."[8]

A patient of mine was in the 'sandwich generation' position, having a severely ailing mother plus an emotionally troubled daughter who occasionally behaved in a reckless, self-endangering manner. My patient felt that she was not up to the task of helping either one, and our work focused on helping her to take better care of herself. During this difficult time, in which she felt that her recently deceased father was communicating with her in a supportive manner, she had a dream. In the dream she had a plate of food in front of her, and was given a fork with no handle and therefore couldn't eat.

Whether this was what her soul saw when traveling outside her body, whether it was what the spirit of her father was noticing and trying to communicate to her or whether it was a product of her unconscious mind, the dream accurately crystallized her dilemma. I asked what it meant to her, and she said it meant that she couldn't 'handle' what was happening in her life and still nurture herself – and therefore was doomed, along with her daughter and mother. After we talked about these feelings for a while and I felt myself clearly present at the scene in her dream, a question for her arose. I asked, "Why didn't you pick up the food with your fingers and eat without the fork?" This simple question broke open the dream and spontaneously began to bring in other solutions. She explained that she had always felt she had to do things the right way, and eating with her hands would have violated the rules she lived by. Yet, if she could violate the rules and manners by which she was trapped, she could better take care of herself and her mother and daughter. She recognized her rules were stripping her strength, and exploring solutions outside of them was the direction to take.

In the Piman system of diagnosis, actions that violate taboos can bring about symptoms, such as stepping on a bear track and experiencing the punishing effect of the *bear strength*. In psychoanalysis, violating the unspoken rules of one's family of origin, and the introjects that are reflective of them, can lead to similar punitive symptoms.

In the case of the emotional suffering of babies and young children, shamans and psychoanalysts both agree that the patient is innocent of committing any violation, but suffers nonetheless. Another similarity between the two metaphors of causality is that there is often a separation in time between the causative factors and the appearance of symptoms. For instance, if the patient has a particular cluster of symptoms known to the Pima as 'whirlwind sickness,' the shaman assumes that as a child, the patient ran inside of a whirlwind and the consequences of that trespass took several years to 'reach' and sicken the victim.[9] Likewise, psychological theories pose that traumatizing events in childhood (being caught in an emotional whirlwind, so to speak) may take years to 'reach' and sicken the patient. Both shamanic healing and psychodynamic psychotherapy work to uncover any wrongful past transgressions of a parent through the analysis of the symptoms and history of the child.[10]

Considering the object that is making someone ill as separate from that person allows patients to feel more intact and better able to mobilize personal strengths to fight the symptoms of the disease, instead of squandering energy with self-recriminations. The idea of 'externalizing' the illness,[11] which we see in the indigenous diagnostic systems and in many psychotherapies, allows the healer-patient dyad to release the patient from the grip of the illness. In his description of Tibetan shamanism, Tenzin Wangyal says,[12] "When we identify with our suffering and illness, it becomes difficult to heal because the healing means giving up our identity. If we can shift our identity, the sickness or suffering can be left behind."

Another aspect that psychotherapy shares with shamanism is that the practitioner serves as an emissary and a negotiator with the forces in non-ordinary reality. In indigenous medicine, such negotiation on behalf of the patient has special importance in cases where the patient's illness is seen through the metaphor of possession. In the Korean *kut* ritual, for instance, the shaman negotiates with and beseeches ghosts and spirits who are thought to be making the patient ill in order to encourage those unseen forces to loosen their control over the 'possessed' patient.[13]

In Tibetan shamanistic practice, a 'ransom' can be offered to the spirits who possess the ailing patient. A life-size effigy of the patient, dressed in his or her clothes and packed with food or gifts for the spirits, is given to the spirits as ransom in exchange for releasing the patient from illness. [14]

Following a similar formula, a Korean shaman (*mansin*) who senses that a 'death messenger' has come to claim the patient's soul, instructs the patient's family to make a straw doll to represent the patient, make traditional funeral preparations for the doll, and then bury it to mislead the harmful spirits away from the patient so the healing can begin.[15]

In psychoanalytic psychotherapy, there is also a possession-like metaphor in the concept of introjected objects. Interventions can be designed by the therapist to attempt to fool or to negotiate with such introjects to stimulate them to show themselves. If this succeeds, the previously invisible phenomena become a 'felt presence' in the therapy sessions, often causing the patient to say and do surprising things that make them feel as if they are indeed 'possessed.'

For instance, one patient recently reported to me that she felt possessed by her mother's persona when she suddenly stood up and yelled and cursed me during her session, pointing out my supposed malevolence, and wishing death upon me. She quickly recognized that this force had power over her but was 'not her.' Furthermore, she realized that the control that this object had over her had to be fought wholeheartedly. Through such recognition, and with guidance, she could now begin to affect these forces on her own behalf.

The dark side: inherent dangers in non-ordinary reality

One advantage that indigenous medicine wisdom has over psychodynamic psychotherapy practice is in its recognition of the dangers inherent in journeying into non-ordinary reality. In indigenous metaphors, the realm of non-ordinary reality is not an exclusively safe playground of health, light, and helpful spirits. In that realm darkness, shadows, and sickness also exist.[16] Korean shamans view these forces through the metaphor of restless and hungry ancestors and ghosts (*chosang malmyong* and *yongsan chapkwi*) who "wander angry and frustrated, venting their anguish on the living,"[17] as well as 'death humors' and 'invisible arrows' which can invade a home.[18]

In psychoanalytic metaphors, these darker forces are often associated with internalized representations of frightening or punitive figures from the past, accompanied by strict rules for the patient and punishments for the patient's transgressions against such rules. These are known as 'bad objects,' and can lead to a debilitating inner struggle between parts of the patient's mind, generating symptoms of emotional illness.[19]

For example, I have a patient whose family members lived victimized and self-destructive lives, including drug and alcohol abuse, brushes with the law and promiscuity. Whenever this patient violates that family legacy (e.g., she chooses *not* to get drunk or refuses to have a one night stand with a stranger), she feels the compelling urge to carry out self-mutilating behavior such as cutting her legs with a razor knife. It could be said that these symptoms came from a violation of the bad objects of the family 'way' and the punishment for this trespass is carried out by the family 'strength' in her that makes her cut herself.

If a psychotherapist encounters such bad objects or punitive family strengths when interacting with entities within the patient's unconscious realm, there could be potential harm if these are misinterpreted or taken at face value without thoughtful evaluation. For instance, if a therapist finds information that portrays the patient in a very negative light, or sees that the patients needs to confront something, or needs to try something he or she is hesitant to try – how is that therapist to know that this information is being provided by good or bad objects, or by helpful or harmful spirits?

One safeguard in addressing this question is the training that psychoanalytic psychotherapists receive regarding 'countertransference,' an inner process of the unconscious realm of non-ordinary reality. Countertransference can be thought of as part of a reciprocal set of non-ordinary experiences that psychoanalysts call the 'transference-countertransference' relationship and through which information is transmitted or received. When, during the course of treatment, the patient falls into a 'transference,' he or she can experience the therapy relationship as if key elements are the same as those of a past significant relationship. This re-experiencing of a past reality in the present reality of the treatment reactivates the set of emotions, thoughts, predispositions, expectations and manner of interaction reflective of that past relationship and the therapist is seen through that lens.

When the therapist receives this transferred set of experiences, he or she has reactions to it – 'countertransference' [20] – that could helpfully inform the treatment if recognized and used wisely by the therapist. On the other hand, countertransference could possibly misguide the treatment if this non-ordinary experience goes unrecognized, is mistaken for ordinary information or stimulates the therapist's own unresolved past conflicts biasing his or her interpretation of information from the non-ordinary realm. Not only psychotherapists, but all helping professionals would be wise to stay alert to what they 'intuit' or glean from non-ordinary means for any subjective bias they may have. Such biases may promote the therapist's accepting as valid messages from harmful or misleading forces regarding the patient or the treatment.

In contrast to modern healthcare practitioners, indigenous shamans have held respect for helpful and harmful powers of non-ordinary reality and are careful to evaluate the information they bring to the patient from that source. Sometimes this caution can be lost in modern health disciplines as well as neo-shamanic health practices where some schools of thought encourage sharing the information discovered in non-ordinary ways without first evaluating that information's impact upon the patient. This rosy view of non-ordinary forces may be a cultural artifact of our modern society in which there is sometimes a loss of humility in the face of forces beyond our control. There is a wealth of positive healing information to be gleaned in non-ordinary ways, and this wealth can be put to use in helping the patient only if it is evaluated and utilized wisely and with discretion.

Evaluating non-ordinary knowledge

With the practitioner's use of non-ordinary ways of knowing on behalf of a patient comes additional responsibility towards that patient. In all healing arts, we are first and foremost committed to the dictum that we 'do not harm.' Instead of sharing what is learned from non-ordinary reality without restraint, holding that hard-won knowledge inside while calling it to empower the techniques of treatment may be in the best service of the patient's progressing health. The act of our internally experiencing the information can also benefit our ability to understand the patient as well.

"In a therapy session with a patient I had been seeing for some time, I was struck by a strong urge to be more giving. As the session progressed, this feeling distilled into the impulse to give the patient a small print of a Japanese woodcut that I had been carrying in my appointment book for some weeks. Following the principle that such information was to be evaluated and not taken as an instruction to act in any way, I studied the feeling to see if it was at all . . . related to anything the patient was discussing that day, but saw no connection. The same experience overtook me in the following session and still there was no clarity. . . Finally, in the session after that, it all became clear when the patient entered and handed me a rolled-up sheet of rice paper stating that he had been intending to give me this piece of artwork for a few weeks. I opened the paper to find a woodcut print. It seemed now that my desire to give may have been a resonance and an experience of exchange about his desire to give. My restraint allowed his process to go to completion and there was, in retrospect, some wisdom in awaiting some empirical evidence before infusing any intervention with the giving impulse rather than allow untamed or wild resonance into the treatment."[21]

Shamanic trances and Ogden's reverie

Shamans may access non-ordinary reality through the use of plant-based mind-altering substances and/or through a spiritual practice that allows them to enter into a trance-like state of consciousness. Essie Parish, a California Kashaya Pomo healer, describes her experience of the shamanic trance as follows: "While the disease is coming to me, I'm in a trance. It speaks to me firmly saying, 'This is the way it is. It is such and such kind of disease. This is why the person is sick.' But when I come out of the trance, I no longer remember what the disease told me."[22]

Psychoanalysts glean similar experiential knowledge when they engage in a close empathic connection with a patient, to the point of exchanging their own reality for the patient's unconscious-realm reality. This can bring a curative element, similar to the shaman's trance, into the treatment. In our psychoanalytic shift of consciousness to this non-ordinary reality, we employ free-floating attention, or what Thomas Ogden describes[23] as a 'reverie' within the analyst's mind during the session—a process that could be viewed as a form of healing trance.

According to Indian psychoanalyst Sudhir Kakar,[24] "Empathy, and the meditative state that underlies it, may well be the sluice through which the spiritual enters the consulting room and where it flows together with the art and science of psychoanalysis."

A patient of mine had a session immediately after attending the funeral of his sister with whom he had been very close:

"During this session, he expressed his sense that there was a heavy feeling of 'loneliness in the room' and that he felt it was coming from the office itself or from me. I felt it too. I experienced a palpable hollow, unsettling sense of loneliness, but I did not say so out loud. It seemed that something was in delicate balance and I did not want to disturb that balance. My patient then moved to the analytic couch that he had usually occupied during our previous sessions, and I could no longer see his face. He spoke in a halting manner, talked about how odd it felt to come into town without his sister being here, and then fell into complete silence. My sense was that the hollow, lonely feeling now pervaded the room even more. Often when a patient falls silent, it is good for the analyst to say something to feel them out in case they need contact in their silence. However, in this session, I felt somehow guided to remain respectfully silent but receptive to and connected with the [pervasive] feeling that was ongoing. After some time, I found myself feeling very sad, noticed my eyes were tearing up, and soon I began gently crying. At that same moment, I experienced the feeling of loneliness in the room disappear completely from me. Nearing the end of our session, my patient sat up and turned to look at me. I could see that he, too, had tears streaming down his face. On his way out, he told me how good it was to see me and, as I sincerely felt likewise, I told him how good I felt to see him."[25]

Through this experience of connection in non-ordinary reality, it seemed that this man was able to open into his process of grieving.

It is particularly hard to deny the similarity between our work and that of indigenous medicine when noting a shamanic technique among the Navajo medicine men and women called 'listening.' According to Walter and Neumann-Fridman,[26] such listening has similarities to the kind of receptive, non-judgmental, open attention many of us practice during our psychoanalytic work. "The listener would bless his ears and those of his patient with powder made from dried badger eardrums. He would then go outside away from the patient and chant and the listen for telltale sounds in the environment. Based upon the pattern of what he heard (lightning, a rattlesnake, a coyote howling, whatever it might be), he would render a diagnosis.

Becoming the patient: a common thread

Michael Harner describes[27] an indigenous healing ritual that is striking in its similarity with the experience we have as psychotherapists when understanding our patients through our empathy and compassion for their history and suffering. In the 'becoming the patient' technique used by Coast Salish shamans of British Columbia, the shaman takes upon himself the harmful effects of the spirit world that are making the patient ill. The shaman interviews the afflicted person to learn about the experience of the patient and about what it is like to be the patient. This resembles the process of interview in psychoanalytic psychotherapy except that it lasts only a few days, while the psychoanalytic version takes place over many sessions and becomes a continually renewed process during the length of the treatment.

When the Salish shaman knows enough about the patient that he or she feels capable of identifying with the inner experience of the patient, they both go to the wilderness to perform the ritual. During this ritual the shaman and the patient slowly exchange clothes, and with each article of clothing borrowed and put on, the shaman contemplates taking upon himself more of the patient's hurts and symptoms. Then the patient and shaman perform a dance in which the patient moves and the shaman imitates each movement and gesture of the patient. At first the movements are just empty imitation, but eventually the shaman feels his consciousness changing and feels "waves of sickness or pain passing over him." [28]

Like the shaman, the psychotherapist who is open to non-ordinary elements welcomes and even cultivates the transfer of psychological toxins such as despair, helplessness, aggression and self-punitiveness. If the therapist has discovered what it may be like to be the patient through touching the non-ordinary realm of the unconscious, a small trace of that knowledge begins to inhabit his tone of voice and infuse the supportive words he speaks. The patient receives this other-than-conscious message by a sense of feeling understood, making the psychological intervention more meaningful.

Shamanism without drama

Psychotherapists need not carry a rattle, beat a drum, chant, or lie on the floor beside the patient in order to access a patient's unconscious realm. In our version of the healing rituals, we are subtler in our empathic pyrotechnics than our shamanic forebearers.

Despite the reputation of shamans for chants and rituals, drama was not always a required element of healing. In some indigenous cultures, shamanic healings were often performed simply through "a conversation between the sick person and the shaman in which the shaman would induce hope of recovery in the patient by referring to similar cases where the ill person became well again, or by narrating the happiness in the Otherworld."[29]

A smooth and non-jarring access of non-ordinary reality of the unconscious mind, which doesn't disrupt normal discourse, is key to our work. It can be understood as a form of shamanism, quietly accessing non-ordinary knowledge without telegraphing it to the patient or anyone else who might see the interaction.

Sharing the tradition of "eyes that see in the dark"

David Cumes[30] has posited that the most complete treatment emerges from combining science and shamanism. The shamanistic and scientific aspects of psychotherapy have already begun to meet in innovative approaches to countertransference, therapeutic resonance, and other accesses to non-ordinary reality. For the psychotherapist, integrating shamanism and psychotherapy means keeping one foot in the realm of the surface interaction and another foot in the realm of the non-ordinary – called by whatever metaphoric label the individual therapist prefers.

Finally, as imperfect as we are, and as incompletely enlightened as we tend to be, the in-touch-ness with non-ordinary ways of knowing can be expected to come and go as we work with our patients. We cannot expect to be firmly planted in both realms at all times. Instead, a window can open and close in our sessions, and through that window we can access what is important to know to help the patient. Such windows can be likened to a form of what Zen Buddhists refer to as 'kensho' experiences,[31] a momentary opening into the interconnectedness of all things. Such openings during psychotherapy may well be enough to help the patient toward health in a deeper manner than can otherwise be achieved.

The two metaphors explored in this paper, those of shamanic healing and of psychodynamic psychotherapy, both point to the notion that health is mediated through non-ordinary reality. If so, the legacy of psychotherapy extends thousands of years into the past, and could well be a continuation of ancient and indigenous healing practices. The Inuit and Innu peoples who reside close to the Arctic Circle refer to shamans as "those with eyes that see in the dark."[32] Through such eyes, the extraordinary knowledge gleaned from the elusive, mostly invisible, non-ordinary is never far from us.

References

[1] Grosman L., Munro N. and Belfer-Cohen A. "A 12,000-year-old Shaman Burial from the Southern Levant (Israel)." *Proceedings of the National Academy of Sciences* 2008; 105: 46: 17665-17669.

[2] Bahr D., Gregorio J., Lopez DI. and Alvarez A. *Piman, Shamanism and Staying Sickness.* Tucson: University of Arizona Press; 1974; 28.

[3] Weininger O. *Melanie Klein: From Theory to Reality.* London: Karnac Books; 1992; 27.

[4] Bahr D.; 21.

[5] Bahr D.; 42.

[6] Walter M., Neumann-Fridman J. *Shamanism: An Encyclopedia of World Beliefs, Practices, and Culture.* Santa Barbara: ABC-Cleo Publishers; 2004; 293.

[7] Freud S. *The Interpretation of Dreams.* New York City: Avon; 1980; 647.

[8] Bernstein JH. *Spirits Captured in Stone: Shamanism and Traditional Medicine.* London: Lynne Rienner; 1997; 59.

[9] Bahr D.; 74.

[10] Bahr D.; 76.

[11] White M., Epston D. *Narrative Means to Therapeutic Ends.* New York: Norton; 1990; 38.

[12] Wangyal T. *Healing with Form, Energy and Light.* Ithaca, NY: Snow Lion Publications; 2002; 55.

[13] Kendall L. *Shamans, Housewives, and Other Restless Spirits: Women in Korean Ritual Life.* Honolulu: University of Hawaii Press; 1987; 87.

[14] Wangyal T.; 55.

[15] Kendall L.; 87.

[16] Donden Y. "Tibetan Medicine: Buddha Wisdoms and the Healing of the Mind and Body." Trans. Thurman R. *The Journal of Traditional Acupuncture.* 1983; 7: 2: 22-26.

[17] Kendall L.; 99.

[18] Kendall L.; 104.

[19] Fairbairn W. *Psychoanalytic Studies of the Personality.* London: Routledge; 1994; 62.

[20] Silverberg F. "Resonance and Exchange in Contemplative Psychotherapy." In Kaklauskas FJ., Nimanheminda S., Hoffman L., Jack M.S., eds. *Brilliant Sanity: Buddhist Approaches to Psychotherapy.* Colorado Springs, CO: University of the Rockies Press; 239-257.

[21] Silverberg F.; 247-248.

[22] Tedlock B. *The Woman in the Shaman's Body.* New York City: Bantam; 2005; 19.

[23] Ogden T. "Reverie and Metaphor." *International Journal of Psycho-Analysis,* 1997; 78: 719-732.

[24] Kakar S. "Psychoanalysis and Eastern Spiritual Healing Traditions." *Journal of Analytical Psychology,* 2003; 48: 659-678.

[25] Silverberg F. "The Tao of Self Psychology: Was Heinz Kohut a Taoist Sage?" *Psychoanalytic Inquiry,* 2011; 31: 5: 483.

[26] Walter M.; 322.

[27] Harner M. *The Way of the Shaman.* HarperSanFrancisco; 1990; 132.

[28] Harner M.; 133.

[29] Walter M.; 301.

[30] Cumes D. *The Spirit of Healing.* Minnesota: Llewellyn Publications; 1999.

[31] Fenner P. "Spiritual Inquiry in Buddhism." *ReVision* 1994; 17: 15.

[32] Tedlock B.; 25.

About the Author

Farrell Silverberg, PhD, NCPsyA, is a clinical psychologist, a certified psychoanalyst, a member of the Society for Shamanic Practitioners and the first Western student of Taopsychotherapy master Rhee Dong Shik in Seoul, Korea. Silverberg began integrating psychoanalysis, Buddhist-Taoist philosophy and shamanic thought thirty years ago. Having served in hospitals and clinics over the years, Silverberg is currently a Supervising and Training psychoanalyst at the Philadelphia School of Psychoanalysis.

IV

Medicine Stories: Shamanism and Personal Narratives

Carin Roberge, PsyD

Many clients who seek psychotherapy and shamanic healing are feeling overwhelmed by the circumstances of their lives and hope to have their symptoms of anxiety and depression eased. Some struggle with the natural transitions through life stages, while others report unfortunate experiences of addiction, illness, loss of loved ones, unemployment, financial strain, divorce, or abuse. Adding to their distress is the media's exposure to real time views of the horrors of war, terrorism, and natural disasters. Their personal experiences, exacerbated by the rapid pace of social, cultural, and economic changes in today's society, have left many feeling vulnerable and unprepared to cope effectively. The breakdown of social networks and the resulting loss of resources for emotional support and practical assistance further contribute to their sense of being overwhelmed. Many report being disoriented and disconnected from themselves, from others, and from the larger community that otherwise might have fostered hope and meaning in their circumstances.

From a shamanic standpoint, what these clients are describing is soul loss, a dissociative response to trauma in which a part of the soul's essence leaves the body, numbing the person and enabling them to survive the experience. Such trauma can be overt and brutal as in childhood sexual abuse or exposure to violent death, or subtle and pervasive as when it stems from social upheaval or the loss of critical social support. When the soul essence fails to return, soul loss occurs and results in diminished vitality.[1] A person with soul loss describes feeling anxious, depressed, or says that they have never felt the same since a particular event happened. Families, communities, and even whole societies can experience soul loss as well as individuals.

The importance of stories

Soul loss is expressed through stories of distress and disconnection, and recovery is hindered by a lack of life-supporting narratives. The rupture of the vital web of community life in today's society has led to the loss of healing stories, forgotten or left behind as old-fashioned, inapplicable, and of little value today. It is these life-supporting stories, 'medicine stories,' that nurture and guide us in making wise, affirmative choices. Such stories bestow a sense of security that one has a place among loved ones and a connection with the transcendent.

In indigenous societies, people learned what to expect, how to feel and how to respond to the circumstances of their lives from medicine stories. These stories reminded people of the rituals and traditions that had guided them safely through the thresholds of development to realize their place in society and in the great web of life. Medicine stories were passed from mother to daughter, father to son, from village and community elders to each new generation.

Mythologist Joseph Campbell describes this phenomenon: "When the story is in your mind, then you see its relevance to something happening in your own life. It gives you perspective on what's happening to you . . . These bits of information from ancient times . . . have to do with the themes that have supported human life, built civilizations, and informed religions over the millennia. [They] have to do with deep inner problems, inner mysteries, inner thresholds of passage; and if you don't know what the guide-signs are along the way, you have to work it out yourself."[2]

Narrative has always occupied an important place in shamanic healing. The shaman's journey to the spirit world involves a basic narrative structure that includes a beginning, middle, and end. Every journey has an originating point, a landscape through which the shaman travels, a destination in non-ordinary reality, and an eventual return to ordinary reality. Narrative also plays a central role in what Joseph Campbell refers to as the archetypal myths or dreams of the world's major civilizations,[3] connecting people through metaphor to their own nature and the natural and social worlds which they inhabit. In the past two decades psychologists have demonstrated the importance of narrative as both a basic cognitive structure by which people interpret their experience[4] and as an organizing principle by which they create a unitary sense of self.[5] Narrative psychology has spawned novel psychotherapeutic approaches that aim at 're-storying' clients' lives by changing the linguistic self- and other-descriptions.[6]

Medicine stories

Medicine stories are stories coauthored with the spirits and developed from one or more core, evocative metaphors. Such metaphors are often raw and undeveloped, appearing as fragments of images, phrases, personal memories, sounds, or colors. Nevertheless, clients usually respond to these elements with a sense of mysterious recognition, as if they were being reconnected with something of vital importance lost long ago, the significance of which they have yet to comprehend. Medicine stories typically contain mythic elements of both a personal and transcendent nature and are 'stories within the story,' explaining particular historical and contemporary events within a client's life. At a personal level these may involve interactions and developments with family, friends, lovers, neighbors, associates, and colleagues. At the transcendent level they may describe and explain a client's involvement with the broader community, social or spiritual groups, or with a philosophy. What gives these stories a mythic dimension is the manner in which they invest everyday events with a greater meaning, linking them with specific people and the larger fabric of the client's world.

Medicine stories are narratives of human ascension that promote the expansion of personal potential, realization of greater life possibilities, and maturation. These stories have the potential to sustain healing on three levels: relationship of individuals to themselves; relationships between individuals, their families, and their communities; and relationships between individuals and the broader physical, social, and spiritual realms.

At the individual level, medicine stories promote a healthful redefinition of self, personal history, and future possibilities. At the family and community level stories help to redefine the nature of these relationships, forgive past transgressions, revitalize lost connections, and explore new community roles and responsibilities. At the transcendent level stories point to new ways to link personal purposes with the needs of the larger world and give new opportunities to define oneself in relation to spirit. The impact of these stories lies in their capacity to provide healing on all levels simultaneously through the rich potential of the story's core metaphor and the collaboration with spiritual guidance.

Finally, medicine stories are lived stories, open-ended and infused with spiritual power. Their significance is only fully realized by clients through a complex dialogue which typically develops through the interplay of communication with spirit allies, personal review and self-reflection, and the integration of new learning and self-experience via interactions with others and the world at large.

For years I have asked my spirit allies what makes the difference between clients for whom healing sustains itself over time and those for whom it does not. I have come to understand that medicine stories can be a key to sustained healing through their restoration of soulfulness. These stories, combined with traditional shamanic healing methods, work in tandem as each creates fertile ground for the other to take root. Shamanic healing methods are the vehicle through which the work occurs and by which people grow stronger and more open to recognizing and accepting new narratives. Medicine stories, in turn, establish a meaningful context for clients to understand and anchor shamanic healing in their lives.

Framework for medicine story creation

My work with clients typically proceeds through four phases: (1) orientation and education; (2) exploration and preparation; (3) revelation and recognition; (4) development and integration. While these phases generally follow a loose sequential order, they may also overlap and repeat themselves. Throughout the healing process I create and hold sacred space for clients to engage with spirit allies, offer myself as a vehicle through which the spirits enact healing, and teach clients to journey for guidance and healing.

(1) Orientation and education

The orientation and education phase begins during the initial telephone call and continues in the early sessions. I listen and watch for the stories that describe clients' experiences and pay attention to the words they use to describe why they are seeking help and what they are hoping to receive from our work together. I share with them a brief history and description of shamanic healing, answer questions, and describe what they might expect during our work together. This includes both possible outcomes and the fact that there can be no guarantee of outcome.

From the beginning, I emphasize the importance of working with strong intention for healing. I invite clients' input and active participation, discuss the significance of personal life stories and begin to sensitize them to narrative as a vehicle for healing. My hope is that from the beginning of our work together they will experience themselves as empowered partners in their healing experience. When clients can feel this way, it increases their sense of personal security in a process which can involve the disassembling and rebuilding of significant elements of their personal identity. It also encourages them to begin to coauthor their experience in the healing that follows.

During the initial session with a client I invite him or her to join in the setting of sacred space in which we lower the veil between the ordinary reality of daily life and the non-ordinary reality of the spirit world. I usually light a candle and smudge to invoke plant spirit allies for the cleansing and preparation of sacred space. If the client has sensitivities to scent or smoke, we find other ways to prepare the space. Since shamanic healing traditionally includes community members who provide information, support, and bear witness to the work, I encourage clients to bring trusted loved ones with them. In some cases I encourage clients to bring therapists and other healthcare providers, and I consult with these providers on ways they might support the healing work.

Claire, aged forty-one, requested a combination of psychotherapy and shamanic healing. During our initial meetings we became acquainted with one another, clarified her hopes and goals, and talked about what she might expect. She described herself as having long-term depression and indicated that she felt stuck and unable to heal. She attributed her ongoing feelings of depression to her 'dead-end' job and said she wanted to learn how to stand up for herself, feel more confident, and get others to take her seriously. For several months she had been suspicious that her boss brought her ideas to his superiors and took credit for them himself. When she communicated her suspicions to him, he denied having done so and grew derisive. The following week he upbraided and shamed her in a staff meeting. Humiliated, she left the meeting in tears. A month later she learned that she had been passed over for a promotion and took a leave of absence rather than terminating. She actually liked her job and most of her colleagues; her field is small and it is difficult to find employment at her level; and she also wanted to be sure to retain her health coverage and benefits.

(2) Exploration and preparation

Once a client decides to go forward, we enter into the exploration and preparation phase of our work together. During this phase I continue to gather information in both ordinary and nonordinary reality in order to clarify a client's current circumstances and any underlying spiritual imbalances that contribute to the presenting concerns. We also discuss what has helped in the past and possible outcomes of our work. I conduct a brief evaluation in which I explore developmental and health-related history as well as social supports. Most often I do not collect detailed information until after I have received guidance from my spirit allies, other than a risk assessment if the client is in obvious distress. I want to avoid confounding the initial information I get from my spirit allies with any ideas I might have formulated in advance about what might be occurring. I do, however, invite clients to share anything that they want me to understand as we go forward in our work together.

In addition, I explore the existing stories by which a client understands and defines his or her life experiences. I listen for what is working and what is not working. Typically, a client comes in with a primary 'descending story' and a mélange of secondary descending and ascending narrative elements. Descending stories are stories of disengagement, disconnection, self-destruction, and lack of purpose that invite imbalance, distress and figurative or literal disease. Ascending stories are stories of engagement, connection, creation, and purpose that foster healing.[7] I listen for these stories for two reasons. First, consciously articulated stories frequently offer clues to underlying spiritual dynamics of a client's presenting problems. Second, these clues can be useful in posing queries and setting intentions for further exploration. Whether descending or ascending, aspects of these narratives will often be replicated through actions later on during the development and integration phase of our work together. Identifying them early provides material that can be referenced later to remind the client that she is reproducing a familiar pattern of descent, or to point out existing or new ways the client may be supporting fledgling stories of ascent and connection.

If a client is only loosely identified with a primary narrative of descent, I sometimes ask for explicit permission to challenge the integrity of the story. This is a way of inserting a 'wedge of doubt' into the client's conscious belief system that holds the story together as a coherent whole. If the client is tightly locked into an identification with the descending story, however, I generally defer to the spirits to challenge it through the introduction of core medicine story material during the revelation and recognition phase of the work.

Claire identified ascending and descending story elements that were part of her experience of self. While she emphasized her strengths in her ability to perform job tasks with colleagues, she noted that initial good relationships often turned bad. She revealed that she had experienced similar dynamics in her marriage as well as in other relationships, and described situations in which people did not take her seriously and discredited her contributions by becoming disrespectful and controlling. Fearing that she might be overlooked and trumped by people she initially trusted, she felt misunderstood, disempowered, small, ashamed, and lost. She recognized her self-narratives as limiting, but felt unable to alter them.

After exploring a client's concerns and hopes, I journey to my spirit allies to learn what healing might be suggested. Sometimes they speak through me directly to my client, and at other times I report what they have shown me. If my client knows how to do a shamanic journey, we may travel together to the spirit realm for direction. We then determine how to proceed based on what healing methods the spirits suggest. Sometimes this plan is well developed, and sometimes it represents little more than a set of guidelines.

Shamanic healing removes what does not belong and returns and heals what does belong. My spirit allies, using me as a conduit through which to work, remove intruding energies and return spiritual power and soul essence. Clients often report restored health and vitality as a result. The methods I most often use are: power animal/guardian spirit retrieval; meeting a spirit teacher; soul retrieval; extraction; depossession; and clearing and rebalancing the client's energy field. The method, combination, and duration of these vary from client to client.

The retrieval or reconnection to power animals and spirit teachers helps clients experience a sense of security. Spirit allies can emanate tremendous compassion, unconditional love, and fierce protectiveness. These spiritual relationships engender in clients a feeling that they are not alone. As their relationships with spirits allies deepen and trust is formed, spiritual power is strengthened. Clients are often deeply moved by the experience of spiritual power and support that enables them to expand their usual frame of reference, engage their imagination in problem solving, and take risks to stretch themselves.

Through soul retrieval, interests and skills that have been unavailable since the soul essence was lost may be remembered. Clients feel more grounded, curious, and open to the seed metaphors of medicine stories.

In some instances, spiritual intrusions fuel the ongoing enacting of descending stories. Removal and healing of intrusions, especially when combined with the construction of ascending medicine stories, serves to enhance clients' receptivity to healing. Depossession works in much the same way. If a possessing spirit is confused, misguided, or intends harm, I work with spirit guidance to offer healing to the spirit and guide it back to the spirit world. When there is interference from a possessing spirit, shamanic healing and ascending narratives will not be effective until the possessing spirit is attended to first.

With my spirit allies, I continuously monitor a client's energy field, clearing and rebalancing it as needed to augment the shamanic healing and the receptivity of clients to the medicine story metaphors.

I explored with Claire what she was hoping for from our work together and described shamanic healing work and what she might expect. I called to my spirit allies who showed me that there was a large energy cord from her solar plexus to a shadowy figure in the distance; as a result she was losing much of her life force.

I also saw some of the same shadowy energy in her abdomen and realized that she had significant soul loss. With guidance from my spirit allies, I suggested to Claire that she might benefit from extraction, guardian spirit retrieval, and soul retrieval.

When I told her I had seen intruding energy and an energy cord that I wanted to clear prior to soul retrieval, she wanted to know more. I explained that I do not like to say very much about what I am shown, as I do not want to cause distress or reinforce negative energy by initiating a story of descent. Claire spontaneously offered that she had experienced stomach pain related to digestive problems since early childhood.

After shifting into a shamanic state of consciousness, I discovered that the cord was connected to her father with whom she had been close during early childhood. She explained to me that when she was eleven, her father sustained an injury and was unable to walk or fully care for himself. Her mother worked to support the family, and Claire's job was to help care for her father who had become quite critical of her and emotionally controlling.

During the soul retrieval, I discovered Claire's eleven-year-old soul part tied to her father with a cord attached to her solar plexus. She was trying to free herself by pulling at the cord, but each time she came close to being free, she stopped pulling and gave up. She sat down on a curb and held her head in her hands.

My spirit allies worked to remove spiritual intrusions that held in place core beliefs that she was not good enough, did not deserve to have her needs met, and that if she asserted herself something terrible would happen. When she was ready, they worked with Claire to gently release the cord that bound her to her father in an unhealthy way. They then educated her about more healthful ways to enhance her relationship with him. Next, I retrieved a guardian spirit to help return her eleven-year-old soul part. Because I had no way to know whether the shamanic journey information was to be taken literally or metaphorically, I reported the images and asked Claire about their meaning. She indicated that for years she had felt herself to be in a tug-of-war with her father to regain his affection and stated that she "had always given in" because of fears of hurting or losing him.

(3) Revelation and recognition

The revelation of a seed metaphor in a medicine story often occurs during shamanic healing or journeywork, although it may also come in a night or day dream. Either way, it is a gift from the spirits. It most often appears in a flash: a quick seeding of a thought, a phrase, a sentence or a question, sometimes a single word or sound. Other times it comes as a color, a scent, or a familiar feeling.

When it is nurtured, it can restore health-promoting, ascending narratives in clients' lives.

I have learned to listen and watch for the initial seed metaphor that heralds the beginning of a new or remembered story of ascension. It resonates with clients at a deep level, and they instinctively recognize it as a taproot calling forth potentials which until that moment have been unrealized or forgotten. When they recognize such a metaphor some people feel a rush of excitement, an 'aha' moment, or a sense of deep relief as they reconnect with something more vast than themselves. For others, the recognition may be less dramatic but powerful nonetheless. With little or no prompting, these seed metaphors evolve into an ascending self-narrative from which the embryonic medicine story develops.

During her soul retrieval, Claire's spirit allies introduced a seed metaphor. She saw a flash of yellow-and-black light and felt a sense of great wellbeing. As she heard her power animal singing a song that was vaguely familiar, she recalled that as a young child she and her father had written a song about a honeybee. The song spontaneously reconnected her to a powerful self-narrative from earlier in her life as she remembered herself loved, valued, and worthy. Thus, her seed metaphor came in the form of a flash of light and a song about the ways she brought sweetness into his life.

(4) Development and integration

Traditional shamanic healing methods can restore the client; however she runs the risk of losing these gains if they are not integrated into her ongoing life. By coauthoring medicine stories with spirit allies, a client engages in an inner dialogue that is integral to her healing. The introduction of core medicine story metaphors provides the raw ingredients for building healing narratives of ascension, but they can only be integrated into the client's repertoire over time. The development of a medicine story involves taking a seed metaphor and combining it with ascending story elements. Some of these are available from the client's repertoire of life-story elements, and others are introduced either through ongoing work with spirit allies or through exposure to new personal stories. As these metaphors gain additional ascending story material they can become quite elaborate, representing changes in self-experience and self-definition. Still, at this stage, these elaborated positive personal narratives can have a tentative quality about them and remain unrelated to one another, so that the client may doubt the full integrity of these stories. They can also be easily undermined by the resurgence of a more powerful descending story triggered by events in the client's life.

Only with integration of these story elements into a more secure primary ascending story can the client begin to gain confidence in the integrity and coherence of these positive story elements. Integration is the product of much interplay between the client, spirit allies, and significant others. It occurs as ascending narrative structures come to form mythic elements that explain key events and episodes within the client's current and past life in a more positive light. These elements weave together many life threads to form a strong and durable fabric that stretches to encompass personal meaning-making between the client and self, client and others, and client and the world. As she connects these mythic elements, coherence develops and allows for the emergence of a primary ascending story around which to form a revitalized personal identity.

This phase often seems unpredictable and chaotic for both the client and healer. Unexpected obstacles, surprising developments and breakthroughs, even serendipitous revelations from the spirits occur with great regularity. Throughout this process the previous two phases of exploration and preparation and revelation and recognition may be repeated. Sometimes the progress seems unbearably slow; at other times, clients will proceed rapidly in their growth and development. A client may heal a part of herself and then in the everyday world get feedback, and through that process experience herself differently. When she returns for additional shamanic healing, more medicine story elements may reveal themselves. These will need to be developed and integrated recursively into an already developed primary ascending story.

In subsequent sessions, Claire journeyed to meet her spirit allies and her eleven-year-old soul part to rework a primary limiting self-narrative. This proved to be a challenging time of self-examination in which she gradually recognized the ways her dominant self-narrative negatively affected her relationships not only with her father, but also with her husband and others. She also focused on how it affected her experience at work with her boss and came to understand that she held a deep-seated fear that if she asserted herself she would lose affection, love, value, and status and eventually be discredited and abandoned. Each time this happened, her limiting self-narratives were reinforced and her self-esteem eroded. Organizing her life around a descending life story of negative self-identity had left her feeling disconnected from both herself and others, and placed her at risk for further soul loss. As she understood her own role in keeping these limiting self-narratives alive, she experienced periods of deep grief.

With a lot of hard work, Claire developed new self-narratives that further defined and strengthened her medicine story. She forgave her father and others who had treated her badly. She became self-confident enough to assert herself without fear of losing the respect of those important to her. After she regained her health she negotiated a promotion at work, noticed that she could bring sweetness to her family and friends and that she could cultivate playfulness in her relationships without compromising her power or effectiveness. Her experiences with spirit allies gave her a feeling of being loved and held in esteem, and thus she no longer felt alone. These experiences translated into fulfilling relationships with several people in her community. Over time, Claire had coauthored a powerful medicine story.

Conclusion

Claire's experience exemplifies how remembering and developing a medicine story in combination with traditional shamanic healing can serve to both deepen and sustain the effects of therapeutic work. In the pervasive soul loss of today, there is often inadequate social support and practical assistance to sustain one's wellbeing. I believe the spirits have responded by reintroducing the stories that foster connection, balance and soulfulness into our world to bring meaning and context to the healing process.

References

[1] Ingerman S. *Soul Retrieval: Mending the Fragmented Self.* HarperSanFrancisco; 1991.

[2] Campbell J. *The Power of Myth.* New York: Doubleday; 1988; 2.

[3] Campbell J. *The Hero with a Thousand Faces.* New Jersey: Princeton University Press; 1973.

[4] Bruner JS. *Acts of Meaning.* Cambridge, MA: Harvard University Press; 1990.

[5] Crossley ML. *Introducing Narrative Psychology: Self, Trauma, and the Construction of Meanings.* Buckingham, UK: Open University Press; 2000.

[6] McNamee S. and Gergen KG. *Therapy as Social Construction,* London: Sage; 1992.

[7] Bonnet J. *Stealing Fire from the Gods.* Los Angeles: Michael Wiese Productions; 1999.

About the author

Carin Roberge, PsyD, is a clinical psychologist and shamanic practitioner who has integrated various spiritual practices into her healing and teaching work for over two decades. She is a graduate of the Foundation for Shamanic Studies 3-year program and has trained with native North American healers, anthropologist Larry Peters, PhD, and with Tibetan and Nepali shamans in Nepal. She is co-director of Center of the Circle, an organization sponsoring programs in shamanism and shamanic healing in the greater Boston area, and maintains a private practice in Arlington, MA.

V

Shamanism and Psychiatry: Initiation to Integration

Stephen Proskauer, MD

In our society, mainstream healthcare is divorced from spiritual healing. When clinicians enlarge the scope of their practice to include shamanism, they must find a way to embrace two seemingly incompatible worldviews and systems of intervention. The official 'standards of care' in modern medicine do not include spiritual factors in health and disease, let alone the possibility of invoking spirit's help in treating illness. In allopathic healthcare, spiritual issues belong to the domain of the clergy, and many clinicians are therefore ambivalent about introducing shamanism into their practices. Must we shrink back from using everything we know to help our patients just because shamanism challenges the cultural biases separating spirituality from scientific medicine?

Biological sciences are still limited by the culture-bound belief that what one can't see or measure doesn't exist, or is at least irrelevant to an evidence-based scientific system. According to Shakyamuni Buddha 2,600 years ago, and confirmed with awed consternation by modern subatomic physics, not even what you *can* see and measure can be proved to have any fixed existence. Quantum theory casts doubt upon even the most fundamental assumption of objective science, that the observer is separable from the observation.

Like most people in our culture, I was detoured away from developing a personal rapport with spirit until one day I heard its voice speaking directly to me. Faced with the choice whether to label myself psychotic or blessed, I chose the blessing and decided to deepen rather than deny my relationship with spirit. Contact with native diagnosticians and medicine men as a psychiatrist on the Navajo reservation helped me to make a decision that changed the course of my life.

Now, after forty years of psychiatric and spiritual practice, I can perceive five developmental stages of integration through which I passed as spirit impacted me ever more profoundly. Each stage resembles a phase of human emotional development and involves a corresponding shift in the relationship with spirit, until finally all sense of separation vanishes.

First stage: Initiation

Through shamanic training, I first met my power animals and teachers. These vivid experiences quickly overcame any remaining skepticism about the existence of non-ordinary reality. In this stage I began the long process of surrendering to spirit guidance, feeling excitement and gratitude at being able to directly perceive the presence of spirit. The impact of my initial encounters might be compared to the relief an infant feels after waking from a nap when mother comes into the room. The helpless baby has been awake for a while crying fitfully, wet and hungry, but nobody is there. Since the infant is too young to trust that mother still exists when she cannot be seen, need and fear give way eventually to helpless rage and grief, then to hopeless despair if she never comes.

This is the vulnerable spiritual condition in which many people survive in our materialistic culture, largely by clinging to power, money, food, sex, drugs or whatever activities are available to numb existential terror or divert attention with fleeting gratifications. An underlying anxiety afflicts our society, contributing to chronic disease and unhappiness. This immature state of mind distorts our relationship with spirit, adding to inner impoverishment and disempowerment.

Skeptics and agnostics may decide to rely only on rationality and science to make sense of the world, believing there is nothing divine, while others find fragile solace in a religious faith. They pray like helpless infants to an all-powerful god for deliverance, but this god acts like an unreliable parent and hardly ever appears. To avoid this, we ordain priests and elevate gurus to whom we yield our power. At least they are clearly visible, will tell us what to believe and do, and provide the comfort of their presence. We gladly surrender to them rather than face the terror of being alone in the void.

Second stage: Experimentation

After completing advanced shamanic training, I knew how to conduct healing journeys, extractions and soul retrievals. I realized that these powerful shamanic interventions might be helpful with patients, but would shamanism be compatible with psychiatry? How would my colleagues feel about my assuming the role of shamanic healer? With which psychiatric patients and in what settings would shamanic interventions be practical and effective? And which shamanic skills would be most appropriate for psychiatric patients?

Unlike some shamanic practitioners, I was not drawn to the model of shamanic counseling that depends on the readiness of patients to journey. I felt this approach would not be appropriate for most psychiatric patients, since severely unbalanced people have a tenuous grasp on ordinary reality and have difficulty moving in and out of non-ordinary states without severe anxiety, disorientation, and even psychotic symptoms. Best to err on the side of caution and journey on their behalf, I thought, at least until they have been stable for some time.

So I embarked on a period of experimentation with less disturbed patients who were open to shamanic healing, and the positive results from this encouraged me to complement clinical approaches with shamanic methods. As I learned by trial and error when and how to conduct ceremonies with them, I found myself unwittingly influenced by assumptions from psychotherapy that did not apply to shamanism.

For example, I was treating a depressed patient who complained of feeling empty and incomplete. She was haunted by the sense that something was missing inside that she couldn't identify. Her condition sounded like a classic case of soul loss, so I proposed a soul retrieval for the following session. I congratulated myself for having carried out this complex journey successfully in my office with no one else present except the patient and me. But even though it appeared to go well at the time, the soul retrieval did not help very much. What went wrong?

Three key requirements had been ignored: I gave the patient very little time to prepare for the ceremony, no friends or family had been invited to attend, and no one was present to drum for me and help hold the space. I introduced soul retrieval casually, as if it were just another psychotherapy technique rather than a complex celebration that is inappropriate to attempt unassisted. In the name of protecting her privacy and accelerating her treatment, I had attempted single-handedly to conduct a profoundly transformative event that should have included at least one friend or relative. I had not even discussed the implications of the ceremony with her or asked her to commit herself in advance to proper self-care after the soul retrieval, underestimating the support she would need to nurture and integrate her newly reclaimed soul parts.

My arrogant attitude during this stage had adversely affected my relationship with spirit. I thought I knew better than my guides what would be best for the patient and had treated spirit as my servant, like a bossy toddler with his parents. I even believed I'd be the best person to do soul retrievals for my patients because I would know in advance when and why soul loss had occurred. I was taking my guides along just to help me find the lost soul parts in the spirit world.

Trusting professional knowledge more than spirit resulted from deep-seated resistance to giving up control. My unawareness resembled that of a willful preschool child who feels powerless and overcompensates by acting out omnipotent fantasies. Such egocentric spiritual exploitation is uncomfortably reminiscent of imperial colonization, during which spiritual traditions and native social structures are destroyed and natural resources plundered. Many indigenous peoples understandably regard the expropriation of their shamanic ceremonies by foreigners, however sincere, as stealing all they have left of their native cultures – in other words, spiritual colonialism. Much to my chagrin, I found an immature imperialist colonizing my unconscious mind and running the show from behind the scenes.

It took time for me to learn to trust spirit guidance as much as psychological training. My human teacher Jen Tarchin observed that professionals and academics are more prone to preempt spiritual power in a disrespectful and undiscerning way than are lay people, who do not bring the egoistic baggage of their expertise with them into shamanic training.

In retrospect, I realize that the overconfidence of this period compensated for feelings of inadequacy and insecurity about my unfamiliar role as a shamanic healer. Like any beginner, I wasn't sure I could do it or that it would work. As I began to feel more trusting of spirit and more at ease with shamanic interventions in the office, I noticed that some patients responded with dramatic and lasting recoveries.

For instance, during a healing journey I undertook on a patient's behalf, my spirit guide retrieved a tiny golden scepter from the bottom of a pond as an empowerment for him. Spirit instructed me to tell him that he would find a real scepter like this in ordinary reality. I hesitantly suggested he watch out for this unusual object and perhaps look for one in a toy store. The possibility that the scepter might manifest for him effortlessly never occurred to me. After searching for weeks without finding it, he suddenly spotted the exact object lying on the sidewalk right in his path, gleaming in a shaft of sunlight.

This experience enhanced my faith in the interpenetration of ordinary and non-ordinary reality. Feeling skeptical about spiritual power, I'd preempted control by instructing my client where to find the scepter rather than trusting it would appear when the time was right. I was not quite ready to let myself function as an empty vessel through which spirit could flow. Integrating shamanism into my work was not just a matter of adding new methods; it required years of dedication to empty myself of the self and its ideas to make room for spirit to enter.

Third stage: Apprehension

The issues in this stage of development resemble the concerns of the six- to ten-year-old child who is learning to follow the mores of society outside the home by relating to teachers and peers. School children can't get away with rebelling against authority in the same self-centered way toddlers can. Their challenge involves learning rules and skills more than dealing with emotional issues. Helping spirits serve as mentors in non-ordinary reality, just as school teachers help us to learn the ways of the wider human world beyond the family.

The underlying emotion surrounding any attempt to incorporate something new is apprehension. In talking with professional colleagues who were also attempting to bring shamanic healing into their practices, I learned that there is a point at which most faltered, especially if they were *purists* by nature rather than *synthesizers*. Purists adhere to a single tradition, faithfully practicing exactly as instructed, and do not readily use what they've been taught outside a ceremonial setting. For purists, maintaining the context is an intrinsic part of honoring the tradition.

Purist healthcare professionals struggle harder than synthesizers with identity issues and fears of criticism from spiritual and professional teachers and peers. When purists do make the tough decision to introduce a shamanic healing ceremony into a clinical situation, the problem is how to do it right without violating the integrity of either the ceremony or their professional role. Purists tend to regard synthesizers as being careless and disrespectful of tradition, whereas synthesizers look upon purists as overly rigid and preoccupied with insignificant details. Both types of practitioners are important: faithful purists to maintain the integrity and continuity of spiritual traditions, and innovative synthesizers to help introduce the unique benefits of these traditions into new settings.

Healthcare professionals begin like everyone else by learning shamanism outside a professional setting. Purists may deny the validity or practicality of attempting to integrate shamanic healing into their work, or they may attempt to keep a foot in both worlds and respect the boundary between them by sending their patients to other practitioners when shamanic healing is indicated. One practitioner I know came to the drastic conclusion that she had to give up her professional license and career if she wanted to practice as a shamanic healer anywhere, even outside a professional setting, because the problems of harmonizing these two roles seemed insurmountable. For purists, the chasm between cultures can seem too deep and wide to bridge.

As a synthesizer rather than a purist, my path was easier to negotiate. I also had the advantage of conducting a solo practice in my home office, free from the judgments of professional colleagues. By the time I began to call myself an integrative psychiatrist, I was experienced in shamanic healing practices and comfortable working with my spirit guides, but I remained anxious about applying shamanic healing in mainstream professional settings.

During the stage of apprehension, struggles over power and control diminish, and it becomes easier to maintain a neutral task-oriented relationship with spirit guides in helping patients. We just need to be clear about the different rules that apply in dealing with ordinary and non-ordinary reality, as though we were attending a progressive school in the morning and a military academy in the afternoon: potentially confusing, but possible if we keep a clear head and remain mindful of the environment. Once we feel more confident and relaxed about what we are doing, it's easier to work comfortably with colleagues in a clinical setting. If the social worker in the next office complains about the odor of incense or the sounds coming through the wall, it's no cause for alarm. Just burn less incense and drum or rattle more softly.

Toward the end of this stage, after becoming comfortable with shamanic practice in a clinical setting, we may begin to experience the subliminal fear of an impending transformation. This formless anxiety resembles the restless confusion of eleven- to thirteen-year-old children at the threshold of adolescence.

Fourth stage: Transformation

Whether we are purists or synthesizers, we are evolving through disciplined task-oriented apprenticeships in which our helping spirits and human mentors teach the skills we need to resolve problems. Meanwhile, our prolonged engagement with spirit is changing us in profound and unanticipated ways, leading to the fourth stage in which spirit catalyzes a deep transformation. Like adolescents leaving childhood behind, we don't recognize ourselves anymore.

After I had practiced shamanism for a number of years, strange things started to happen. Wisdom from the spirit world began to flow into my therapeutic decisions and interventions even when I wasn't consciously calling upon the spirits for assistance. The lines between shamanism and other healing practices began to blur, and ordinary and non-ordinary reality began blending into one another in spontaneous, creative synthesis. Shamanic interventions happened on the spot to suit the patient and the situation, in accord with healing intent, but not always in a familiar form. Insights and interventions occurred that were fresh and new, not clearly derived from any known theory or tradition. I felt like I was moving into uncharted territory.

Once I saw a severely disturbed patient with her family physician in a busy medical clinic. The patient had been complaining of a dark spirit trying to choke her. Repeated physical and sexual assaults starting in early childhood had caused soul loss and torn big holes in her energy field, making her vulnerable to spiritual attack by negative thought forms and predatory spirits. The setting required speed and simplicity, so I rattled around her body while explaining that I was sealing up her aura. Given the severity of her psychiatric condition, I was surprised when this simple intervention fended off the black spirit, and amazed when my rattle appeared in her dreams. Unbeknownst to her, she had inherited shamanic dream medicine from her deceased grandmother, giving her the ability to move objects between ordinary and non-ordinary realities. Somehow I had begun to dwell in the borderland between the worlds, and could see the significance of what was happening in both realities.

Healing interventions flowed effortlessly and the results seemed to be excellent, but I questioned myself. Was I running unacceptable risks with patients? Was I still in danger of misdirecting spiritual power? After all, I was cutting corners and conducting makeshift, freeform interventions. Was I irresponsibly ignoring conventional practice in both shamanism and medicine? The voice of my inner purist was whispering anxiously in my ear. For a while, I could reassure this voice that I was just responding to direction from my spirit helpers, but then I found myself saying and doing things without any awareness of being guided. I thought I'd finally gone over the edge, but the interventions kept feeling right and having a healing effect, even if I couldn't explain how or why. In reflecting afterwards what had happened, I always found wisdom.

For example, sometimes I felt prompted to choose something for a patient from my altar as a spiritual gift. Often an object would draw my attention or ask outright to be chosen. Once when I picked an eager stuffed otter, the patient's eyes widened and she asked, "How did you know that otter is my favorite animal?" She was delighted to hear that the otter had also chosen her.

My work with dreams was dramatically transformed during this period. A patient who was going through a traumatic divorce recounted a vivid dream of being trapped in a snowbound rural house trying to escape from threatening men next door. Some other people stood around a fire in her back yard. She tried to escape by the front way in her truck, but it slid into a snow bank and the scary men grabbed her. Not enough time remained in the session to work with her dream, but a few days later while taking a shower, I saw the dream scene suddenly appear before me in amazing detail. I noticed a trail leading off into the woods behind the house and sensed that the people standing around the fire were friendly allies. When my patient returned for her next appointment, I told her about my experience and suggested she do a waking journey into the world of the dream, an active imagination exercise that involved visioning without formal journeywork. Escaping through the back door this time, she found that the people around the fire were friendly guides telling her to take the path into the woods and keep going. This event was the first in a series of spiritual experiences that empowered the patient and freed her from a failed marriage. Six months later she mentioned that she was still following that path through the woods and learning something new around each bend.

A spontaneous glimpse into the world of one patient's dream taught me that dreams could function as portals into other realms, the remembered dream being like the framed portion of a much larger picture. If we enter the picture and explore beyond the limits of the frame, we can find hidden treasure in the simplest dream. This inspired me to include shamanic dreamwork in my practice. Many breakthroughs with patients and several exciting workshops developed out of that vision in the shower that one morning.

Fifth stage: Integration

What was going on? This certainly was not shamanism as I had known it, but my patients kept having breakthroughs, so the change in my work seemed unlikely to be unbalanced or inappropriate. Transformation had opened me to the next stage of development: seamless integration, a state of pure undifferentiated healing that was creative and spontaneous that went beyond form into the unknown.

This practice can't be labeled as a particular brand of healing; it's not a definable discipline. Its flavor is unique for each healer since it involves an equal partnership among mind, body and spirit – the very essence of the healing process as it manifests moment to moment in the encounter between patient and healer.

My clinical work now includes the occasional use of standard shamanic rituals during psychiatric treatment, but more frequently takes the form of spontaneous interventions beyond any familiar shamanic, psychotherapeutic or psychiatric reference points. For me, it's not so important where interventions come from as long as they serve the patient well.

Is it still 'shamanism' if spirit operates directly through me without the appearance of intermediary spirit guides and teachers making their presences consciously felt? Some purists might say no, but the process has the same subjective qualities of clarity, ease and fluidity as shamanic journeywork. It functions the same way and gets the same favorable results. I'm no longer aware of discontinuities between formal shamanic healing practices and these freeform responses. The difference is that I have to take full responsibility for everything that happens. While I cannot defer to higher authorities, my guides are always ready to show up if I call on them. To remind me about staying on track, I keep a seven-foot wooden carving of my primary power animal, the giraffe, in the corner of the office. Since he has a long neck, he can always see what's happening.

Negotiating the transformation stage is like passing through the turbulence of adolescence that dispels old patterns, dethrones idealized parental images from childhood, and opens the way for a new synthesis. Integration ushers in spiritual adulthood. We create a fresh identity, a unique blend of life experience with personal temperament, newly evolved ideals, and self-directed destiny. Stable self-confidence cannot manifest until this level of maturity has been established.

Experience teaches that human spirituality is expressed through the filter of personal ego. That is why spiritual maturation into clarity and discernment cannot take place without psychological maturation into differentiated and integrated adulthood. When this maturation process fails, spiritual power feeds into immature narcissism. Personal charisma masquerades as wisdom, attracting gullible followers. The confusion between spiritual power and psychological maturity sets the stage for sorcery and the tyranny of cults. All of the ugly stuff hidden in the shadows of the personality must be raised up from the dark depths into the light of consciousness before any human being is capable of becoming a clear channel for spirit. This is why I had to go into psychotherapy for myself, to clean the smudged lens that was interfering with my discernment and magnifying the harm I could do to myself and others in exercising spiritual power. Our integrity as healers depends on remaining constantly vigilant to detect signs of distortion that can arise throughout our lives.

Integration has changed my perception of reality. I began to see my patients and the whole world with a panoramic vision that included all six dimensions of human experience – physical, psychological, relational, karmic, energetic and transcendent – all distinct, yet intimately interconnected.

With all the change that has come about over many years of spiritual practice, some things remain the same. Each morning I offer incense and call in the spirits of the six directions with gratitude, invoking their healing power and feeling a rush of warm energy flowing through my body. The Bodhisattva of Compassion, Kanzeon, appears at the still center of the six directions, extending a loving hand to me and to all suffering beings. I call upon Kanzeon to dwell in my heart and help me offer unconditional compassion and wisdom to all who come through my door that day. After that invocation, I relax and respond to each patient with whatever is appropriate to the moment: prescription, meditation, insight, story, journal assignment, healing ritual, nutritional supplement, breathwork or past life regression. I often find myself listening to what comes out of my mouth with amazement as I receive teaching and healing along with the patient. I trust the flow of this process and no longer think as much about how to integrate psychiatric, psychological and spiritual methods, except perhaps when I am writing about the process or trying to explain it to others.

Conclusion

Unconditional love always has been the true healer. If I do not have to do the healing, there's no mental effort. The process unfolds naturally, unobstructed by the doubting mind. The art of integrative healing depends on but also transcends the mastery of many techniques. I function merely as the lens through which healing energy passes on its way to the patient. The issue then becomes how and where to focus that energy in order to restore balance most effectively.

After many years, I feel free to allow various perspectives and the techniques that go with them to shift from moment to moment as the need arises. I have stumbled into the mysterious terrain beyond the limits of familiar shamanic ritual, psychotherapeutic methodology and mainstream psychiatry. I will never be the same nor will reality ever look to me as it once did. The union of healing and transformation has become both teacher and spiritual practice. By the grace of spirit, the Inner Shaman now comes forth to help me realize and express an all-inclusive wholeness.

About the author

Stephen Proskauer, MD, is a psychiatrist, psychotherapist, family therapist, breathworker, past lives therapist, Zen monk, and shamanic healer. He practices child, adolescent, and adult psychiatry at the Sanctuary for Healing and Integration in Salt Lake City, Utah. He is author of *Karmic Therapy: Healing the Split Psyche*; *Big Heart Healing: Multidimensional Treatment of Trauma and Abuse*; and is preparing to publish his first novel, *Gaia's Web,* a near future science fiction saga in which the major character practices shamanism as well as visionary computer science.

Shamanism in Conventional Healthcare Settings

VI

Reverent Participatory Relationship in Integrative Medicine

Evelyn C. Rysdyk

Modern healthcare as it is currently practiced often does not meet the needs of either patients or practitioners. Patients complain of feeling rushed, ignored as a person, and not listened to, while practitioners feel they haven't been able to give the kind of care they dreamed they would be able to offer when they were in training. An atmosphere of suspicion and mistrust frequently exists among practitioners of widely differing disciplines as well.

Into this setting we began an experiment of sorts: introducing into a multidisciplinary healthcare clinic a time-tested, shamanic perspective that relationship with 'other' is an intrinsic source of power. We understood this perspective could potentially offer a framework within which to create a more functional and effective healthcare model for all participants and for the clinic's organizational governance and operation as well.

Historical relationship with 'other'

The model for this experiment dates back over 12,000 years. Historically, the earliest magico-religious way human beings interacted with the world was through animism. First coined by English anthropologist Sir Edward Tylor in 1871, animism comes from the Latin word, *anima*, or soul. It describes the belief that everything that surrounds us is alive: plants, animals, birds, landscape features such as rivers and mountains, forces such as wind and rain. Animists believe that each part of the environment has a vital essence or spirit.

Archeological evidence suggests that prior to the Neolithic Era of twelve thousand years ago, before the development of agriculture, all human beings practiced a hunter/gatherer lifestyle. In this earliest form of social organization all members of a tribal group participated in the ultimate survival and wellbeing of the whole.[1] Anthropological evidence reveals that these ancient hunter/gatherer peoples viewed the world from an animist perspective, perhaps stemming from a need to better understand the 'others' that human beings depended on for survival beyond the human community. Seeing all of the elements of the landscape as living beings implied the necessity for communication with them in order to facilitate relationship. In such cultures, the one charged with the job of communicating with these 'others' was the person identified as what we now refer to as a shaman or facilitator between the human realm and the other spirits that inhabit the environment. Since shamanism is a global phenomenon and these understandings about relationship and interdependency are part of this way of being, this suggests that that the shamanic way of perceiving the world is a part of our collective human history.

The many spirit beings that are available for relationship are also potential sources of power for the shaman. Since the shaman's ability to heal is based upon the power-filled relationships he or she forges with the spirits,[2] an attitude of harmonious give-and-take becomes the guiding principle in exchanges within those associations, reflecting the hunter/gatherer understanding of mutual interdependence and the necessity to work cooperatively. The Quechua-speaking pacos or shaman-healers of the high Andes refer to this idea of mutual, respectful interaction as ayni, a word that is translated as sacred reciprocity. They believe that this state of being is the basis for health and wellbeing and must always be monitored and lovingly attended to. Referring to this mutually beneficial interchange as sacred helps us appreciate that there is a kind of holiness to being in right relationship that puts us somehow more in alignment with the fundamental framework of existence.

Since shamans have successfully worked with the conceptual framework of sacred reciprocity and its impact on health and wellbeing for many thousands of years, it seems useful for deliverers of healthcare to pay attention to this perceptual model.

The community of people that gathered together for the experiment that eventually evolved into the unique, multidisciplinary health center known as True North consisted of a very diverse group of practitioners. It became clear early on that it was critical to establish common ground for this community — who belonged to different healing 'tribes' as individuals — if they were going to be able to work well together. Each healthcare modality represented in the group had its own way of perceiving the patient and his disease, a different education, different terminologies and inherent prejudices about what constituted 'good medicine.' Like members of a hunter/gatherer society, we found ourselves in an environment of 'others' with whom we needed to relate in a mutually beneficial way to create a healing container for our patients and for each other as practitioners. We needed a cultural model for our interactions that would promote harmony and health.

The modern English word 'culture' is based on a term used by the Roman philosopher Cicero, who wrote of the cultivation of the soul or *cultura animi*.[3] So our term 'culture' actually relates to a collective experience reflecting the consciousness of the people it connects.

In the midst of the thousands of volunteer hours the multidisciplinary group donated in planning our new cultural model, circle member Sister Mary Consuela White coined the phrase 'reverent participatory relationship' to describe the way of being we were trying to develop. This phrase subsequently became a fundamental guiding principle in all of our interactions. The word *reverent* implies feeling and expresses a profound respect or veneration as well as a willingness to show consideration or appreciation. *Participatory* means that we engage in participation which the Merriam-Webster Dictionary of Law defines as, "the action or state of taking part in something: as in association with others in a relationship or an enterprise usually on a formal basis with specified rights and obligations." In our context, the obligation may be seen, at least in part, as remaining considerate and respectful while taking part in any interaction.

David Reilly, MD, has shown that an effective therapeutic encounter where a healing response has been engendered is based in such an understanding of relationship. In his April 2005 presentation "Creating Therapeutic Encounters," he suggests that, "traditional and indigenous healing systems including shamanism have spent a long time learning about these things. Translating it to our world is the challenge." He noted that human recovery is a built-in potential that can be modified for good and bad by human interaction and that being considerate and respectful and really listening to the patient can become a primary healing modality. Among traditional shamanic healers, this approach is widely understood as pivotal to having effective outcomes. For instance, traditional Central and South American shamanic practitioners or curanderas(os) speak of the *pláticas*, or heart-to-heart, as a method to "uncover the real root of the problem, not what the person thinks is the problem."[4]

Maintaining a reverent attitude in all interactions is, in and of itself, a challenge when we consider that in our current Western culture we do not generally respect one another's perspectives nor do we see the fundamental interdependencies with nature and with each other. Furthermore, our societal perspectives on relationship are skewed by unhealthy relational manifestations such as power abuse or codependency. Our group posited that putting a supportive framework in place at True North to encourage both reverence and participation would be key to addressing this challenge.

The resource we chose for facilitating reverent participatory relationship was the use of *circle process*.[5] Using the circle as a modern organizational structure appeared in the book *Calling The Circle: The First and Future Culture*, by Christina Baldwin; however, the circle as an organizational and societal structure is actually quite ancient. Echoes of circles as a uniting principle may still be found among the world's indigenous cultures. Whether expressed as a medicine wheel, circle dance, council circle or in circular dwellings such as Sami *lavuu* or Lakota *teepee*, this form is deeply ingrained into our collective consciousness. Perhaps it's in our genes to be at home in a circle, as our DNA carries direct connections to our indigenous, tribal ancestors. Ursula K. LeGuin once described our genes affecting a kind of immortality as they passed through thousands of generations: "All you can say of it is that it is, and it is, and it is. No beginning, no end. All middle."[6] A perfect description of a circle.

Reverent participatory relationship: an effective, nonhierarchical form of governance

To develop effective and humane ways of delivering multidisciplinary care, it is necessary for hierarchical behavior and modality-centric tribalism among the practitioners to be neutralized so that a deep and reverent participatory relationship can begin. Circle process provides such a framework.

Circle process is not simply holding meetings while sitting in a circle, but rather is a cultural and organizational model that incorporates specific principles and practices. Circle process as practiced at True North incorporates three principles, three practices and four agreements.

Three Principles

• *Leadership is shared*
Each meeting of the circle is facilitated through rotating leadership by a different member of the True North community. In addition, leadership within a circle may shift moment-to-moment based on present need or tasks.

- *Responsibility is shared*
Even though a facilitator is present, every member of the circle helps keep to the form. We also support each other to take action by calling for a moment of silence or breath when the circle becomes unfocused or unbalanced.

- *Center is held by reliance on Spirit*
The circle understands that inspiration comes from all around us, not simply our training or even the collective wisdom of those gathered in the circle. The center of the circle and the objects we place there remind us of Spirit, a higher purpose for our work, and the larger world toward which we have responsibility.

Three Practices of Council

- *Attentive listening*
This includes actually looking at the person who is speaking, remaining still inside and outside physically as she or he speaks, and attending to *hearing* what is said by the person rather than being busy thinking about your reply while you wait for them to finish speaking!

- *Intentional speaking*
This involves taking the time to compose clear communication without judgment or blame. Our contributions to the circle need to have relevance, heart, and meaning for the topic being discussed.

- *Compassionate self-monitoring of one's behavior*
We need to consider the power and impact that our words and actions may have upon others.

Four Agreements

- *Confidentiality*
"What is said in circle, remains in circle." By keeping the circle confidential, i.e., limiting the sharing of any circle content to the True North community, we support people to take more risks and encourage creativity.

- *Listening to each other as witnesses without making judgments*
This means there can be multiple right opinions in any situation. Once all ideas are heard, we can discuss and discern what may become a consensus viewpoint.

- *Asking for what you need and offering what you can*
Each person is encouraged to participate and is also encouraged to take good care of oneself by not over-doing.

- *Pausing at times of uncertainty or when the circle needs a resting point*
Whenever this may occur, we agree to fall into silence, take a breath and ask Spirit for guidance.

Circle Process in Action: The Format of a Circle Meeting

- *Creating the center of the circle with meaningful objects*
Our center changes from circle meeting to circle meeting and may range from a collection of individually contributed objects to a simple candle. Often, we have a teacup and saucer in the center. This object is a symbol of hospitality for the Sisters of Mercy and was contributed to our circle by Sister Consuela. She told the story of how the founder of the order, while on her deathbed, had told those attending her to make sure the weary sisters had a "comfortable cup of tea" after she was gone. So, this teacup reminds us of the need to truly and lovingly receive each other and our patients.

- *Beginning with a time for silent reflection*
In the midst of a hectic day, the ten to fifteen minutes of silence we give each other before a circle begins is a gift. No phones ringing, no talking, no busyness; just sitting together in meditative silence.

- *Taking four breaths together*
We take one breath to let go of whatever it took to get there, one to focus on the present and the work we have to do, one to invite what's next, and one to step into action. Like the meditative beginning, this action provides every person present an opportunity for centering and focus.

- *Opening with a reading*
Whoever facilitates the circle that day usually offers a reading, but anyone can bring a reading to share. The readings are as diverse as the practitioner community itself.

- *Checking in*
This is a brief statement about what energy you bring to the circle. This is not an extended storytelling time, but a chance to gather our energy for the work to be

done. We ask that participants observe compassionate self-monitoring to ensure that everyone has a chance to speak so that we have enough time to complete our tasks. We may also ask to list our agenda before the check-in begins so that all are aware of the tasks ahead.

• *Attending to agenda items*
These are discussed using group process and may include brainstorming and problem solving.

• *Making decisions*
We figure out exactly what needs to be done and who will be responsible for working on it.

• *Closing*
This may be a simple as a breath of gratitude or a reading.

Additional Notes

• *Each person takes responsibility*
Each person asks the circle for the support she or he wants and needs as well as takes responsibility for responding to and acting upon specific requests.

• *Anyone in the circle may call for silence*
The form this may take is to ask for a breath or ritual to establish focus, to center, or to remember the need for spiritual guidance.

• *Agreements can be updated*
If something is not working, we revise the agreement and maintain the process.

At True North, we function by using multiple circles. We have a large circle that meets once a month in which overall policies and concerns are brought up and processed. All practitioners and staff members are included in this circle and all of the voices are heard and valued. In addition, we have several work-focused circles that answer to the larger circle. All members of the True North community are welcome to choose what task circles they wish to participate in based on their interest.

We also create task-oriented circles whenever a need arises. An example of this is our Ethics Circle that created a document that was inclusive of the ethical guidelines of every healing tradition practiced at True North. This document resulted in all members of our community being able to attend the case presentations and occurred prior to the enactment of the new Health Insurance Portability and Accountability Act (HIPAA) guidelines. We found that our document was even more stringent than the one offered by the federal government. A weekly Decision Circle is charged by the larger circle with attending to those administrative tasks that need to be accomplished in a more rapid fashion than the larger circle may be able to provide. Members of this circle are drawn from the entire community of True North and are composed of conventional and complementary practitioners, on-site and affiliate practitioners and office staff.

This framework has become our model for working in community, but no model, however effective, can function well without sufficient attention being paid to the invisible interactions in which we all engage. Humans interact on many levels. While we are most familiar with the obvious ways that we communicate, cajole and even consciously try to influence one another, we also profoundly affect each other through our feelings. Certainly we know these invisible, emotional energies have the ability to disrupt our conscious interactions, but what is now beginning to be understood is how they can impact our individual and collective wellbeing, as well.

Reverent participatory relationship: being conscious and responsible about feelings

"Create a place of peace and healing will happen."[7]

Over the millennia, shamans have gained mastery over the invisible world, and our emotional energy is a part of the invisible world that impacts our visible one as powerfully as any spirit. When we consciously decide to enter into relationship using the circle as a framework, we become aware of how we can affect each other's health and well being through our feelings. Feelings and their effects can have an enormous impact on the effectiveness of circle process. For instance, when we notice if someone around us is in a bad mood, it can very quickly become contagious. This kind of energy may even contribute to illness. *"The shamanic perception of well being...depend(s) on ideas of balance, flow and equilibrium in the environment, and on ideas of giving and withholding, love and anger, and motivation and intention among the spirits which animate this environment."*[8] (my emphasis) So, when presented with situations that may cause us to become angry or anxious, we have opportunities to work with feelings that arise during interactions and not only experience personal growth, but learn another resource for healing others. When we look at the following data through the shamanic lens, we can also see that our feelings affect the very same sphere of reality beyond linear time/space that a shaman would refer to as the spirit world.

Studies by Rein and McCraty of the Institute of HeartMath have demonstrated that the quantum fields generated by our human feelings can influence neurological and immunological functions at a cellular level.[9] In their work, they determined that when we experience deep feelings of love, compassion or gratitude, we radiate coherent frequencies throughout the body that promote health and vitality. Conversely, when we experience feelings such as anger, anxiety, fear and rage, we directly affect the body in harmful and damaging ways. Laboratory analyses measuring the levels of SIgA (salivary immunoglobulin A), an easy-to-measure immune system indicator, have proven that a ten-minute expression of anger produces a six-hour decline in a test subject's SIgA. Conversely, a ten-minute period of feeling compassion, love or gratitude produces a measurable six-hour boost in this immune system indicator.

Other research by Glen Rein, Ph.D. and Rollin McCraty, Ph.D. has shown that our feelings are broadcast as both measurable electromagnetic energy and also as a non-Hertzian quantum field.[10] Indeed, these non-local quantum field effects have been measured over distances of half a mile.[11] In lay terms, that means that our feelings produce measurable energetic effects that are not limited by either time or space, and these feeling-generated energies affect not only the spaces inside our bodies but the world around us.

Additional research[12] by Rein and McCraty shows how our feelings affect the conformation of our DNA. When we are feeling love, gratitude, appreciation and compassion, the DNA molecule in our cells assumes a perfect conformation of the now-familiar spiral ladder. When we feel angry or afraid, our DNA molecule winds tightly onto itself. This alteration of its structure can negatively affect how well the DNA can do its job. These researchers also discovered that a person generating strong feelings changes the configuration of a sample of someone else's DNA, as well as their own. In other words, if we are angry or anxious, our emotional energy can have the effect of shutting down the overall health potential of our bodies and also of those around us! On the other hand, those people who cultivate feelings of love, gratitude, appreciation or compassion not only protect the healthy function of their own bodies, they also produce measurable beneficial effects on others and develop physiological and psychological resilience in the face of stressful situations.[13] This suggests that, as healers, we have a responsibility for developing a practice of generating coherent, harmonious energies such as those produced when we experience gratitude.

As the circle learned about the power of gratitude and began practicing this way of being, we realized that loving kindness, patience, and true caring flowed effortlessly from a grateful heart. This attitude also made it far easier to reduce any sense of separateness or separation from others, be it separations between patient and practitioner, between conventional or complementary practices or practitioners, or even between the aspects of life that might be defined as either sacred or profane. If indeed everything and everyone is sacred, then even the most arduous task or difficult interpersonal situation can be met with more grace. We discovered that this shift in attitude changes everything, and members of the circle have worked to be more conscious and aware of their feelings and attentive to transforming disruptive emotional states.

Reverent participatory relationship: interdisciplinary consultations and diagnoses

The complexities of our patients' presenting issues often leave us wondering if we have gathered all the data we need to help them on their road to healing. One key to providing the very best multidisciplinary holistic care is to access the collective wisdom of all practitioners in the group. This means setting up opportunities to hear the perspective and approaches of different modalities. For instance, an osteopathic physician may see a different path of healing for a patient than an allopathically trained physician or one that uses a Functional Medicine approach. An acupuncturist has a completely different viewpoint of patients' presenting issues than may be offered though energy medicine, and a shamanic practitioner's methods (such as the shamanic journey process) offer opportunities to access the information that lies just beyond the reach of our ordinary perceptions. How best to combine the scientific and complementary healing approaches into a powerful resource?

Accessing the breadth of combined medical and complementary healing knowledge requires a format within which to share it. One possible venue can be a case presentation; however, a typical medical case presentation is frequently fraught with competitiveness, ego and criticism. It also does not necessarily offer opportunities for creative input or the input of practitioners of complementary disciplines. In addition, typical case presentations do not offer the opportunity to support the primary practitioner in her or his care of the patient. Even more importantly, the 'case' usually focuses on the patient as a collection of symptoms, rather than as a whole person.

At True North, we practice a new way of entering into a reverent conversation with each other about patient care. This involves replacing the typical format of a case presentation used in hospitals to one that not only includes all the same pertinent data, but also offers opportunities to include psychosocial and spiritual information about the patient in a respectful atmosphere that encourages multidisciplinary collaboration. Our ultimate desire is to eventually have the patient actually present for his or her own case presentation and to receive real time input from the group.

Relationship-Centered, Patient Case Presentation Process

Before beginning, we remind the assembled group to:

• Pay attention to process as well as content

• Review Circle Process rules and covenants

• Recognize that we all learn as we go

• Use a bell or some other pleasant sound to signal phases

The format includes 10 minutes at the end of the presentation for feedback on the process itself, and all participants have an outline of blinded patient information.

Actual Process Format:

1. Assign a facilitator
Do this at least initially, to keep the process on track.

2. Take breaths –5 minutes
This is a time for short silent meditation for transition, grounding and setting the intention for the consultation including what the presenting practitioner wants from the presentation.

At this point, we bring the patient's and gathered group's Higher Selves into the room by asking that this be for the best and highest good for all persons that are involved. We take time to remember that this patient is a not a collection of symptoms, but rather a human being deserving of our respectful attention. The practitioner introduces the patient to the circle as though he or she were introducing a friend. We learn about what kind of person he or she is, what ties and responsibilities he or she has, the patient's emotional connections, his or her presenting health issue and what interventions the patient has already been pursuing. This is quite powerful, as we then have to look at our communications from the standpoint of feeling that the person in question is actually present. To aid in this connection to the person, we visualize connecting our hearts with the patient's heart like spokes on a wheel.

We then ask for our own intuition and non-local intelligence to be present for assistance towards the highest healing of the patient. This reminds each of us to not only rely on our brain, but on our own whole being. We also remind each other to use as little technical jargon from our individual disciplines as possible and to speak both plainly and with compassion. This is also the point at which those who have the skill employ the shamanic journey process to check on the patient and their condition.

3. Information Gathering Phase –15 minutes
At this point we silently review the patient information (one page, blinded to patient's specific identity) that has been handed out. Then the presenting clinician or complementary practitioner reviews the highlights and what information about the person stands out most for him/her. At this point in the process, no problem solving occurs.

The circle considers the information that was presented and allows each person present to connect head and heart. At this time, practitioners become clear about what wisdom they want to share.

4. Brainstorming/problem-solving –20 minutes
During this part of the process, we go around the circle, each offering our perspectives on the patient's issues. By proceeding in this fashion, we ensure that each voice is heard and all wisdom is gathered.

5. Close consultation circle
At the close, the circle offers gratitude to the patient's Higher Self, to Spirit and each other for compassionate wisdom. We then release patient's Higher Self. In this way the patient's spirit is only present for the initial work and not the final processing of the material.

6. Feedback about process – 10 minutes
At this phase, we get input from the group, the facilitator, and the presenting clinician about what was useful or not useful, how best to support the clinician/

practitioner, what it may have stirred up for clinician/practitioner and the larger circle, etc. We added this section to the process to be able to recognize and facilitate the possibility that in a healing interaction the healer, as well as the patient, may be impacted.

7. Close session with breaths
This format has provided the opportunity to support patients in ways that might not be possible without True North's unique approach. One example of this collaborative case presentation approach is a woman in her fifties who experienced a temporary psychosis upon having a profound spiritual experience while in New Mexico. The patient was exhibiting marked disconnection from reality and behaving in accordance with an illusionary perception of the world. She also expressed a fear of self-harm, so the True North shamanic healers and a True North psychotherapist collaborated in having her hospitalized. Upon her release, the healers referred her to the True North psychiatrist and presented her case with the intent to access the wisdom of the circle. The assembled practitioners provided suggestions that included supportive nutritional supplementation, gentle massage, continued shamanic support and regular psychotherapy. While visits with the psychiatrist and pharmacological solutions were included in the plan, through the additional support of her shamanic healers, massage therapist and osteopathic physician, the client was able to stabilize and return to ordinary living without the need for medication. Since her initial episode, and in spite of subsequent flashbacks to severe childhood abuse, the patient has had no return of her perceptional delusions or destructive behavior.

Conclusion

As True North continues into its second decade, it is clear that the challenges any group faces in creating a truly integrative medical center may be aided by using the shamanic perspectives of reverent participatory relationship, as well as attending to the participants' invisible, spiritual and energetic interactions. The shaman's viewpoint recognizes that every thing and every being is interconnected and that our relationships with 'others' can be a source of power and healing. In writing about the effectiveness of the healings provided by indigenous shamans, Hyman says "The role of community in the healing process created a container for the sick to be cleansed, free, and able to see and know meaning and purpose in the family of human beings. The process created balance and realignment. It addressed body and soul sickness at the root." [14]

In keeping spirit on equal footing with mind-body medicine, we continue to have shamanic practitioners work side-by-side with conventional medical, mental health and complementary practitioners to provide a uniquely supportive and whole way of delivering care. Recent publications about integrative health care support the need to embrace collaborative care that includes a 'full spectrum' of effective modalities.[15] At True North, we have shown that combining shamanic healing with a relationship-centered approach that respects the efficacy and importance of differing modalities of care is effective for those we serve and for practitioners as well.

References

[1] Pringle H. "New Women of the Ice Age." *Discover Magazine* April 1998; 19: 4: 62-69.

[2] Vitebsky P. *The Shaman*. Boston: Little Brown & Company; 1995; 22-25.

[3] http://en.wikipedia.org/wiki/Culture.

[4] Avila E. *Woman Who Glows in the Dark*. New York: Jeremy P. Tarcher/Putnam; 1999; 213.

[5] Baldwin C. *Calling the Circle: The First and Future Culture*. New York: Bantam Books; 1998.

[6] Le Guin U. *Dancing at the Edge of the World: Thoughts on Words, Women, Places*. New York: Grove Press; 1989; 39.

[7] Sister Mary Consuela White. Personal communication.

[8] Vitebsky P.; 99-100.

[9] Much of the scientific research in this section may be found in *Science of the Heart: Exploring the Role of the Heart in Human Performance*, a bound overview of research conducted by the Institute of Heart Math. http://www.heartmath.org/ Access to electronic copies of their research is also available on this site.

[10] Rein G. and McCraty R. "Effects of Conscious Intention on Human DNA." *Proceeds of the International Forum on New Science*. Denver CO; October 1996; 5.

[11] Rein G. and McCraty R. "Local and Non-Local Effects of Coherent Heart Frequencies on Conformational Changes of DNA." *Proceeds of the Joint USPA/APR Psychotronics Conference*. Milwaukee, WI; 1993; 4.

[12] Rein G.; 2-6.

[13] Childre D. and Rozman D. *Transforming Stress.* Oakland, CA: New Harbinger Publications; 2005; 97-98.

[14] Hyman M. "The First Mind-Body Medicine: Bringing Shamanism Into the 21St Century." *Alternative Therapies in Health and Medicine* 2007; 13: 4: 10-11.

[15] Thayer L. "The Adoption of Shamanic Healing Into the Biomedical Healthcare System in the United States." Accepted doctoral dissertation, University of Massachusetts Department of Anthropology, Amherst; 2009; 228-232.

About the author

Evelyn C. Rysdyk is a teacher of shamanism, healer and artist in joint practice with C. Allie Knowlton, LCSW, DCSW at *Spirit Passages,* their training center for advanced experiential shamanism. As founding members of *True North,* an integrated medical center in Falmouth, Maine, they also collaborate with physicians, nurses, a psychiatrist, naturopath and other complementary health practitioners. Ms. Rysdyk's latest book, *Spirit Walking, A Course In Shamanic Power,* (RedWheel/Weiser, Spring 2013) focuses upon the pivotal role healthy and vibrant relationships play in a shaman's ability to be effective in the world.

VII

Shamanism in the Surgical Suite

Carol M. Tunney, MD

Modern surgical practices have profoundly enhanced our ability to restore health and extend life. While the surgical process is increasingly attentive to the mind-body-spirit connection, surgery is ultimately a physical solution for a physical problem. Introducing shamanic practices into the surgical setting provides a framework for addressing both the underlying spiritual cause of illness and the traumatic impact of the surgery, and fosters healing on all levels: spiritual, emotional, and physical.

Just as shamanic practices support surgical work, surgery contributes to the power of the shamanic healing. For shamanic practice to be effective, bridging the work on the spiritual plane to physical reality is crucial. In turn, the surgery itself can anchor shamanic healing when the surgeon and the surgical team consciously perceive the surgery as a sacred ceremony held in a sacred space.

Surgery as sacred ceremony

When viewing surgery as a sacred event, it is important to remember that shamanism is a spiritual practice, not a religion. The principles of shamanism can easily be applied within the context of one's own (or the patient's) beliefs. When surgery is recognized as a sacred ceremony, the surgeon or surgical team becomes the shaman or 'priest;' however, neither surgeon nor the surgical team requires any special training to create this ceremony. What is required to infuse the surgical procedure with the power of the sacred is conscious awareness of the energy or intention that they are creating, and the focusing of their energy entirely upon the patient and the procedure at hand.

In *The Rites of Passage,* anthropologist Arnold van Gennep identified the criteria that are consistently found to be present in sacred ceremonies. These aspects of ritual include the performance of the ceremony at a special location, specific clothing particular to the ritual, special language distinct from ordinary conversation, highly trained and respected practitioners, and the inclusion of unusual and often highly vulnerable behaviors as part of the ceremony. Deviation from any condition is strictly taboo and results in immediate, and possibly dire, consequences.

Surgical procedures meet the all of these criteria. The operating room (OR) is a special location, used for no other purpose other than surgery. As in rituals, the room undergoes special preparation before and cleansing after procedures, and only 'initiates' of the ceremony – the doctors, nurses, technicians, and patient – can enter the space. In order to enter the space, special costumes and masks must be worn. Any violation of the OR dress code results in immediate consequences.

As an intern, immediately after scrubbing I absent-mindedly scratched my masked nose with my newly gloved hand. Though a simple change of gloves or even gloves and gown would have been sufficient to restore sterility, I was chastised by the scrub nurse and 'banished' from the OR until I 'purified' myself by scrubbing for another full five minutes.

Purification is a common element of ceremonies, and because interrupting the integrity of a sterile field endangers the patient, it is an appropriate taboo that the surgical initiate must honor at all times. In breaking the sterile field I violated a taboo, thus the simple solution to restoring the sterile field was not an option. The sanction for violating this taboo required public chastisement and that the purification ritual be reinitiated from the beginning.

To enter the OR all participants must wear special clothing, and the surgical team wears masks, gowns and gloves. Masks and costuming are important aspects of ceremony and are often utilized in shamanic cultures and healing to signify the transition of the practitioner from the realm of the ordinary to an empowered state, merged with divine helping spirits. In contrast, the patient is wearing a flimsy short gown that highlights the vulnerability of the 'initiate,' seemingly stripped of protection, status, power, and modesty.

Ceremonies include special language, and medical jargon is its own language to allow practitioners to communicate efficiently with their peers, but which can be alienating to patients and often requires translation. At times it is deliberately cryptic to avoid unduly alarming a patient in a tense or emergent situation. Jargon effectively separates the practitioners who hold the power from the patients who are dependent upon the practitioners to assist them through their health crisis or passage.

As for special behavior, there is no other situation in Western culture where it would be even remotely deemed sane for people to consent to relinquish control of their essentially naked and unconscious body to a group of masked individuals who will then cut into their bodies with knives!

Most importantly, the surgeon and the surgical team are trusted because of their status as the 'priests' and 'disciples' of the ceremony. Rigorous training and licensing empowers the surgical team to perform acts strictly forbidden by law for the uninitiated (i.e. untrained). Recognizing the surgical team as 'high priests' of the OR underscores the importance of the words and actions of the surgical team and their subsequent emotional and psychological impact upon the patient. For this reason, the surgeon or the surgical team is responsible for establishing a sacred space.

Spaces are designated as sacred when they exist for a specific purpose or because of special events that occur at a particular place. While that definition applies to the OR, there is a much more powerful context for sacred space. A place can be made sacred by the energy generated in a group when they are united in intention, focus, and love.

In *Medicine for the Earth*, Sandra Ingerman states, "Creating sacred space, as I refer to it here, means the vast energy created by people's individual energies joining together in a room.... When everyone in a room is focused on using their energy to support, love, and heal others, that is exactly what occurs, and this is the energy that supports miracles."

Traditionally, shamanic healing is a community event, precisely because of the power that can be generated and accessed for healing when people gather in groups with open hearts and focused intention. The surgical team is such a community. Ideally, it is a community that will be expanded to include the presence of a spiritual healer to be present from pre-operative procedures through the recovery period to attend to the spiritual, energetic, and emotional needs of the patient.

Inclusion of a healer is critical, for although the attention of a surgical team is certainly focused upon the procedure, too often the atmosphere in the OR from a patient perspective is chaotic, rushed, and impersonal. Hectic OR schedules, emergencies, the technical demands of surgery, and medical economics limit the availability of the surgeons and nurses to the patient during the surgical process. Often, most people on the surgical team are unknown to the patient. The presence of a healer would provide the patient with emotional security and continuity of care in addition to the power of the spiritual healing work.

Diane's experience is a powerful example of patient perception and the impact of perception on the reality of the patient's experience. She underwent an emergency Cesarean section for a birth complication and suffered profound soul loss. Below is her account of her pre-operative experience and her impassioned plea for a designated surgical attendant to be strictly present with and *to* the patient at all times.

> I was wheeled to the OR in a knee-chest position. My face was in a pillow and my hips, covered only by a sheet, were up in the air. The surgical team had been called in emergently, and I had never met most of them. I was stripped of my support; my husband and even my midwife weren't allowed in the room. I felt acutely ignored, isolated, and angry during the chaotic rush to begin surgery. . . . most of the people in the room hadn't even seen my face, and I had no idea who they were or what they were doing. The energy was awful, and that was the last thing I was going to feel before they put me to sleep. Someone had to take charge of it, so I yelled out "Who here believes in God?" The room fell totally silent and then one by one, everyone walked up and looked me in the face and said "I do," " I do." So I said "Well, you better let her in the room."

While interviewing Diane after her experience, she implored:

> You need to tell them [medical personnel] that their most important job is to safeguard the patient throughout the surgery, and that means more than just taking care of the physical body. It's about connecting with and providing a lifeline to the soul of the patient. You have to look at and see and know the patient. No one looked into my eyes [after the surgery] and saw that I wasn't there, that I hadn't come back!

Diane's story is an important reminder that what to the medical community is a well rehearsed and efficient hustle to save precious time can easily and reasonably be perceived as disconnected chaos by the patient. Surgical and emergent settings are intense arenas where orders are barked, tempers flare, and black humor abounds as staff attends to their role or job, but has limited time to acknowledge, comfort, or connect with the patient. From a patient perspective, just as he or she is being asked to extend the greatest trust to the surgical team, the team is focused on the procedure and may appear most unavailable to the patient. In Diane's case, soul loss may have been averted or recognized and addressed promptly had a spiritual healer been present at the delivery.

The benefits of sacred spaces within hospitals, clinics, spas, and offices are well documented and reflected in the marketing of healthcare facilities. Primarily these spaces are interfaith prayer or meditation rooms where one can seek solace, pray, or go inward to heal. In an address to the 2003 graduating class of Duke University School of Medicine, Vice Dean Dr. Edward Halperin urged the graduating physicians to create sacred space *wherever* they stood. Nowhere is that more important than in the surgical setting.

As an obstetrician/gynecologist and shamanic practitioner for many years, I have found the following simple steps a starting point to make powerful changes. First and foremost, empower the surgical team and the patient by acknowledging surgery as a sacred ceremony and honoring the sacred trust between the patient and the surgical team. Use the time at the scrub sink to meditate or pray, clearing the mind of all extraneous concerns – particularly anger and frustration – and become fully focused and present in the moment. Be responsible for monitoring the energy in the room and, if the head of a surgical team, for directing that energy and keeping it focused. Eliminate all disrespectful conversation, including unnecessary or unkind remarks about the patient, angry or disrespectful comments between members of the surgical team, and inappropriate topics of conversation. Patients are hyper-alert to the atmosphere in the OR; their lives depend upon what is happening there. They notice tension among the staff and recognize it as a distraction potentially deleterious to their wellbeing, and therefore it generates insecurity. While it is fine to converse during surgery, be aware of the energy that the conversation is creating. Would you be comfortable with the conversation if you were the patient? For example, as an intern I was horrified to assist at a delivery where the attending physician discussed a particularly brutal rape that had been in the paper that morning – while he was standing between the patient's legs looking at her exposed genital anatomy waiting for the infant's head to crown. Anesthetized or not, if you wouldn't want the patient to hear it, it shouldn't be said. Maintain a connection to the patient and speak to the patient even while anesthetized. The impact and benefits of such communication are profound. Finally, invite a shamanic, spiritual or energy healer to be present throughout the surgical process to guide the patient through the spiritual perils of surgery.

The risks of surgery from a shamanic perspective

The second step in integrating shamanism into the surgical setting is to address the risk of surgery from a shamanic perspective. Classic shamanism views illness as spiritual disharmony. When spiritual disturbances are not recognized and corrected, illness will eventually manifest on the mental, emotional, and physical planes.

Soul loss and intrusions are the most common spiritual complications of surgery. They can have profound impact upon the patient, particularly if they go unrecognized. Awareness of the potential for soul loss and intrusions can alert a practitioner to consider spiritual post-operative complications, particularly where there is no clear medical explanation for a patient's post-operative symptoms or concerns.

Anesthesia

When people are unaware they are journeying, they are unaware that they are in non-ordinary reality and unaware that they need to know when to return. Surgical patients are particularly vulnerable to these complications because of the alteration of their state of consciousness by anesthesia and amnesia-inducing drugs. When anesthesia is administered, there is always the potential that an 'untrained shaman' (i.e. patient) will be launched upon a journey without a pilot (intention), without the knowledge that he or she is journeying, and without the ability to return. When people do not return from a journey into non-ordinary reality, the result is soul loss. When people journey without intent, the nature of the journey is akin to a roll of a roulette wheel. Whether the journey is peaceful or a veritable nightmare will depend upon their mental state, and most likely will reflect the last concerns on the mind immediately before the journey began. Thus, patients' mental states immediately prior to surgery impacts their experience while under anesthesia, reinforcing the importance of the surgical team ensuring that the atmosphere or energy of the OR is as serene, reassuring, and safe as possible.

In addition, the surgeon, anesthesiologist, or spiritual attendant must establish a strong connection with the patient so that his or her voice can be easily recognized. Traditionally, the anesthesiologist is the person to awaken and call to the patient after surgery. However, the patient may have only met the anesthesiologist briefly prior to the surgery or met one of his or her colleagues at a pre-operative consultation. From a shamanic viewpoint, it would be preferable to have the person who calls the patient back to ordinary reality be someone well-known and emotionally connected to the patient – someone who knows the patient well enough to *know* that the patient is not only physically awake, but spiritually present. The body may awaken before the spirit has returned. A spiritual attendant/shaman would be available to accompany the patient from the operating room and throughout his or her stay in the recovery room to insure that the soul has fully returned to the body and to assist in that return when necessary. Most importantly, the spiritual attendant would be able to maintain a spiritual connection to the patient in both physical and non-ordinary reality. The stakes are high, for without the patient's complete return there is soul loss.

Soul loss

From a shamanic standpoint, 'soul' is considered to be one's essence or vitality or life force. People experience soul loss when a soul fragment leaves their body and is no longer accessible to them. Most commonly soul loss is a response to physical or emotional trauma, and the soul fragment leaves the body in order to assist the person to survive the emotional impact of the trauma and/or lessen the pain. After trauma, this soul essence may be unable to return or unaware that it is safe to return. Throughout the surgical process there are multiple triggers for this type of soul loss: the pain or trauma necessitating the surgery, fear about the surgery itself, the physical and emotional stress induced by the surgery, and the post-operative pain and stress.

The type of soul loss that is incurred during anesthetic alteration of consciousness, as discussed above, is best explained as 'soul wandering,' where the drugs enhance the likelihood of spontaneous journeying and a portion of the soul wanders from the body. Whether the soul loss is caused by trauma or wandering, the presentation of soul loss will include common features that vary significantly depending upon the individual and the degree of soul loss involved. People suffering from soul loss may exhibit chronic illnesses such as depression, chronic fatigue syndrome, fibromyalgia, autoimmune disease, or unusually frequent colds. They express feeling deeply fatigued, powerless, numb or deadened. They may refer to being 'beside themselves,' 'spacey,' 'trapped in a fog,' 'lost,' or 'not all here.' They may experience memory loss or memory gaps. Though they may remain able to function, they may feel as though they are watching their life from outside of themselves, or that they are just going through the motions without experiencing life. Profound soul loss, such as occurred in the case of Diane, can present as post-traumatic stress disorder (PTSD).

Diane experienced profound soul loss after her emergency Caesarian section, as the birth was extremely traumatic for her. When her baby's heartbeat began dropping precipitously just before delivery, everything happened very fast. She was separated from her husband and midwife, neither of who was allowed in the OR during the surgery.

Diane developed PTSD after the delivery. She had panic attacks if she passed a hospital, or even if she simply saw someone wearing scrubs. She was having night terrors in which she kept reliving the experience. Though Diane had no knowledge of soul loss or soul retrieval, she described how she felt after surgery in the following terms:

> I just didn't come back from the surgery. I never got back into my body. I know I crossed over into another place during anesthesia . . . My body woke up and was functional, but I wasn't there. It took tremendous energy to try to stay in my body even while nursing the baby. I couldn't sense the presence of my body below the bridge of my nose. I had almost no peripheral vision.

Diane came to see me for soul retrieval 10 months after the delivery of her daughter. In my journey to retrieve Diane's soul, I found her lying on a table floating near the ceiling of a green operating room. She was positioned as though she lay in a coffin. Deeply asleep, her essence was clearly still under general anesthesia. I gently awakened her and returned with her essence, which I blew into her crown and heart chakras. Diane had a very similar journey during the soul retrieval. Independent of my experience, she saw herself lying in a coffin, where she could see, but not speak or move. Immediately after her soul retrieval, the panic attacks and night terrors stopped. Diane wryly recalls being startled to discover, "I have legs!" Her visual perception returned to normal, as did physical sensation and the awareness of being present in her body.

Three years after the soul retrieval, Diane says that she has very little memory of the first 10 months of her daughter's life, but remembers everything after the soul retrieval. She felt that the soul retrieval also was a major shifting point in the healing of her sense of loss and anger around the birth experience. Prior to the soul retrieval, she had been receiving counseling and working hard to heal the wounds around the delivery, but "it didn't stick." Afterwards, "it was as though all the other work clicked into place and healing occurred."

Diane's experience is a classic example of a surgically-related soul loss and the immediate and profound healing that can occur upon restoration of the lost soul fragment. I didn't ascertain whether her soul loss was the result of the trauma of the birth, soul wandering or a combination of both. From a healing standpoint, the mechanism of the soul loss was not relevant. What mattered was finding and returning what was in this case a very significant portion of this woman's essence. As in this case, the onset of symptoms with soul loss is abrupt and clearly related to a specific event. Complications in the patient's life may compound over time because of decreased functioning related to the missing essence, but with surgical soul loss the underlying shift occurs at the time of the surgery.

Also typical of soul loss, the patient generally has a poor response to more conventional therapies such as antidepressants and psychotherapy. Though Diane was working diligently to recover after her surgery; her grief and anger simply did not resolve or lessen. As long as a large portion of her soul remained 'anesthetized' in non-ordinary reality, she was unavailable to respond to treatment. When she learned about the concept of soul loss, she immediately recognized that she needed soul retrieval. Afterward, her physical symptoms such as the numbness, visual disturbances, and anxiety attacks abated immediately. She *knew* that she was 'back.' Her emotional issues of anger and grief did not resolve instantly; however, the healing process and resolution of the emotional issues began upon the return of her soul.

Following soul retrieval, a person may feel a vast array of emotions. For Diane, there was relief and joy to be back fully present, but there was also additional grief to be processed over the loss of both the birth experience and the memory of the first 10 months of her daughter's life. People typically don't recall what occurs during anesthesia, and from a shamanic perspective, the vast majority of Diane's soul was anesthetized in non-ordinary reality during those months.

Intrusions

Soul loss is frequently accompanied by spiritual intrusions. These intrusions are not possessions by evil spirits. Most frequently they are energies generated by negative thought forms unconsciously sent by others or by our own self-deprecating thoughts. When a part of someone's essence is missing, there is an opening or vacancy within the body that is available to be filled by an intrusion. When intrusions enter a person who has lost power or experienced soul loss, they block the movement of energy within the body, causing localized illness or pain.

While suffering from depression, Beth awoke crying, feeling exhausted and hopeless. As she got in her car, she shouted in frustration "I need a break, I need a break!" Five miles down the road she hit a patch of black ice, totaled her car, and broke her ankle in two places. Her state of exhaustion and loss of power left her open to intrusions that she had then inadvertently created and directed towards herself. The intrusion extracted from Beth reflected the belief that she could rest only if she were injured or ill.

Intrusions, which manifest as diseases, mood disturbances, pains, or as injuries and accidents, can be perceived in non-ordinary reality. A shamanic worker who identifies such an intrusion would offer a healing ceremony in the form of an extraction to remove the intrusion from the body of the client.

Similar to surgical soul loss, an intrusion acquired during a surgical procedure will usually be marked by the abrupt onset of symptoms that correspond to the date of the surgery. In the following case of Sarah, it was the clear association of the onset of her pain and concerns with the date of a surgery that led me to suspect an intrusion. In order to confirm that an intrusion was present, it was necessary to perform a diagnostic journey and confer with my helping spirits.

Sarah is a feisty and delightful woman of action. As she is by nature optimistic and pragmatic, I was surprised when she called and said everything in her life was falling apart and she didn't know what to do. She felt angry, depressed, and irritable all the time. Her business and relationship were falling apart, and she had a constant, nagging pain in her upper back. Her symptoms had begun so abruptly that she was able to pinpoint the day they had begun. It was on the day two months earlier that she had undergone general anesthesia for eye surgery.

Since the surgery her once thriving cleaning business had been plagued by a loss of clients, employee theft, and a high rate of employee turnover. These were all unusual problems for her. She was considering selling her business and starting over in something new, perhaps buying a franchise or selling her house and moving out of the area. Everything about her relationship with her boyfriend had become an irritation.

At her healing, I removed an intrusion from her back that was clinging to and partially embedded in her upper and middle back. Sarah physically felt something leave as I energetically pulled it from her body in non-ordinary reality. She reported an immediate relief of pain and a shift in her emotional state as the intrusion was extracted. After the extraction, Sarah's own essence was able to fill and move freely through her body. It seemed that the intrusion had been blocking the flow of her energy and had displaced some of her essence. I guided her in transforming into her divine self (her pure essence, free of ego and limiting beliefs) to restore balance and harmony and fully fill her body. In this transformed state she reconsidered her urge to sell her business, buy a franchise, sell her house, and end her relationship.

After she returned to ordinary reality, she reported feeling optimistic and content. "I love my house and my business. I'm not going to sell either." Her relationship again seemed to be worth working on. A year later, Sarah reported that the problems with her business ceased very quickly after the healing and the business was again thriving. The back pain had never returned. Her relationship had ended about three months after the healing. Though the breakup was difficult, she felt that she was well equipped to move on with new confidence in herself and clarity in what she seeks and deserves in a mate.

Notice that the onset of symptoms for Sarah was strongly associated with the date of the surgery. In her case, the intrusion and associated soul loss manifested as physical pain in her back, uncharacteristic mood disturbances, and general havoc in her life. Sarah physically felt the intrusion being pulled from her back. She described it as a very odd, though not painful or uncomfortable, sensation. It was distinct enough that she called out during the healing "What was *that?*" Many, but not all clients will physically perceive something being removed from their body as the intrusion is extracted. When the intrusion has been present for a relatively brief period in time (weeks to months as opposed to years), and has not yet caused physical tissue damage, the relief of discomfort is usually immediate as it was in this case. In her case, both the physical and emotional symptoms were immediately relieved upon extraction.

Extraction of an intrusion after physical changes or disease have occurred in the body will remove the spiritual cause of the disease, but not necessarily the physical manifestation of a long-term intrusion. However, the physical manifestation of the intrusion may respond more effectively to treatment after the removal of the intrusion.

It is worth noting that the site of the intrusion was not related to the surgical site, nor were any of the client's symptoms. This is typical. The site of attachment of an intrusion is more likely to correspond to a general area of weakness that is specific to that individual. When unrelated problems or symptoms occur after a surgery it is worth considering the possibility of an intrusion.

Possession

Similar to an intrusion, a possession occurs when a disembodied spirit (usually of a deceased person) enters the body of another individual. Possessions will only occur when an opening or vacancy exist for that possessing spirit to occupy. When people are whole, filled with power and unaffected by drugs, they do not become possessed.

Unfortunately, the term possession tends to conjure fear or Hollywood horror scenes. However, possessions do occur, and it is important to begin correcting the misconceptions that surround it. A possessing spirit is not a demonic entity; it is merely a soul that has lost its way and is looking for a place to live. As hospitals are places where people die, they are also places occupied by spirits of deceased persons. When someone dies traumatically or unexpectedly, the spirit of the person may be confused and unaware that he or she is dead. Possessing spirits are not attacking their hosts; they are looking for a home. In performing a depossession, the shaman is assisting both the patient and the possessing spirit. Generally, possessing spirits are gently brought to the realization that they are deceased and assisted in crossing over to the spirit world. The patient is then freed of the possessing spirit and will usually require either soul retrieval or a power animal retrieval to fill the void that the possessing spirit had occupied.

I have encountered several surgically related possessions. When I saw Tom, he was about 45 years old with a history of chronic depression. He always felt a pervasive underlying sadness. He had had multiple surgeries as a young child, and the depression had begun after a surgery that took place when he was about 5 years old. He recalled the post-surgical time as having been very traumatic. As typical many years ago, his parents were not allowed to be with him in pre-operative holding or recovery room, nor were they allowed to spend the night with him in his room. His family always said that he was "never the same" after that surgery; he lost his joy and playfulness. That was all that I was told before beginning to journey.

In the journey, I was shown a sobbing child in a cage-like bed. The child left his body and began to run through the halls of the hospital looking for his mother. I was then shown another child, a sad three-year-old who was confused and unaware that he was deceased. The three-year-old saw the body of the first child and 'crawled' into his body seeking warmth and comfort. When the first child returned to his body, he could not get back in. As my journey continued, my helping spirits arrived with great love and light and offered to take the possessing child spirit home. Held in the arms of a guide, the spirit of this child became radiant and turned to my client to express his appreciation for helping him to go home. The journey finished with the retrieval of my client's soul.

Tom was deeply moved during the healing, feeling the presence of angels, and feeling something heavy and sad leave his body. Afterwards, I was guided to share what I had seen. Tom then told me that in fact another child had died the day of his surgery. He remembered being scolded by the nurses for getting out of bed. When he persisted in getting out of bed to look for his mother, he was put in a barred crib.

After the healing, Tom felt that he was in a 'state of grace.' Physically he felt much lighter, emotionally he felt deeply loved and awed by the presence he had experienced in the room, and he was able to recognize that some of that presence was truly his own essence returning home. The key point in this case is that though the healing involved a depossession, it was an extremely gentle and loving experience for both the client and the possessing spirit.

Soul loss, intrusions, and possessions can cause significant morbidity. Only by being aware of the possibility of spiritual illnesses can they be recognized and healed. When undiagnosed, spiritual illnesses will persist and manifest physically, often in forms that elude allopathic diagnosis or are resistant to conventional therapy. As surgical patients are at high risk for spiritual illness, it is particularly important that spiritual illnesses are acknowledged within the surgical community. As the diagnosis and healing of spiritual illnesses require a trained shaman or spiritual healer, there is a clear benefit to including healer as part of the surgical team to assist in the prevention, recognition, and treatment of spiritual illnesses.

Other benefits of shamanic healing during, before, and after surgery

During surgery

There are other significant benefits of having a shaman present in the operating room. By maintaining a connection with the patient's soul in non-ordinary reality, the shaman facilitates communication between the surgeon and the patient's higher consciousness (or divine self) during the procedure. Such communication potentially reduces complications and operative times by minimizing blood loss, stabilizing vital signs, and optimizing exposure of the operative field. Furthermore, the patient's soul would be able to communicate messages to the surgical team through the shaman such as warnings of aberrant anatomy, problems not directly in the surgical field, or impending shifts in vital signs.

As an example, early in my surgical practice and before I had begun to study shamanism, I adopted practices mentioned by Dr. Bernie Siegel in *Love, Medicine, and Miracles* and began to speak to my patients while they were under general anesthesia. Usually the messages were calming reassurances that everything was going well and that they would have minimal pain and a quick recovery. On one occasion as I started a hysterectomy, I observed that the patient was bleeding noticeably more than usual from small vessels at the incision site. The anesthesiologist assured me that the woman's blood pressure was fine and her blood clotting studies were within normal limits. I remember thinking that the case would be simpler if the bleeding was minimized. I decided to enlist the patient's assistance and addressed her by name aloud. After reassuring her that everything was fine, I told her that I would like her to redirect her blood flow away from the surgical incision, the pelvis, and pelvic organs that I was removing.

I explained that the redirection of blood flow would assist me in performing the surgery more easily and minimize her exposure to anesthesia and blood loss. My request was accompanied by laughter and overt ridicule from the assisting surgeon and anesthesiologist, though I perceived an immediate decrease in bleeding. At the close of the case, the anesthesiologist reported total blood loss for the hysterectomy as 25 milliliters (ml), including what had been absorbed by sponges and suction. Ordinarily, blood loss would range from about 125 ml on a 'dry' case to 500 ml with moderate to heavy blood loss.

Though not delivered with shamanic awareness, the message to the patient above incorporated many of the elements present in healing practices: clarity, focus, intention, concentration, and love were all present. As I generally used my time at the scrub sink to meditate and clear my mind of everything but the procedure at hand, I entered the OR grounded, fully present in the moment, and asking for spiritual assistance on behalf of my patient. Although I was not yet aware of the shamanic power of my role, enough elements of the sacred were present that some aspect of this patient was able to respond with dramatic results.

Imagine the potential of working with a healer as an integral part of the surgical team to facilitate communication between the surgeon and the anesthetized patient. As vital signs, blood loss, length of procedures, and other intra-operative variables can be measured, there is a tremendous opportunity to study the efficacy of shamanism in the operating arena.

Before and after surgery

A discussion of the benefits of shamanic healing before and after surgery must be acknowledged as speculative. There are no studies on the impact of shamanic healing on surgical outcomes. But we can consider the potential benefits of shamanic healing from a classic shamanic perspective.

Pre-operative shamanic healing would optimize patients' preparation for surgery by restoring their power through soul and power animal retrieval. A patient with significant power loss pre-operatively is more prone to intrusions, which manifest on a physical level as surgical complications and prolonged recovery times. If an intrusion contributed to the development of the pathology that is to be treated surgically, its removal pre-operatively heals the underlying spiritual imbalance so that the likelihood of the pathology recurring post-operatively is decreased or eliminated.

On the physical level, pre-operative shamanic healing yields multiple benefits such as decreased pre-operative anxiety and depression, decreased hospitalization and recovery time, decreased pain medication requirements, and fewer complications. The patient experiences an enhanced sense of wellbeing which bolsters the immune system and results in increased satisfaction with their care. In addition, there is the possibility that spiritual healing may generate spontaneous healing on the physical level, reducing the complexity of a required surgical procedure or even eliminating the need for the procedure entirely.

Post-operatively, shamanic healing assists in clearing anesthesia from the body, accelerates the return of body functions, and significantly reduces the requirement of narcotic pain relief. It may also provide a context for patients to understand the occasional extraordinary spiritual experiences that may spontaneously occur during or after surgery.

The following cases illustrate a range of impact and benefits observed with shamanic healing before, during, and after surgery within my practice.

Case study: Janie

Janie, a woman in her mid-forties, underwent a diagnostic laparoscopy to evaluate a persistent ovarian cystic mass. As she suffered from anxiety and depression, surgery was a particularly stressful proposition for her. She prepared for the surgery by receiving Reiki (a form of spiritual energy healing) and working with a therapist. She received additional Reiki immediately prior to the surgery and went into the surgery confident, calm, and relaxed. Her surgery was seemingly uneventful, and a benign ovarian tumor was removed. She was discharged home the day of the surgery and recovered quickly and easily.

Two weeks later, she came to my office for her two-week post-operative check. Her wounds were well healed and she had no complaints about the surgery itself, but she was upset that she had woken up during the surgery and could hear and see everything. This didn't seem possible, as at no time during the surgery had she appeared to be inadequately anesthetized. Her vital signs were stable, there was no movement to indicate the anesthetic was wearing off, her eyes had been lightly taped shut to prevent them from drying out, and drapes blocked any possibility that she could see the surgical field. When I asked if she could have been dreaming, she was adamant that this was no dream, and she then proceeded to describe in detail and with astounding accuracy exactly what had occurred in the operating room.

Though she was under anesthesia when I came into the operating room after scrubbing, she was able to describe my position on the right side of the table. She had seen me insert a long sharp pointed instrument (trocar) into her navel with my left hand as I held up the skin around her navel with my right hand. To my amazement, she then repeated exactly what I had said as the trocar was secured "Oooooh, that went in nice and easy; this is going to go well." She remembered being surprised that she had 'awakened' during the surgery, but that she felt so safe when she heard me speak that she just went back to sleep. When Janie confirmed that she had experienced no pain, I explained that she had journeyed out of body.

As Janie talked about the experience, she realized that during the event she had felt unconcerned and relatively detached from the events that she observed. It was only after the surgery that she began to feel annoyed that she had been allowed to awaken during the surgery and believe that something improper had occurred. She became excited as she realized that in that state she had been anxiety-free, and she now *knew* not only what it was to be serene, but that it was possible for her. She was truly inspired by the experience and began to expand and explore her spirituality. As she began to meditate and deepen her spiritual connection, Janie grew in confidence and in feelings of joy.

What strikes me most powerfully about Janie's experience is how easily the transformative opportunity could have been missed. It seemed that the explanation and understanding of what transpired for her in the operating room was necessary to fully activate her transformation. Had the true nature of her experience not been revealed, or had it been dismissed, she could have remained stuck in a place of fear or anger believing that something had gone wrong.

As a surgeon, I was humbled by the experience. First and foremost, I was relieved and grateful that my words, blurted enthusiastically and unedited, had been reassuring and positive. I became acutely aware that not all words I spoke in an operating room were. Secondly, Janie had received a drug that interferes with remembering events that occur while under its influence. Her remarkable account of the surgery was *not supposed to be possible* and unraveled what I thought I knew, and called into question much of what I had been taught. While I had believed and practiced surgery based upon the idea that a patient was *unconsciously* aware of events in the operating room, I had never considered that an anesthetized patient could be *consciously* aware while under anesthesia! This realization made me distinctly uncomfortable, which in turn forced me to acknowledge that I was not behaving one hundred percent of the time in a way in which I would want the patient to observe. I needed to change.

Ultimately, Janie stimulated me to examine myself, to heal myself, and grow. The patient acted as healer; the physician received healing.

The patient as shaman

In *Spontaneous Healing*, Dr. Andrew Weil points out that patients actively involved in their own care, as a group, fare better than passive patients who simply accept their diagnoses and treatments. In addition to the positive impact on their own health, empowered patients can also have a direct impact on the well being of their health care providers. By recognizing the innate healing power of patients, all parties benefit.

By acknowledging patients as shamans, patients are spiritually and emotionally empowered to take ownership of their own healing and to become an integral part of their own health care teams. They may literally or figuratively act as in a shamanic role. My first exposure to the healing power of shamanism was with a patient literally acting as a shaman. The encounter permanently etched upon my being that healthcare and spirituality are ultimately inseparable.

Case study: Susan

Shortly after completing my obstetrical residency, I attended Susan's delivery. As we hadn't met during the course of her pregnancy, her genuine and enthusiastic greeting as I indicated that I was the doctor on call surprised me. The labor went well and a healthy infant was safely delivered, but shortly after the delivery, Susan experienced a life threatening post-partum complication. Even within the midst of dealing with the emergency, I was struck by Susan's serenity, her seeming total lack of fear. She radiated complete confidence that she was going to be fine, confidence that I didn't feel as this was the first major crisis that I had dealt with as an attending physician. I was aware that her demeanor was grounding and inspiring, allowing me to focus and work swiftly, clearly, and beyond my level of experience.

After the crisis had a positive resolution, I reflected upon her unusual affect in such challenging circumstances. It was clear to me that she had not hoped, thought, or believed she would be all right; she truly *knew*. Instinct told me that there was something extraordinary happening here. Much later, Susan told me that prior to the delivery, an ancestor had come to her in a dream and prepared her for the events that then came to pass at the delivery. She had been told that I would be the attending physician and that both she and the baby would be fine.

Susan's dream was what I call a 'big dream,' a dream that is vivid and often brightly colored in which the dreamer is conscious that they are dreaming and aware that they are receiving important information. Such a dream is similar to a divination journey in which a shaman might journey to an ancestor to obtain assistance or information. The longstanding relationship with an ancestor, coupled with a history of reliable information, provides the shaman with deep confidence and trust in the information provided. As this was not an unusual experience for her, Susan completely trusted her dream and knew she wouldn't suffer any serious consequences from complications.

In reviewing this experience 25 years later, a feature that stands out now is the caution that both Susan and I exercised in talking about an obviously spiritual experience. I had learned quickly in medical school and residency that it was not safe or wise to discuss my own psychic or intuitive experiences within the scientific/medical community. Susan's reluctance to reveal her dream before the delivery reflects a similar reservation on her part. In *A Conversation About the Future of Medicine,* Larry Dossey, MD, states "Modern medicine is one of the most spiritually malnourished professions that has ever existed." Patients are acutely aware of this separation of spirituality from the science and technology of allopathic medicine. They rarely discuss their religious or spiritual beliefs with health care providers who, until recently, rarely inquired about their patients' beliefs. Patients will not share with their doctors what they fear will cost them credibility. When beliefs are not shared or elicited, the power of spiritual healing is not accessed and utilized. Fortunately, the value of spirituality and prayer in healing are becoming more widely recognized and accepted, opening the door for conversations between patients and physicians that would not have occurred in the past.

Had Susan felt comfortable telling me about her dream when I first arrived, or had I immediately pursued my intuition that there was a specific reason that she wanted me to deliver her baby, preparations could have been made to prepare for the possibility of a complication. Anesthesia could have been consulted early in the labor. Consents could have been explained and signed at leisure in case they would be needed, rather than in the midst of an emergency. Simple measures taken for high-risk patients, such as placing an intravenous line and cross-matching blood type, could have been made. Though the complication still wouldn't have been prevented, there would have been the potential for less drama and increased efficiency when the emergency occurred and the potential to reduce anxiety for the patient throughout the labor.

Susan's story underscores the potential of tapping into the patient's shamanic wisdom and knowledge. For other patients, such as Janie, an opening to discuss spiritual experiences and beliefs may provide an opportunity for patients to address a spontaneous spiritual experience that occurred in conjunction with a surgery that they have no context to understand or that has generated fears. Too frequently, when patients have extraordinary experiences, they perceive that it is not acceptable to discuss them with medical personnel. Alternatively, if they attempt to discuss the events, patients often discover that many health care providers are uncomfortable or unfamiliar with such spiritual experiences and ignore or invalidate the patients' experience, or pass it off as a hallucination from medication.

Case study: Rita

Recently, I worked with a woman simultaneously diagnosed with breast and colon cancer. Rita was admitted to the hospital when her colon perforated from the as yet undiagnosed cancer. Upon her admitting examination, a large breast lump was found which was confirmed by biopsy to be breast cancer. During her hospitalization, while awaiting the colon resection, she received both soul and power animal retrieval. She was also assisted in connecting with her own spiritual guides. Journeying to her guides, she came to understand that she was at a crossroads and had the opportunity to choose to live or leave. Facing the possibility of death allowed her to realize that despite all the difficulties she faced, she chose to live. She began a powerful personal transformation, changing beliefs and behaviors, opening to receive the support and love of both the spirits and her many friends. Her newfound clarity so grounded her in love and gratitude that her request the night before her colon surgery was that I journey and pray *on behalf of her doctors and the surgical team*. We visualized the surgery and the joyful celebration that would occur among the surgical team after the surgery went well.

One year later Rita was doing extremely well and completed the radiation and chemotherapy prescribed for the cancers. After working with multiple shamanic healers and prayer groups, Rita had returned to the hospital six weeks after her colon surgery to have the breast cancer removed by lumpectomy. A large volume of tissue was removed from her breast because of the size and nature of the tumor identified on biopsy. To the amazement of her doctors, no cancer was found in the lumpectomy specimen.

Many health care providers exposed to Rita became inspired and deeply affected by the privilege of working with her. Rita, in particular, was very open about the impact and importance of her spiritual care as a key component in the treatment of her cancers. Rita's rapid recovery, positive attitude, and graceful presence led one of Rita's oncologists to bring in his son, then currently in a surgical residency, to meet and learn from her.

Rita, Susan, and so many others are touching the hearts and opening the minds of the medical professionals, and opening the door for spiritual healing to resume its critical role in health and healing. Observing the impact of patients like Rita and Susan, it becomes evident that empowered patients not only thrive, but create a new paradigm for the relationship between patients and health care providers. There is no longer an imbalance of power. Instead, power flows freely, purposefully between the patient and health care providers; the physician healing the patient as the patient heals the physician. Just as the shaman is at once student and teacher, patients and providers alike are simultaneously student and teacher.

Conclusion

Ultimately, patients heal themselves. As health care providers, we can do nothing more than support the patient while they heal. It is no longer sufficient or appropriate to support the physical body alone; the mind and spirit must be supported as vigilantly and skillfully as we attend to the physical form. Shamanism, as a spiritual practice, provides a framework to reintroduce the sacred into medical and surgical practice. The integration of surgical and shamanic practices enhances the effectiveness of both, restoring balance and harmony within all aspects of the individual and restoring the balance between the provider and the patient.

The surgical setting is a profound place to begin. The inherent nature of the surgical setting calls forth the power of sacred ceremony. The shamanic and physical risks of surgery create high stakes where there is much to be gained by integrating the separate benefits of healing and surgery in a synergistic way, such that the combined benefit is greater than the sum of the benefit from the individual modalities. As there are many measurable parameters within the surgical setting to effectively monitor the efficacy of treatments, the surgical setting provides a dynamic opportunity to study the impact of shamanic healing on surgical outcomes. Finally, in expanding the role of the shaman to be in the domain of the patient as well as the health care providers, the patient is empowered in a way that enhances their own wellbeing and encourages the emergence of a powerful new paradigm for the delivery of health care.

References

Alandyly P. et al. "Using Reiki to Support Surgical Patients." *J Nurs Care Qual* 1991; 13: 4: 89-91.

Associated Press, Washington. "Doctors Must Double-Check Before Surgery." June 21, 2004, http://www.intelihealth.com/IH/ihtPrint/WSIHW000/333/7228/387821/html?hide=t&k

Dossey L. *Healing Words: The Power of Prayer and the Practice of Medicine.* HarperSanFrancisco; 1993.

Dossey L. "Do Religion and Spirituality Matter in Health? A Response to The Recent Article in the Lancet." *Alternative Therapies in Health and Medicine* 1999; 5: 3: 6-18.

Dossey L. "A Conversation About the Future of Medicine." http://www.dossey dossey.com/larry/QnA.html

Durkheim E. *The Elementary Forms of the Religious Life.* Trans. Swain J. New York: The Free Press; 1915.

Harner M. *The Way of the Shaman.* San Francisco: Harper & Row; 1960.

Halperin E. "Cathedrals and Their Icon." Address to the 2003 graduating class of Duke University Medical School, http://medschool.duke.edu/modules/som_deanofc/index.php?id=11

Ingerman S. *Medicine For The Earth: How to Transform Personal and Environmental Toxins.* New York: Three Rivers Press; 2000.

Ingerman S. *Soul Retrieval: Mending the Fragmented Self.* San Francisco: HarperCollins; 1991.

Jonas W., et al. "Investigating the Impact of Optimal Healing Environments." *Alternative Therapies in Health and Medicine* 2003; 9: 6: 36-40.

Kreiger D. *The Therapeutic Touch.* New York, NY: Fireside Book; 1979.

Levin J. "Spiritual Determinants of Health and Healing: An Epidemiologic Perspective on Salutogenic Mechanisms." *Alternative Therapies in Health and Medicine* 2003; 9: 6: 48-57.

Micozzi M. *Fundamentals of Complimentary and Integrative Medicine, 3rd ed.* St Louis: Saunders Elsevier; 2006.

Miles P. and True G. "Reiki – Review of a Biofield Therapy. History, Theory, Practice, and Research." *Alternative Therapies in Health and Medicine* 2003; 9: 2: 62-71.

Rand W. "Reiki Research." http://reiki.org/reikinews/reikin24.html.

Siegel B, MD. *Love, Medicine and Miracles: Lessons Learned About Self-Healing From a Surgeon's Experience With Exceptional Patients.* New York: Harper & Row; 1986.

vanGennep A. *The Rites of Passage.* Translated by Vizedo M, Caffee G. Chicago: The University of Chicago Press; 1960.

Wardell DW. and Engebretson J. "Biological Correlates of Reiki Touch Healing." *J. Advanced Nursing* 2001; 33: 4: 439-445.

Weaver A., et al, "Spirituality, Health, and CAM: Current Controversies." *Alternative Therapies in Health and Medicine* 2003; 9: 6: 42-45.

Weil A. *Spontaneous Healing: How to Discover and Enhance Your Body's Natural Ability to Maintain and Heal Itself.* New York: Ballantine Publishing Group; 1995.

About the author

Carol Marie Tunney, MD, graduated from SUNY Stony Brook School of Medicine with Distinction in Research, completed her internship and residency training in obstetrics/gynecology at Wesson Women's Hospital of Baystate Medical Center in Springfield, MA, and had a private practice in upstate New York. Former Chair of the Division of Science and Technology at Southern Vermont College in Bennington, VT, she is presently faculty at the Community College of Vermont. In addition to her private shamanic healing practice, she is a member of the Integrative Medicine Task Force of the Gladys Taylor McGarey Medical Foundation and hosts a weekly radio show entitled "Natural Instincts: Health, Healing, and Conscious Living."

VIII

Hospital-Based Shamanic Practice

Alan Davis, MD, PhD

The successful transformation of a healthcare practitioner into a *shamanic* healthcare practitioner requires addressing the emotional, cognitive, and spiritual barriers that one's training, experience and personal history construct. When not addressed, these barriers tend to distance healthcare providers from their own innate healing abilities. A while back, I was shaken to the core to realize how much I had left behind of what initially motivated me to pursue medicine as a career path to help others. It seemed I had become focused on the career goals expected of medical academicians: take care of patients, write papers, teach residents, and plan programs. My personal life seemed to have the same heaviness of my professional life. Everything felt disconnected and often distant from the center of who I had wanted to become: a healer.

But I soon realized that psychological insight into my own behavior and emotions alone was not enough, so I began to pursue the study of shamanism. That training helped me experience the power the spiritual dimension has to catalyze intellectual, emotional, and behavioral shifts necessary to live in accordance with the principles of holistic healing. Walking the path of the shaman extended from the pilgrimage I began in my youth in search of something greater than myself, something that connects all things. I started looking for those moments when daily life seemed imbued with consciousness and connectedness, and I realized that being in that state created a natural response of reaching out to offer healing to others.

This path eventually led to my bringing shamanic practice into the hospital. I initially focused upon acquiring new shamanic healing skills in the same way that I had learned and practiced my medical skills. But it soon became clear that the techniques weren't enough. To integrate shamanic practice into hospital-based medical practice, I needed to address my own fears of ineffectiveness or of being discovered, my lack of clarity as to the appropriate needs of the patient, my tendency to withhold healing hands (as it was not a part of my allopathic medical training), and my tendency to focus only on practicalities rather than allowing the healing process to unfold.

As a physical medicine and rehabilitation physician, I see ample opportunities for spiritual healing and for teaching about spiritual practice. Most rehabilitation patients have a significant element of spiritual illness due to the profound nature of their medical, physical, or emotional impairment. My patients are admitted after stroke, heart attack, brain injury, spinal cord injury, multiple orthopedic trauma or severe debility.

Research supports the importance of the spiritual dimension of health and illness. In one study, patients with a sense of spirituality overall had better life satisfaction and quality of life.[1] In another, cardiac rehabilitation patients who were offered some kind of spiritual practice experienced increased wellbeing, enhanced meaning in life, improved confidence in handling problems, and decreased tendency to become angry.[2]

Dialogue to healing

As my personal view of illness shifted, I found I needed a parallel shift in my listening skills and my use of language. Through my shamanic training, I began to discover the joy of connecting with patients in hearing their stories, recognizing that embedded in these stories is the key to their desired healing.

In the hospital, the clinician has the benefit of visiting with the patient on a daily basis and so can easily discuss the person's challenges to returning home considering their illness, trauma, and loss of function. This daily contact also provides an opportunity to begin to deeply hear the patient's story. Common symptoms of spiritual illness can manifest in the language that rehabilitation patients use to describe their present situation: sadness, immense tiredness, loss of drive, not feeling that they are 'in their body,' being out of balance, fearful, disconnected, or a sense that something is profoundly wrong and that they cannot get back to who they were. Because these are such frequently voiced concerns in the hospital setting, the shamanically-trained clinician has an opportunity to enter into dialogue with patients about whether or how these may represent a spiritual dimension of their illness.

Unfortunately, religion and spiritual discussions are excluded from training for most hospital clinicians and therefore present barriers to responding to the patients' spiritual needs. In studies evaluating why clinicians do not discuss their patients' religious and spiritual beliefs, most cite lack of knowledge, discomfort with the subject, lack of time, or worry that the patient would ask the clinician to pray with them.[3] Yet most patients would like their physician to ask them about these very personal subjects, as it does affect their decisions regarding medical treatment. When the clinician engages in this dialogue, a whole series of events occurs: the patient understands that his or her treating clinician cares enough to ask about their personal beliefs and values; the therapeutic relationship deepens; and better compliance with treatment plans occurs simply because the message given is one of caring and compassion. The physician enters into the role of a healing companion,[4] integrating the patient's stories into the care plan and extending his role beyond that of technical collector of information to diagnose and treat.

Multiple tools are available to bolster the clinician's skills and open the door to dialogue about spirituality without compromising the flow of regular clinical routine or causing bedside anxiety. These tools are open to all healthcare providers and offer key psychosocial information to add to the medical history. The FICA spiritual assessment tool developed by Dr. Christine Puchalski[5] provides a well-tested, simple questionnaire that allows the clinician to remain within comfortable boundaries. Each letter of the mnemonic cues the clinician:

- What is your **Faith**?

- How **Important** is your faith to you?

- What is your spiritual or religious **Community**?

- How do these beliefs **Apply** to your health? And how do you want me, your clinician, to **Address** your spiritual needs?

In a similar approach, the American College of Physicians and the American Society of Internal Medicine consensus panel suggests posing four questions to patients with serious medical illness.[6]

- Is faith (religion, spirituality) important to you in this illness?

- Has faith been important to you at other times in your life?

- Do you have someone to talk to about religious (spiritual) matters?

- Would you like to explore religious (spiritual) matters with someone?

These two questionnaires require only a few minutes of time to administer and are part of the patient social history. The clinician then uses this information to guide patient care and medical decision making, to request involvement of the person's social support system, and to bring in others as needed who provide spiritual and religious needs outside the experience and comfort level of the clinician. In the hospital there is a wealth of resources available: visiting clergy of many faiths, pastoral counselors, hospital chaplains. Thus, broaching the subject of spirituality and religion need not cause anxiety for the clinician. Rather, a brief dialogue provides an opportunity for patients to tell how their personal religion and spiritual practices support their adjustment to the challenge of impairment or illness.

Shamanic training allows the physician who attends hospital inpatients the option of ministering to some of their spiritual needs as well as to their medical care. Since shamanic practitioners have traditionally used healing stories to inspire and in some cases even heal the ill, introducing the possibility of discussing the spiritual dimension of their illness with a patient encourages these stories to emerge in the medical encounter and strengthens the clinician-patient bond.

Shamanic healing at the hospital bedside

My own approach to using shamanic healing in the hospital remains quite simple. If a patient's story hints to me that there is a significant component of spiritual illness to their present illness, I explore this in our daily visits. I inform the patient that in addition to being their attending physiatrist, I can provide spiritual healing as an adjunct treatment. I use a spirituality and religion assessment tool to elucidate the patient's spiritual and religious values and to avoid a potentially awkward interaction if my own interests in healing are in conflict with their belief system or personal practices. I am not invested in whether the patient chooses shamanic healing or not. I am not engaged in 'selling' my healing modality at the bedside. If the person has a sense of spirituality and religion that is positive and supports their healing, I see my role as a facilitator for this rather than pushing an agenda for being the spiritual healer for all of my patients. Some patients choose specific religious rituals for healing; others simply want prayer or visits from their community. Some find their own religious background negative and prefer either to refuse spiritual healing or to work with the hospital chaplain.

In our sharing the story of the patient's illness, words play an important role. As dialogue about spiritual illness and shamanic healing is introduced, the words chosen should support the healing process rather than prolong the trauma.

For example, instead of using the term 'soul loss,' I usually describe to patients the possibility of a temporary loss of life force or life essence. This frames their circumstance as a means of self-preservation instead of focusing on how the trauma of illness or accident led to the problem. Loss of personal power is relatively easy for most patients to relate to while hospitalized, lacking much of their own autonomy. Because the core of shamanic healing is to bring a person back into balance spiritually, emotionally, and physically, patients may welcome shamanic work as an opportunity to explore more deeply the profound adjustments they confront following major medical illness or trauma.

Once the person has given me permission to do spiritual healing work, I do a shamanic journey to examine what healing work needs to be done and explain this to the patient in neutral language. Patients next want to know what this would look like. I explain that to prepare for the healing I might listen to an audio recording to help me maintain my concentration, or that I might sing or simply sit in silence by their bedside. I tell them that I may float my hands over their body, touch them over specific points, or even lightly scrape and scoop material off the surface of their body. I tell them that I may need to put something into their body such as power or life force by blowing it into their heart. Since the terms and techniques may be unfamiliar to the patient, I explain that the intervention is dynamic and flexible for each person and their situation. In the hospital setting, personalized healing work, rather than a rigid form, affords more comfort for both the patient and practitioner. Once the process has been explained and the patient still desires the healing, I ask them to invite friends or family to be present to witness, support the process, and help provide a container of sacred space in which the healing can occur.

The bed where the patient spends much of their time usually ends up being the place of healing work. Because the austere hospital environment calls for a minimalist approach, I use few shamanic supplies. I sometimes use a quartz crystal, a rattle or a chime. I frequently work while singing to maintain my healing state and have learned that for me this works better than most accoutrements. I never burn sage or use essential oils in the hospital, as so many patients and staff members have adverse reactions to strong smells. When invited guests are present, I simply describe what they will see and begin the healing work. The work ends in silence. Once this silence naturally dissipates, all present have time to share their experiences.

The initial session begins the healing process. Continuing work for both the practitioner and the patient then focuses on integrating this healing into recovery and daily life. If the patient feels ready and requests another shamanic intervention, there is specific follow-up healing work. This may mean additional journeywork or a ceremony to welcome back the gifts that the healing brought and to develop a greater understanding of their meaning. For some patients, learning how to journey develops into a regular spiritual practice that supports and empowers the healing on their long journey home.

Shamanic extraction work for recalcitrant pain

Pain remains one of the most common complaints for patients seeking care by physicians. In the hospital, pain accompanies physical trauma, most surgeries, and even the hard work of physical therapy. Pain caused from nerve damage is particularly challenging to the medical team, and often a combination of medications, physical modalities and mobilization may help to manage it. Occasionally this standard regimen alone lacks benefit, and when this occurs I have suggested to the patient that I simply take the pain away and neutralize it at the bedside using shamanic extraction. This has been effective for overused muscles, back pain, pelvic pain, headache, and as an adjunct to wound healing. Though it appears to have a limited duration of effect at times, it remains a simple treatment without side effects. It may be repeated during the routine course of examining a patient and provides another means of affirming to the patient that you do indeed care about their pain and that you desire to alleviate their suffering.

Therapeutic drumming

One program that has been well liked by most individuals admitted to rehabilitation is therapeutic drumming. Drumming has a long history of use as not only a means to facilitate entering an altered state of consciousness supporting shamanic journeying, but also for its healing properties. In a contemporary study of group drumming in healthy subjects, Bittman and colleagues[7] found that drumming enhanced immune function. On the rehabilitation unit of an affiliated community hospital, the rehabilitation psychologist and I facilitated a one-hour therapeutic drumming circle for patients and staff once or twice per month for approximately three years. This was held in the therapy gym and offered as an adapted recreational activity. Each patient was given a choice of percussion instruments: a shared powwow drum, hand drums, rattles, click sticks or tambourines. If an individual needed assistance holding or playing the instrument, staff would assist. For example, an individual with weakness on one side of his body would receive help holding the drum while he played it with his able hand and arm. A single person started each round of percussion by picking a simple rhythm, and the group was instructed to support that rhythm or to fill in the spaces between beats. A staff person facilitated the first round to demonstrate. Patients would then start the remainder of the drumming rounds. Each round continued until it naturally dissipated, and then another person would pick the next round's rhythm. Patients and staff reported how this raised everyone's energy level and alertness. For many patients returning to visit after discharge home, this was remembered as one of the highlights of their stay in the hospital; they would return simply to participate again. This was a very lighthearted endeavor that elevated 'spirit' and set individuals up for success in a non-threatening and non-judgmental milieu.

A healing song after stroke in a new mother

Stroke comes to people of all ages as a silent, symptomatic brain attack. Occasionally pregnant women suffer a stroke if they have eclampsia, a condition of extremely high blood pressure induced by their pregnancy. Mrs. B was a 35-year-old woman who had a massive stroke after delivering her first child. The right side of her body became totally paralyzed, and she was left with mildly slurred speech, impaired thinking, and an inattention to the right side of her body. She was admitted for rehabilitation with the goal of returning home to care for her new son with the help of her husband and family. This was quite a lofty goal, given the severity of impairment from the stroke. Because she no longer had the insight to see the huge barriers she needed to overcome to do this, her mood was lighter and allowed her to participate more fully in her rehabilitation. Over the course of nearly two months, she regained a limited ability to stand and walk with a cane.

Her husband and baby lived in her hospital room and were part of the rehabilitation process. As a family this supported her self-care activities of not only learning to toilet herself, but also trying to respond to the needs of her baby: nursing, diaper changes, and simply holding him. She did regain partial use of her weak arm and hand, but she continued to need constant cues to watch what she was doing to prevent her from dropping things due to inattention. Well into her rehabilitation she started feeling discouraged and depressed that she was never going to return home and care for her baby.

Her participation in therapy waned, and she became easily upset. In addition to supportive counseling and the use of anti-depressant medication, we started a discussion of the spiritual aspect of her illness. She wasn't particularly religious or spiritual, but she wanted to explore alternative healing in the hope that her rehabilitation might become a bit easier. I offered her a healing song to help keep her motivated whenever she became sad or discouraged. She sang it in bed, in therapy, and with her family who were still living in the hospital room with her. She found comfort in using it, and indeed found it helpful to sustain her full rehabilitation effort. After a prolonged rehabilitation of nearly three months, she finally returned home with her child and husband. On follow up visits in my clinic, she still spoke of the healing song and remembered it for years afterward whenever challenges arose. This experience underscored for me that shamanic healing doesn't need to produce miracles to have positive effects.

Shamanic healing after brain injury

Mr. J was a 47-year-old man living an active life in the mountains of Utah who enjoyed mountain biking and wind surfing. In a rollover car accident he sustained severe brain injury, a skull fracture, and subsequent blood clot on the brain surface that required immediate neurosurgery to remove and mechanical ventilation to support his breathing. The next stage of his recovery was in a nursing facility for supportive care where he made steady progress, and a month later, he was admitted to participate in intensive hospital-based rehabilitation with the hope of returning him to a home setting. At the time of his entry into rehabilitation, his breathing tube was removed and he quickly regained his ability to speak audibly. He then made a rapid recovery of mental and functional skills during the next few weeks.

Once he was interacting well, Mr. J and I spoke about how he felt somewhat 'off' and a bit 'clouded' in his thinking and action. In our talks he wondered if he could get back to his recreational passions of mountain biking, wind surfing, and playing guitar. When he left the hospital he was speaking well, walking without difficulty, and able to provide his own physical care. He was left with a mild thinking impairment that affected his organization and planning, and his wife provided supervision for a period after discharge.

On the surface, all seemed well. From a rehabilitation perspective, he was an incredible success story. He had nearly returned to his pre-injury baseline after a severe brain injury and was functioning independently in the community without any special equipment or accommodation. Though he returned to work as a waiter in an upscale restaurant, he soon found himself surprised by how difficult it was to perform adequately. Additional attempts to work proved challenging; he was unable to keep his old job and went on to pursue a series of others. Unable to maintain employment, he began to believe that his deficits were quite profound because he was simply unable to complete the tasks of each different job.

In our clinic visits together, he still felt he wasn't quite himself. He felt that his previously high energy level hadn't fully returned. He expressed this by saying that his songs got stuck in his throat and he just couldn't bring himself to play his guitar. He felt very emotional and admitted to symptoms of depression. He wasn't feeling well enough to return to his recreational pursuits of wind surfing and mountain biking, despite being medically cleared to do so. Although we discussed how his rehabilitation had been a great success, he admitted something was still missing. He sensed his life was void of passion, and his wife reported a change in his personality toward more dependence and insecurity. We reviewed his rehabilitation plan and confirmed that everything medical rehabilitation could offer from therapies to vocational rehabilitation had been pursued.

We spoke of how his brain injury had elements of spiritual illness in the way he was feeling the sense of being 'off,' fatigued, and depressed. He agreed and was open to explore shamanic healing as a modality that might support his recovery and restore more of his vitality.

The initial shamanic work consisted of soul retrieval and power animal retrieval. Over the next few months he reported his mood had improved and that he observed a reawakening of love for his wife. He was able to return to work and again hold a steady job as a waiter.

I saw him again a few months later with his wife, at their request, because his shift toward a more demonstrable love was new and uncomfortable for her. The next healing session was for both my patient and his wife whereby each one of them received shamanic healing. This healing was focused on support for their relationship as it shifted to accommodate both my patient's new sense of life and purpose and his wife's training in a new profession while adjusting to her husband's personality changes. This was done in conjunction with their couple's therapy. Both were happy with the outcome and have continued in the relationship. Over approximately four years, Mr. J has continued to have intermittent shamanic healing relevant to his life situation. Most of the focus has been toward work and relationships. We initiated his most recent shamanic healing in response to the challenge of feeling dependent and depressed while preparing for a one-year separation from his spouse while she completed an internship. He feared losing her while she was away and couldn't imagine a full life without her. After healing with spiritual light and work with his power animal he reported feeling "bigger and 'badder,' fully connected with who I am, and happy with the time to do what I need to do for myself." He is adjusted in his marriage, teaching new employees at work the way to truly relate to the customers (and receive big tips), and living a full vibrant life including singing, playing his guitar, wind surfing, and mountain biking.

Shamanic healing in a clergyman with congestive heart failure

Individuals with complicated and debilitating medical illness are frequently admitted to inpatient rehabilitation. One such individual was a clergyman admitted to recover from an exacerbation of congestive heart failure. Despite adjustment of his cardiac medications, he was too weak to walk alone or to provide for his own self-care needs without assistance. He made progress in the rehabilitation program, but he continued to require frequent adjustment of his cardiac medications. After approximately ten days of rehabilitation, he had reached a plateau that was not enough to allow him to go safely home without significant assistance to meet his care needs and faced the dilemma of either nursing home care or home with 24-hour care if he could not improve.

It appeared his condition called for a spiritual healing response that might assist his moving beyond the present barriers to return home independently. My own awkwardness delayed, but didn't prevent, my offering spiritual healing to a clergyman. As I broached the subject, we spoke of the heart as the seat of emotions. In response to my offer of spiritual healing, he said he had already received all of the healing ceremony and ritual his religion had to offer while in the hospital. Yet he said he would be open to my praying over him. I received his permission to sing my prayer. I used song to enter into a state of transfiguration in which I become a healing companion by simply removing the barriers between myself and the rest of creation. In this state of mystical union, the healer and the client sit in sacred space together bathed in the light of creation. I sang over him and placed hands over his head and heart during the healing session. Afterward we shared the need for spiritual healing in the hospital, and his final words to me at the end of the healing session were, "My boy, you've got to heal more than the body."

During his subsequent days of hospital rehabilitation, he suddenly had better endurance and improved so rapidly that he was able to leave the hospital independently two days later. He was able to move back home into the company of his fellow clergy and live his life fully. When I saw him again approximately one year later, we remembered our experience together as a supportive, positive, shared healing and learning moment.

A deaf, mute patient with Parkinson's disease, depression and debility

An elderly man with Parkinson's disease was hospitalized for a heart attack and pneumonia. After completing his acute medical treatment he was referred to rehabilitation to retrain his walking and self-care. On admission there, he was very fatigued and appeared depressed. He communicated by using notes, complied with his therapy program, but didn't exhibit any excitement about his progress. I spoke to his family who stated that he had become progressively more depressed and withdrawn over the previous few years as his age, medical illness, and Parkinson's disease rendered regular tasks more and more difficult. He remained in this state despite regular gains in his function through physical therapy and supportive counseling. When I shared my concerns about his mood with him, he agreed that he was depressed. He lived alone and was further isolated by his medical illness and difficulty communicating. It seemed that even if he could regain adequate function to return home, he would remain lonely and sad. We wrote notes to each other sharing how his illnesses had taken away some of his power and life force so that living had become very difficult. He liked my proposal to focus healing work on returning his personal power and vitality. He asked how this could be accomplished, and we began another discussion of what this would look like at the bedside. When he agreed to it, I asked him to invite family members to come in support.

His daughter was present at the bedside for the power animal retrieval and soul retrieval. The logistics of sitting at the bedside listening to music and then finally reaching over and blowing his power animal and soul parts into his heart were quite subtle. We then all sat in silent reverie at the end, allowing time for him to experience the healing in sacred space.

The effects of the healing were profound and clearly observable. The shift in his rehabilitation was quite remarkable. His mood improved as evidenced by a greater attempt to communicate and to even make jokes with the staff and his family. The greatest surprise for both staff and family occurred when he began speaking. He could read lips and speak, but his mood had been so depressed that he simply didn't have the energy to communicate with words until after the healing work. He made more rapid gains in his walking and his ability to care for himself. His family reported that the healing had prepared him to return home alone with minimal assistance instead of a planned admission to a nursing home. This improved mood and desire to communicate persisted over the next year that I followed him. Both he and his daughter attributed this to the shamanic healing work.

Ethics

Healing in health care settings requires considerations of permission to do the healing work, respect of the person's values and beliefs, and the need to do no harm. For the licensed health care practitioner such as a physician, nurse, or hospital chaplain who attends the patient on a regular basis, one could argue an implicit request for healing occurs on all levels once the patient has been admitted to the hospital under their care. In this scenario every interaction between the health care provider in the hospital or clinic becomes an opportunity for healing. Through this the attending healthcare provider is implicitly given permission to use every skill he or she has acquired to facilitate healing in the patient. While this argument has merit, and though I agree an implicit healing request occurs upon admission to the hospital or clinic, I believe an open dialogue exploring the patient's religious and spiritual values provides for more effective healing practices and potentially avoids harm. The act of open discussion prevents inadvertently providing healing when the person may be against it. In a study on the use of prayer in patients with alcoholism, it was noted that those who were prayed for did worse overall in maintaining their sobriety than those who were not prayed for.[8] One possible explanation for this could be inappropriate boundaries for those praying when the alcoholic didn't want their assistance in seeking sobriety.

Discussing the need for healing and obtaining permission invites the patient to begin the process of integrating the gifts of the healing. Setting up the healing intervention to include family and friends as witnesses provides another means of integration as the patient's primary community supports the individual's journey to wellness and affirms any observed results of the healing. Shamanic healing also invites changes in the patient's thinking and behavior; for example, teaching the patient how to journey for himself supports the integration of returned soul parts and shifts the patient's focus from disease to wholeness and interconnection.

It is crucial to undertake healing work with the patient's informed consent. As is true of other interventions performed in the clinical or hospital setting, shamanic practices require preliminary discussions and mutual understanding of the intent and expectations. Consent also allows the shamanic practitioner to state clearly that the spiritual healing may be integrated into the flow of Western medical treatment, but does not substitute for conventional medical treatment. In particular, I state that though this spiritual healing may have effects on a person's physical body, emotional state, or attitude, this addresses primarily the spiritual aspect of one's present state. As such it provides a means to restore balance and harmony into a life disrupted by the constellation of impairments associated with a significant medical condition.

Considerations for licensed healthcare clinicians integrating shamanic practice in the hospital or clinic

As suggested by the cases in this chapter, shamanic healing may easily be integrated into the hospital or medical clinic either as a consented, overt healing or simply by the clinician's being a healing presence. For the licensed healthcare practitioner, the first step to bringing shamanic work into mainstream healthcare would be to explore if spiritual healing is regulated by the practitioner's state licensing board. For many states it is not regulated nor described as part of the scope of practice. For a few states there must be a separation of shamanic practice from the licensed healthcare practice. Contacting one's state licensing board may help release any anticipatory concern around this.

Institutional culture and policies provide another path to bring shamanic healing into the hospital. As integrative, complementary and alternative therapies have become regularly requested by patients seeking healing, more hospitals and clinics have adjusted their policies to reflect their acceptance of these modalities. One can speak to the hospital administration to ask if there are policies to address this. Often there is a significant difference between a non-licensed practitioner coming into the hospital to only perform their healing work and the licensed healthcare practitioner integrating it into their customary care. In the latter scenario it is often less problematic, as the employee or staff person has an understanding of how care is rendered in the hospital and is unlikely to apply the healing work in a way that could interfere with regular care. The best practice for licensed shamanic healthcare practitioners would be to provide his or her usual high quality care as a physician, nurse, or therapist, and then to integrate the shamanic healing into the care plan when appropriate, agreed to by patients, and in a way that doesn't detract from other responsibilities. One must remain sensitive to the individual hospital culture. Even if integrative therapies such as shamanic healing are allowed by hospital policy, the better part of prudence would be to use discretion in its application, discernment and caution in its discussion, and the use of language that doesn't offend the values and beliefs of others.

Healing presence

Clinicians face challenges in the current health care system to get through their overwhelmingly busy days and nights. All too often, healthcare practitioners are trained to leave behind their own emotional needs when responding to the needs of their patients so that they might focus on the most urgent clinical decisions and treatment plans. In these interactions, both the clinician and the patient may feel emotionally neglected. Yet both the patient's and clinician's story, the community, the environment and the intelligent energy of the Creation all play a role in the healing process. The transformation of a clinical practitioner into a shamanic healthcare provider entails extensive training and completing a series of initiations that require re-evaluation and adjustment of the practitioner's world outlook and beliefs, conscious use of language and metaphor, implementation of listening skills, and shedding the barriers to healing that contemporary healthcare training may have instilled. With this transformation, the shamanic health care practitioner becomes a healing presence at the bedside, whether or not specific shamanic healing techniques or ceremonies are used. This occurs through integrating the emotionally open and attuned spiritual heart with the well-developed intelligent mind to restore balance and allow healing.

References

[1] Tate DG. and Forchheimer M. "Quality of Life, Life Satisfaction, and Spirituality: Comparing Outcomes Between Rehabilitation and Cancer Patients." *Am J Phys Med Rehabil* 2002; 81: 6: 400-410.

[2] Kennedy JE., Abbott RA. and Rosenberg BS. "Changes in Spirituality and Well-Being in a Retreat Program for Cardiac Patients." *Altern Ther Health Med* 2002; 8: 4: 64-6, 68-70, 72-3.

[3] Ellis MR., Vinson DC. and Ewigman B. "Addressing Spiritual Concerns of Patients: Family Physicians Attitudes and Practices." *J Family Practice* 1999; 48: 105-9.

[4] Kane J. *The Healing Companion: Simple and Effective Ways Your Presence Can Help People Heal.* San Francisco: HarperCollins; 2001.

[5] Puchalski DM. and Romer AL. "Taking a Spiritual History Allows Clinicians to Understand Patients More Fully." *J Palliative Medicine* 2000; 3: 129-37.

[6] Anandarajah G. and Hight E. "Spirituality and Medical Practice: Using the HOPE Questions as a Practical Tool for Spiritual Assessment." *American Family Physician* 2001; 63: 1: 81-8.

[7] Bittman BB., Berk LS., Felten DL. et al. "Composite Effects of Group Drumming Music Therapy on Modulation of Neuroendocrine-Immune Parameters in Normal Subjects." *Altern Therapies* 2001; 7: 1: 38-47.

[8] Walker SR., Tonigan JS., Miller WR., Corner S. and Kahlich L. "Intercessory Prayer in the Treatment of Alcohol Abuse and Dependence: A Pilot Investigation. *Alternative Therapies in Health and Medicine* 1997; 3: 6:79-86.

About the Author

Alan M. Davis, MD, PhD, is an academic physician board certified in Physical Medicine and Rehabilitation (also known as Physiatry). He is Clinical Associate Professor at the University of Utah School of Medicine and serves as Medical Director of rehabilitation units and long-term acute care facilities. He obtained his medical degree at the St. George University School of Medicine in 1987, postgraduate training at the New Jersey School of Medicine and Dentistry for a Physiatry residency, and a neuroscience PhD. He began studying shamanism in 1999, and in 2004 helped establish the Society for Shamanic Practitioners, a nonprofit organization dedicated to bringing together shamanic practitioners from all traditions and paths. Currently he serves as its founding Board President.

IX
Tending the Spirit of a Medical Clinic

Krista Farey, MD, MS

I practice family medicine in a large county outpatient department in an urban 'war zone' in California. A 1960's government-issued building with a sometimes-functioning elevator houses the crowded health center, surrounded by acres of dilapidated asphalt parking lots. The neighboring strip malls are semi-vacant. Nearby oil refineries intermittently leak toxic gas or ignite raging fires with choking smoke. The community is vibrant: along with the catastrophes there are currents of great vitality in art, music, politics, environmental activism, and spirituality. The people we care for in the health center have backgrounds and lives as varied as one could imagine: affluent and destitute, insured and uninsured, sober and addicted, of sound mind and with profound mental illness. We see immigrants from every continent, often with histories of trauma: refugees of domestic, economic and political adversity, and survivors of war and their descendants. Impressive art posters adorn the otherwise drab and beat-up health center interior. One hanging in the staff office quotes the folk saying, "a great doctor always has a great angel by her side," an idea that the twenty family doctors and nurse practitioners based here take to heart.

Since starting there in 1989, it has been a near ideal place for me to work. My interest in health care emerged as a teen when my father developed an illness laden with mystery and metaphor. It continued as an exchange student in India, watching the smallpox eradication campaign generate dramatic showdowns between those who believed in vaccines, and those who felt it was a spiritual violation to accept them. I considered training in several different healing arts before choosing Western medicine in order to work in the mainstream and be positioned to change it from within. My medical school emphasized public health and medical social science, supported my Master's work in anthropology, and was established to produce 'agents of change' in health care. Somewhere along the way, sent by my two Celtic spiritualist midwife great grandmothers, angels moved into my awareness, leading me to teachings on healing of a different sort.

In the 1980's and '90's, many refugees from war-torn parts of Southeast Asia and Central America sought medical care in our health center. Often they were indigenous people from tribal communities who understood health, illness and healing in shamanic terms. Some were themselves shamans. What they frequently found was a huge disconnect between what the medical clinic had to offer and what they expected and needed. To better care for and support their deeper healing, my colleagues and I explored a variety of ways of working with their cultural beliefs and practices, along with the angels at our sides.

These explorations have created some unique ways of working that are neither Western allopathic medicine nor shamanism but *exist in the interface*. There are four aspects to this blended work: (1) work with immigrants from shamanic cultures; (2) our group prenatal care program and its shamanic aspects; (3) our arts program on healing the building and the land it stands on; and (4) staff development work for our medical staff members which draws on shamanic practices.

Working with immigrants from shamanic cultures

Providers of public sector health care services are expected to develop 'cultural competency' in the cultures they serve. This is not realistic to achieve for all cultures nor sufficient to provide high quality, culturally appropriate care. One cannot assume that any individual will perceive or act in particular ways just because it is traditional in his or her culture of origin. Nor is it feasible for us to develop a complete understanding of all the many cultures we work with. At our health center, we have found it helpful to develop 'cultural humility,'[1] an appreciation that we interface with a broad range of cultures for which we have limited understanding, with the recognition that the perspective of each individual is his or her own regardless of cultural background. Familiarity with 'core shamanism'[2] has been very valuable to me for this, as it provides a general framework for understanding shamanic perception, diagnosis and treatment while not assuming specifics on the views of any individual.

Core shamanism was developed by Michael Harner, an anthropologist who looked at common underlying processes among diverse shamanic cultures across the globe. His framework helps one appreciate that an immigrant from a shamanic culture will probably, but not certainly, understand illness as having a spiritual cause, view diagnosis as intuitive (with the history and physical exam irrelevant or worse) and feel that recovery involves spiritual intervention. It does not suggest what the specific problem is, what is wanted of the doctor, nor what role might be the most helpful for the doctor to play. The two stories that follow are examples of how I have incorporated a 'shamanic humility' and collaborative approach in my medical practice. These stories are based on individuals I have cared for, with changes in identifying details.

Edgar

Edgar G. came from a remote tribal village, grew up tracking and hunting, and apprenticed as a shaman while a young adult. He became a military leader of a CIA operative in his country and was captured and incarcerated as a prisoner of war for 'reeducation.' After some years he managed to escape, despite the risks and odds against his success, only to find himself launched on a circuitous journey as a political refugee that eventually led him to our health center.

He was reputedly a very powerful shaman and in great demand. This was problematic for his health because he drank heavily whenever he performed his frequent ceremonies. Using Western allopathic medicine, my colleagues and I pulled him through several bouts of alcoholic pancreatitis, a painful and dangerous alcohol-induced illness. He thus developed great faith in this form of doctoring.

One day, he came to the clinic and told me that he saw soldiers coming over the hill to get him. Amongst them were a local archbishop and Che Guevara. He requested that I protect him from these attackers.

I viewed this both in Western psychiatric terms as a manifestation of post-traumatic stress disorder (PTSD) with a psychotic break, and in shamanic terms as an encounter with non-ordinary spiritual opponents. I treated both, working in collaboration with a shaman of his culture and with his family. I provided anti-psychotic medication, counseling and other medical care. His family arranged a shamanic ceremony, and they relocated him to a rural area distant from the local scene of the attack he perceived. He recovered completely and was able to stop the medication within a few months.

Fatimah

Fatimah came to our health center shortly after arriving from a refugee camp with her husband and five youngest children. The family members were treated for intestinal parasites and latent tuberculosis, vaccinated, and the children were cleared to attend school.

Fatimah continued to come see me often for symptoms of pain, tiredness, dizziness, sadness and trouble sleeping. She fulfilled Western diagnostic criteria for PTSD and major depression, as do most refugees from her country on arrival. Her own diagnosis was that she suffered soul loss, saying, "I feel I am only a shadow of myself" and "part of me is left behind." I offered her emotional support, education, medications for PTSD and depression, and treatment of other symptoms.

One day during an exam by another physician, she perceived a demon entering her body. Not long after, she asked me for assistance in locating the physician who did the exam so that he might be killed. This was the revenge expected by her people for those who introduce demons into others, and what she felt was necessary to remove this demon from her body.

The language interpreter working with Fatimah took this threat very seriously, recommending that the staff develop a team approach that eventually involved psychiatrists, family doctors, administrators, interpreters and the clergy of her church. The psychiatrist hospitalized Fatimah involuntarily because she was a direct threat to others, but she was not arrested. The congregation of her church prayed for her. Because the Protestant church that she and many of her people had joined forbade the use of shamanic methods, she did not utilize them herself. However, concerned non-Christian 'traditional' people of her community had shamanic ceremonies done, without her consent, to remove the demon and to heal her. She left the hospital after a few weeks, and I then saw her weekly the following year. I treated her chronic pain and depression and worked with the physical, psychological and spiritual aspects of these illnesses. Fatimah gradually became more able to function, felt better, got off antipsychotic and antidepressant medication, and went on to raise her family semi-independently. The staff interpreters and I became major sources of support for her and helped her cope with her husband's acute psychotic break and later sudden unexplained death, the long term disability of one of her children, and difficult interactions with individuals from other cultures.

As both of these examples illustrate, an appreciation of the shamanic world view and a respect for and willingness to collaborate with shamans in the cultures of our patients is invaluable in providing services that are satisfying and helpful to many immigrants. Had these two, and many other, individuals been understood and treated only in medical or psychiatric terms, I doubt that there would have been such successful outcomes or that the clinic would continue to be seen as a source of valuable support.

Group prenatal care

A relatively new method in conventional Western health care, which echoes shamanic practice in many ways, is group care. We offer this alternative method in prenatal care,[3] which has been enthusiastically embraced by our community. We create a supportive healing circle from several staff members and a dozen or so women who are due the same month. The circle meets for ten two-hour sessions over the last six months of the pregnancy. All the elements of conventional one-on-one prenatal care occur in or adjacent to the circle, including vital sign checks, growth measurement, lab screening, ultrasound exams, and hospital childbirth preparation. However, much more than providing these services can be accomplished under this group care arrangement. To help convey a feel for how this type of group care works, the next story describes the specifics of what happened at one group session.

Before the women arrive, Angelica, a community health worker, and I set up the room. We arrange the chairs in a circle and place a table in the center to hold a small light, and later some food. We put on relaxing music. As the women enter, we greet them before each goes to check her own vital signs and record the results in her chart. They chat, help each other, and exclaim about the growth in each other's bellies since the last visit. One woman brought a spectacular rainbow gelatin salad and others ask how she made it. Another brought pungent smelling fritters and a bowl of fresh strawberries. The women sit down and complete a written self-assessment. As they become ready, I invite each woman individually to meet with me on a mat in the corner, briefly checking on her medical issues, measuring the size of her abdomen, listening to the baby's heartbeat and recording the results. I answer personal questions while deferring more general questions to group discussion.

Individual checks completed, we all rejoin the circle. Angelina begins with a guided relaxation, focusing on the light in the center. Next, we do some movement together: stretching, strengthening and expressive movements, sometimes yoga, sometimes dance. Following that, we ask each woman to let the group know what is up with her. One woman remarks that she is feeling very short-fused and gasps with astonished delight to learn she is far from the only one experiencing this. I raise some of the more general questions that came up when I was checking each individual. One was, "My uncle died last week. Will my sadness hurt my baby?"

I ask the group what they think. There are many different opinions on the effect of grief on a fetus, but all agree that the baby must experience something of what the mother experiences and also of how she processes that experience.

We move on to a facilitated discussion of this session's main topic of domestic violence, asking for responses to provocative statements like "men don't abuse their wives when they are pregnant." One woman responds, "I know that's not true; I have lived it." Tears flow, and then hugs.

Angelica passes out colored markers, pencils, and papers and the women are asked to draw an image of what being pregnant feels like. Some choose to share this with the group. One has drawn a large circle of rainbows around a smiling pregnant woman. She says her image expresses her view that pregnancy is a blessing. Two others draw images involving trees and sunrises, each for different reasons. As the group nears its close, we plan the next session. Finally, we stand holding hands, express our wishes for each other until the next meeting, our intentions in caring for ourselves, and our gratitude for all that has been offered today.

As this example illustrates, many methods used in group-prenatal care echo those of traditional shamans. Women sit in a circle around a candle or light. Musical sounds affect the state of consciousness. Deep relaxation is supported. The women share healing and empowering stories. The message is conveyed that individuals have responsibility for their own healing. Movement and artistic expression connect women with concepts and emotions that are subconscious or beyond. They share food with one another. The women build a supportive community that is a source of strength and healing. This community bolsters the informal social and cultural supports women often have in more traditional communities, but are being lost through the isolating forces in our present Western culture. The strengths of some of these supports have been described as 'The Latina Paradox'[4] in the public health literature, to explain why Mexican women in the United States have much better birth outcomes than expected of members of a community with the socioeconomic disadvantages that often come with recent immigrant status.

Women are empowered and healed through their participation in group care. By checking their own vital signs and charting their progress through the pregnancy, they take ownership of their care. The medical monitoring is transformed into a process supporting self-awareness. It ceases to be the fear-provoking experience of submitting to the authority of a doctor whose primary intention is to scan for pathology. Women relax. The stories and music heal.

The creation of art helps process emotional issues that are difficult or impossible to verbalize.

The benefits of group prenatal care are striking in outcome studies.[5] Clinical trials have shown that women in group prenatal care have greater satisfaction with their care, more confidence, greater assimilation of educational information and fewer visits to emergency departments. Even more importantly, they have longer pregnancies, fewer underweight newborns and fewer late preterm deliveries. These outcomes are long-sought goals, as yet unrealized, of conventional prenatal care.

Healing the spirit of place

Many of our staff felt that the health center building we use was haunted. One evening-shift housekeeper would never go into the basement because of the ghost she had heard there. A care coordinator, although practicing a religion that taught it was impossible, was sure she felt in the building the spirit of someone who had died there years ago. Even the CEO of the entire county health care system would repeatedly say in meetings that the problem with the clinic was in the building, there was something about the place, in the walls, in the grout, that made many things very difficult there. Most in the meeting room would nod in agreement when he would say that. I took an informal survey of the staff: eighty-five percent believed the building was haunted.

Our health center has an enormous 'cattle call' waiting room, with centralized registration and a large sitting area where people sit, often for hours, waiting to be called to their clinic appointments. Years ago there was nothing to do there, and nothing to look at but dirty carpet, walls with peeling paint and some bulletin boards with required information about the financial obligations of receiving government sponsored health care. Gradually, we began to make the space more pleasant and interesting, adding a table with toys and books for children, a clean tile floor, colorful multicultural art prints and appealing posters promoting healthy living and community organizations. We realized that our large waiting room could be transformed into a great resource for the community, a wonderful place to display visual art and to hold performing arts events. We organized a committee to develop an arts program, a group that later transformed into an independent nonprofit organization whose mission is to 'transform medical institutions and enliven the work of healing.' The organization has developed a series of in-place displays, traveling exhibits, and performance events. The events often involve audience participation and include food. Some of these highlight the cultures and immigration experiences of many of the communities using the health center. Another series of exhibits looks directly at various aspects of the nature of healing of individuals and of communities.

After learning that the vast majority of the staff were concerned about the haunted building, I felt a need to work more directly on healing the land and the health center on it. A spirit teacher told me in a shamanic journey that this work should include the following four components: knowing the past, sharing what we know, singing and dancing with drums, and eating well. The arts committee enthusiastically embraced the idea of an exhibit featuring the history of the land, and an opening event with good food, music, drumming and dancing.

I researched the history of the land and of the building at the local historical society library, and collaborating artists collected old drawings and photographs of the location. I wrote a history of the place. This was printed on an enormous poster spanning most of the back wall of the huge waiting room. The poster was covered with a beautiful montage of images illustrating the very local history: indigenous people hunting and gathering, fields of poppies and native plants, pear orchards, and urban development. The exhibit was called "Tincture of Time, Place and Healing." All around the waiting room were other large images depicting local history, both natural and human.

Some of the history of the land and building printed on the poster said, "The land that the health center now stands on came into being at the same time as human precursors began to emerge in Africa, about 3.5 million years ago. The Pacific Tectonic Plate in the earth's crust changed direction and jammed into the North American Plate, producing fault lines in the bedrock. Hills emerged from this collision, and creeks rushing down from them deposited soil on the bedrock below, creating the fertile alluvial plain of the flatlands that the clinic is built on.

"People began living here about 6,000 years ago, not long after the Ice Age was over. The people lived near the water, and came to the lush grasslands to hunt tule elk and gather plentiful plants, including horsetail rush and bunch grass, to use for food, medicine and tools. They cared for their sick by calling on helping spirits of ancestors, plants, and animals and used the medicinal effects of local plants and of hot sweats and cold mineral baths for healing.

"Spanish missionaries established a farming outpost here in the early 1800's. Cattle grazed on the grasses, and the people planted grains and vegetables. Within 30 years the indigenous people had vanished; those who didn't die of European diseases like smallpox and measles dispersed and left little trace. Mexico, including California, gained independence from Spain in 1821, and two years later the mission ranch supervisor was granted title to all the land, some of which his descendants continued to farm for the remainder of the century. The land here had vegetable gardens, pear orchards and cattle grazing in fields of evergreen grasses and orange poppies.

"This land was paved over in the 1950's and 1960's with the construction of the buildings and parking lots on county-owned land. The health center building is now home to a broad range of public health and medical health care services. Many of the communities who use the health center extend healing to land and places and believe that the power and history of a place is related to the healing that occurs there. In this respect, it helps to be aware of the history of this place; to remember that under the concrete and asphalt lie remains of orchards and native grasslands; to visualize the actual footprints of indigenous people left in alluvial soil washed down from the hills and deposited on bedrock; to recall the fault lines formed by colliding tectonic plates."

The opening event was an evening celebration with good food. Staff, patients, community leaders, and the artists who had worked on it were there. A storyteller came and told some old local tales. The artists told how and why they developed their pieces. There was a healing drumming demonstration. A staff gospel choir came together for the occasion singing Hezekiah Walker's "I Need You to Survive" to many tearful eyes.

After that, I didn't hear another offhand remark about ghosts in the building for many years. It remains a difficult place to work, but an edge has softened. Discussion about the badly needed replacement facility, which had been stopped by what many considered insurmountable obstacles, restarted with the identification of surprising new funding sources. The arts organization is involved in the design of the facility that includes space for the arts program displays.

Staff group

There is considerable interest in reconnecting with the heart and soul of medicine amongst practitioners of Western medicine. It may be a response to burnout or to the public's yearning for medicine with authentic heart. This response may also be a backlash to the conclusion by the advocates of a purely technical approach that medicine is only science and their related claim that the art of medicine is dead. The popularity of the Institute for the Study of Health and Illness programs for physicians at Commonweal is one manifestation of this renewed interest in the heart and soul of medicine.[6]

For over two decades, our medical staff has held a voluntary monthly evening group during which we support each other in addressing clinical, interpersonal, emotional and spiritual challenges, and in keeping our hearts and spirits connected in our practice. Over the years, we have used a variety of methods to do this, a number of which have interfaces with shamanism: guided imagery, creating clay masks, building altars, singing, storytelling, and writing poetry. We have also explored narrative medicine and shamanic journeying.

Narrative medicine is a popular movement in Western medicine which looks at the story of a patient's experience, works with the patient on seeing and developing his or her own story of illness and healing, and is mindful of the role the doctor may be playing in each individual's story.[7] Our group has done exercises from narrative medicine practice to look at how storytelling can be used to both heal ourselves and to increase our skills as healing practitioners, that is, using story in some of the ways as shamans.

One such exercise is to write and share the story of a serious illness we have experienced ourselves. Like shamans, doctors often find that their own illnesses and healing draw them to the healing arts and contribute to their capacity to help others. Another exercise is to re-write the third-person 'medical history' of a patient as a first-person narrative from the patient's perspective. The health care worker can then go further to look at that story for the 'missing piece' that would turn the story from a tale of illness into a narrative of healing. This process also offers a different lens through which to see their own role in their patient's narrative, and to consider ways to cast themselves in ways more supportive of deeper and broader healing. Another activity of the group is to collect very short parables, songs and poems to give to patients at opportune moments, reminiscent of word-doctoring or song-doctoring traditions in shamanism.

Our staff has also learned about core shamanism and journeying, devoting several evenings to explore non-ordinary worlds and to learn about methods of working with spiritual assistance. Participant family doctors have responded enthusiastically to these sessions, engaging in lively discussions about how shamanic methods might be applied to their lives and clinical work. Some see connections between shamanism and their dreams, premonitions and serendipities. Many have found shamanism to overlap with other traditional and religious practices they engage in such as Kabbala and traditional Chinese medicine. Some have found in it explanations of the synergy between healing and the arts. Others have been impressed by the ideas that the nature of a place would have an impact on healing. All found these explorations helpful in appreciating the shamanic perspectives of many of our patients.

Conclusions

Since shamanism and Western medicine have common roots as healing arts and common objectives in the healing of individuals, it is natural that shamanic methods, which abound in our community, be integrated into our practice of medicine. Shamanic methods have been helpful to us in providing culturally sensitive care to immigrant communities, to providing a group prenatal care program that has shown clinical outcomes superior to those of conventional individual care, to extending healing to the building and land, and in further developing ourselves as healers.

In my shamanic training, one of the primary instructions I received from a spirit teacher was to learn to work in the interface, the border between light and dark, presence and absence, doing and not doing – a powerful context entirely different from the juxtaposed polarities that highlight the edge of each individual interface. Though we frequently use the phrase 'integrative medicine' to describe mixing aspects of other traditions with allopathic medicine, I increasingly find this language inadequate. Integrative medicine suggests little more than the components that have been 'integrated.' The work I've described feels much more like a sort of 'betwixt and between medicine.' With roots in both shamanism and allopathic medicine, this work is transforming into practices that have emerged through the interface. It goes to places and people that neither tradition, either alone or simply added together, is likely to reach.

One more art poster is worth mentioning. The arts committee created scores of large black and white photographic portraits of some of our patients, captioned by a few paragraphs of each of their stories. One of these shows a proud and serious shaman in traditional dress, holding implements used in the ceremonies of her culture. When her elderly father seeks healing for himself, he usually looks to my allopathic medical practice rather than a shaman from his own culture. He comes with expectations of both what shamans do and what Western doctors are thought to do, and gives me the impression that he feels this is usually accomplished. When I see the poster of his daughter, it reminds me (and I like to think it also reminds those who pass by) that our work in the health center is inexorably of both worlds, and of neither.

References

[1] Tervalon M. "Cultural Humility Versus Cultural Competence: A Critical Distinction in Defining Physician Training Outcomes in Multicultural Education." *J Health Care Poor Underserved* 1998; 9: 2: 117-25.

[2] Harner M. *The Way of the Shaman*. New York, NY: HarperCollins; 1990.

[3] Rising S. "Redesigning Prenatal Care Through Centering Pregnancy." *J Midwifery Womens Health* 2004; 49: 5: 398-404.

[4] McGlade M. "The Latina Paradox: An Opportunity for Restructuring Prenatal Care Delivery." *Am J Public Health* 2004; 94: 12: 2062-2065.

[5] Ickovics J. "Group Prenatal Care and Preterm Birth Weight: Results From a Matched Cohort Study at Public Clinics." *Obstetrics and Gynecology* 2003; 102: 5: 1051-1057.

[6] www.commonweal.org/ishi, www.meaninginmedicine.org

[7] Charon R. "Narrative and Medicine." *N Engl J Med* 2004; 350: 9: 862-863.

About the author

Krista Farey, MD, MS, is a graduate of the Foundation for Shamanic Studies three-year program and of the U.C. San Francisco – U.C. Berkeley Joint Medical Program. She is a Clinical Assistant Professor of Family and Community Medicine at U.C. San Francisco and at U.C. Davis. She has been practicing and teaching family medicine for over 25 years and works with the visual and performing arts to support the healing of individuals and of the community. She has written extensively on health care policy reform, and is the co-author of a textbook on physiological medicine.

X

Parallels in Healing: Shamanism and Osteopathic Medicine

Michael Verrilli, DO, MS

Shamanic healing and osteopathic medicine work well together in clinical practice because of their similar, shared beliefs. Central to both are the unity of the body and interrelatedness of all of life, recognition of the divine healing principle inherent in the body, and a natural, noninvasive, hands-on approach to health and healing. Also shared are a knowledge that all things are alive and that movement is essential to all of life. With proper training and practice, shamanic journeying, extraction, soul retrieval, power animal retrieval and divination can be easily integrated and performed during osteopathic manipulative treatment to complement and extend its healing effects.

Origins of an integrated practice

I became interested in osteopathy because of its natural, holistic approach. After graduating from a college of osteopathic medicine, completing a flexible osteopathic internship and a conventional allopathic medical residency and fellowship, I then practiced hospital-based medicine for a decade. However, soon after beginning my hospital practice in 1990, I experienced the gradual onset of a mysterious illness that included unrelenting headaches, fatigue, muscle pain, and muscle tightness. As I began searching for answers outside of conventional medicine, I turned to an art therapy workshop. It fortuitously included mask-making, which connected me deeply to my forgotten Native American ancestry and introduced me to some of the classic shamanic literature. Several years later, I became interested in the high mountain shamanism practiced by the Q'ero Indians of Peru, which matched well with my northern Italian mountain ancestry, my love of nature, and my growing interest in healing. Eliot Cowan's Plant Spirit Medicine training in 1999 (www.plantspiritmedicine.org) taught me how to work with plant spirit allies and their unique healing properties, as well as the energy meridians of the human body from the perspective of ancient Chinese Five-Element medicine. The following year, Evelyn Rysdyk and Allie Knowlton's Spirit Passages Advanced Training Program in cross-cultural shamanism (www.spiritpassages.com) helped me to integrate my previous teachings, deepen my self-understanding, and develop my shamanic practice by allowing me to give and receive shamanic healing. Looking back over this 10 year period, I slowly began to realize that the purpose of my mysterious illness or 'sickness-vocation' was shamanic initiation.[1] Also in 2000 while receiving osteopathic manipulation, my doctor reminded me to practice osteopathic manipulative treatment in a way most natural to me,[2] which stimulated my changing my own practice to one that began to include shamanic healing.

Historical antecedents of osteopathic medicine

Osteopathic medicine is an original field of Western holistic medicine founded in 1874 by Dr. Andrew Taylor Still, a country physician and surgeon in Kirksville, Missouri. His personal experience led Dr. Still to become dissatisfied with the ineffectiveness of the conventional medicine of his time: several of his children died unexpectedly from untreatable spinal meningitis, and he saw other people injured or die as a result of toxic drugs and rudimentary surgery. According to Dr. Still, both divine inspiration and guidance combined with his long and comprehensive study of human anatomy and physiology helped him develop, practice, and teach osteopathic medicine.[3,4] Dr. Still chose the term osteopathy because, as he said, "We start with the bones." He deemed osteopathy a very sacred science, a "healing power through all of nature,"[5] and that "no human hand framed its laws." [6]

Dr. Still was interested in treating the patient's root cause of suffering, saying, "Find and remove the cause, then the effect will disappear." [7] He based this new healing discipline on the following tenets:

1. The human body is a unified organism.

2. The human body has a natural tendency towards health, as well as the capacity to resist disease and heal itself.

3. The human body's musculoskeletal system is central to the patient's health and self-expression. The bones appear at the beginning of our lives, the bone marrow is at our core throughout our lives, and the bones remain at the end of our lives.[8]

4. Palpation (touch) and manipulation are essential to gaining patient confidence, as aids to the diagnosis and treatment of disease, and for reestablishing and developing health.

5. Preventative medicine, such as proper nutrition, exercise, and reducing health risks, is essential.

6. Nature is the source of healing.

As a result of Dr. Still's pioneering work, there are now twenty-three accredited osteopathic medical schools and over 52,000 actively practicing osteopathic physicians today. Recognized worldwide and considered part of mainstream medicine, osteopathy training consists of four years of college premedical study followed by four years of osteopathic medical school. This training also includes an additional 500 hours in the study of the body's neuromusculoskeletal system and training in a unique, natural form of hands-on treatment developed by Dr. Still known as Osteopathic Manipulative Treatment (OMT).

OMT is a natural hands-on treatment of a patient's physical, mental, emotional and spiritual bodies. It is unique in treating the spiritual body as the root cause and location of most illness and is one of the most comprehensive forms of bodywork available. Osteopathic physicians are taught to touch patients with their hands in a kind and caring way in order to create a relationship with the patient and to diagnose and give treatment. Through their trained sense of touch, osteopathic physicians can feel the patient's entire history of health, illness and physical injury since conception and birth as restrictions or strains in the patient's body that prevent normal movement. These restrictions are areas in the body where the tissues are twisted, tight, compressed or stuck. During an OMT treatment, the patient lies fully clothed on a massage treatment table with the physician seated at the head or to the side. The physician first properly positions the patient and then very gently applies a precise amount of force or movement to the restrictions. The patient's body responds by slowly releasing or unwinding the restrictions so that energy and fluids can flow, and the tissues, bones, joints and organs can move properly. Patients typically leave the office after an OMT session feeling relaxed, calm, balanced and energized. They also notice lessening or disappearance of their symptoms for a period of time or permanently. During the office visit, the physician may also give the patient nutritional counseling and advice about stress management and lifestyle changes.

Ancient roots of osteopathic medicine and shamanism

"Osteopathy . . . (is) as old as the cranium itself."[9]

While the concepts of body unity and treatment of the cause of the disease have some of their origins in the teachings of Hippocrates, osteopathic medicine has another ancient source in Native American healing. According to Dr. Lewis Mehl-Madrona, "the Cherokee culture developed a comprehensive and sophisticated bodywork system that encompassed a form of osteopathic massage and manipulation, breath, and bodywork. Some of its fundamental techniques included the use of the breath to reanimate the body and 'draw spirit' into the affected tissues and the alternation of deep pressure and gentle rocking release."[10]

Shamanism is the most ancient and widespread system of healing known to humanity, working to restore spirit and connect with spirit.[11] Its approach and methodologies have survived and flourished because they have been proven to maintain health and strength and to heal illness under both ordinary and extraordinary life-and-death circumstances. Osteopathic medicine shares important beliefs with this ancient system, allowing shamanism and osteopathy to work strongly together in an integrative medical approach:

1. The unity of the body and the unity of life

"All matter is living substance"[12]

Understanding the human body to be one unified being whose true health reflects this oneness, osteopathic physicians believe that all systems of the body are interconnected and influence each other. Adverse changes in one system can alter the function of other systems, so that the symptoms may appear in one location while the cause is actually located in another. Osteopaths therefore see each patient as a whole person and treat the cause of the disease instead of treating only the symptoms. They also recognize that patients have physical, mental, emotional and spiritual needs that are affected by family, by their environments and the surrounding community, and that these needs must be addressed as part of the treatment.

Shamanic healers likewise see their clients as human beings with physical, mental, emotional and spiritual bodies that are connected to other people, to the ancestors, to the place in which they live and work, to the natural world and to the invisible world of spirit. Shamans know that the loss of these connections can lead to illness through feeling separate and isolated. As Chief Seattle said, "Humankind has not woven the web of life. We are but one thread in it. Whatever we do to the web, we do to ourselves. All things are bound together. All things connect."[13]

2. The divine healing principle within the human body

"All remedies necessary to good health exist in the human body" [14]

Osteopathic physicians recognize that the human body has a divine healing principle active and living within it, and they work with this principle during diagnosis and osteopathic manipulative treatment. The divine healing principle demonstrates itself as a natural tendency toward health and homeostasis, so that the body is self-regulating, self-correcting and self-healing in the face of disease. This divine healing principle is the life force itself present throughout the body, though most highly concentrated in the cerebrospinal fluid. It stimulates the immune system, blood and lymphatic circulation, nervous system, and cerebrospinal fluid flow[15] and also enhances respiration and digestion.[16] Osteopaths believe the divine healing principle can be contacted and communicated with through the sense of touch: osteopathic palpation and manipulation help release restrictions in the body so that the divine healing principle can flow and work freely.

The shamanic healer sees the divine healing principle within the body as the person's spirit, understands that spirit is the deepest source of health, and knows that illness can manifest when spirit is damaged or lost. When illness is present, shamans work at the spiritual level to restore health by removing energy blockages or negative energies, and by returning vital life essences such as lost soul parts and lost power animal allies.[17] This type of healing can activate the immune system[18] and accelerate healing.[19]

3. A primary focus on health and its maintenance

"Nature is ever-willing, . . . self-caring, self-feeding and self-protecting" [20]

Osteopaths are trained to be health-oriented and consider their greatest responsibility to be to restore and develop the patient's health and awareness to the highest degree. They use their hands to find and sense the health within the disease, and then help the patient recruit this health and express it for complete recovery.[21] They also encourage preventative medicine through proper nutrition, correct breathing and posture, regular sleep and exercise, and eliminating personal health risks.

Shamans, too, have traditionally focused on health and its maintenance, knowing that the survival of the tribe depended upon the health of its members and their proper relationship with each other, their land, nature, and with spirit.[22] Their many traditional roles have included acting as healers, priests, counselors, mystics and storytellers to their patients and their community.[23] In these roles, they have utilized energy work, herbal remedies, ceremonies, shamanic journeying and other assistance from non-ordinary sources.

4. Life and movement

"Motion is the first and only evidence of life" [24]

In osteopathic medicine, the musculoskeletal system is central to the patient's health and well-being: (a) it is the largest organ system in the body; (b) its upright position makes it susceptible to gravity and outside forces; (c) the most common restrictions to the flow of life force occur here; (d) its rich nerve and blood supply link it intimately with all other body systems; (e) it allows each human the full expression of their uniqueness.

Being born from nature, the entire body including bones is fluid and alive, has its own natural movements and rhythms, and moves toward balance, freedom and health. As good health reflects an alignment with the natural world and its rhythms, so disease is seen as a loss of connection to these essential rhythms.[25] Osteopathic manipulation is designed to restore movement to areas of the body that are meant to move, and to improve the body's function through increased vitality and flow.

Shamans, too, know that the universe is alive and that everything in it moves or vibrates in a natural way as spirit flows through all living things. Shamans themselves are people of action, moving between realities to help others,[26] and using movement (e.g., extraction, dancing) or sound vibration (chanting, drumming, rattling) to restore natural movements and energy flow to the body by unblocking stuck energy or reconnecting a patient to natural sources of healing power.

5. A hands-on approach to health and healing

"The osteopath removes the obstruction, lets the life-giving current have full play, and the man is restored to health" [27]

Because of their training, osteopathic physicians are comfortable with touching patients and using their hands in a sensitive and intelligent way to build a relationship with the patient, to diagnose, and to give treatment. They know that the patient's entire history of health, illness, and physical injury since conception is imprinted into the body structure as both freedom and restrictions to normal movement. Osteopathic physicians are trained to feel the body's living anatomy and work with it.

Shamanic healers also use a natural, hands-on approach. With their hands they can sense the body's energy, detect or remove foreign energies, or reach inside the body to heal. Their hands are used to give back lost soul parts, power animals, or energy pieces. And they also use their hands to 'line up' and direct healing energy, assisted at times by their spirit helpers, power objects, sacred stones, feathers, or shaman's altar (mesa).[28]

Integration

For me, the integration of shamanic healing and osteopathic manipulative medicine occurred over several years as I began to use my hands regularly to help people heal. Applying what I learned from my various teachers in ordinary and non-ordinary reality, I practiced what I knew regularly and often, using what I had learned when I felt ready to do so. Over time, I received a deeper insight into clinical situations at the level of spirit, so that I knew more for my next patients and could approach them differently. Lastly, I did what I was guided to do (or intuitively knew to do) when new and unfamiliar clinical situations arose or I came to an impasse. I pioneered ahead under spirit's guidance without necessarily knowing exactly how to do it, or without knowing the precise outcome, or whether or not it followed 'logic.' Through this process, I came to know that I have a personal style of shamanic healing and osteopathic manipulation that is my own[29] and that works best for me and for the good of the patient.

Currently in my integration process, typical new patients' visits to my office start with a phone call discussing why they are coming to me and what their needs are. Then I talk to them about what I do and educate them about osteopathic manipulative medicine and/or shamanic healing. At the beginning of the first office visit, I ask the patient for written informed consent to treat, whether for osteopathic manipulative medicine, shamanic healing, or both. I also get non-ordinary consent for shamanic work by silently checking in with spirit throughout the session.

After a history and physical examination, I sit down at the patient's head as he or she lies down on my treatment table. I then create a safe ceremonial healing space by opening and expanding my luminous body and by silently calling in the four cardinal directions, my teachers and my power animals to ask for protection, guidance and permission to do the work. This opening ritual is very important in shamanic work, and centering is also a long-standing tenet of osteopathic thought: "Be still and know."[30]

I clear the patient's luminous body of any toxic or negative energies such as spirit possession or aggressive energy and balance the patient's energy meridians in a general way by centering their umbilical pulse. I do this by silently summoning a plant helper spirit, *Artemesia vulgaris* (mugwort) through my hands. Next, I use shamanic seeing to look at the patient's luminous body to check for spiritual intrusions, energy blockages, and energy holes (representing power loss) while I kinesthetically feel with my hands for these same problems and for osteopathic restrictions in the patient's body. Lastly, I use my Plant Spirit Medicine training to take the patient's pulses (pulse diagnosis) to detect energy blockages. I have found through experience that osteopathic restrictions almost always have one or more energy blocks associated with them, and sometimes soul loss and/or spiritual intrusions, too.

Following this integrated diagnostic phase, I use osteopathic manipulation to release these restrictions from the patient's body and *Artemesia vulgaris* to release the associated energy blocks. Sometimes I may be guided to do extraction work or a soul retrieval with the assistance of my power animals or spirit teachers, and when the sessions ends, they counsel me to "say this" to the patient or "have them do this" to integrate the treatment session. I complete the session by giving silent thanks to spirit and by closing my own luminous body.

Case studies

Case 1: M, a 32-year-old man, comes to see me for the first time because of his long-standing headaches. After the initial history and physical, he lies down on the treatment table for an osteopathic treatment. Before I place my hands on him, I expand my luminous body, merge quickly with my Upper World teachers and power animals, and say a silent opening prayer to Viracocha (Great Spirit), Pachamama (Mother Earth), the local Apu (Mountain spirit), the cardinal directions, and the healing spirits of the land as I ask for protection, guidance and permission to work.

Following my opening ritual and prayer, I silently call on the spirit of the energy transfer plant ally, *Artemesia vulgaris*, to enter my hands and clear his luminous body of any spirit possession, aggressive energy, left-right energy imbalances, and to center his umbilical pulse.[31] This preliminary clearing of negative energies from the patient's energy field using a specific plant spirit ally is tremendously helpful in increasing the effectiveness of osteopathic manipulation.[32]

Next, I am shown an image of a video screen that acts as an internal TV monitor of the inside of the patient's body. I journey through his body with my spirit teacher, and I see and feel the osteopathic restrictions that his body is ready to release, some of which contain spiritual intrusions. My teacher and I release the restrictions and intrusions with my hands to another spirit helper who takes them away. In this example, a teacher or power animal can merge with me to see, feel and guide the precision of the treatment, which here is also an extraction.[33] This merging also offers me power and protection.[34]

At the follow-up appointment, the patient tells me he is having an acute episode of his chronic left-sided chest pain. During my osteopathic examination and treatment, I locate restrictions between thoracic vertebra 4 and the head of the left humerus, and between ribs 4 and 5 on the left and the sternum. These I release with traditional osteopathic manipulation. One of my power animals then appears and shows me a dense energetic intrusion in the form of a sword projecting from the patient's heart, which I extract, and another power animal appears and simultaneously extracts another dense energy intrusion from the patient's back near the left shoulder blade. The two power animals silently vanish, taking the spiritual intrusions with them. At the end of the session, the patient's chest pain is gone.

M's case is an excellent example of the benefit of combined shamanic and osteopathic approaches for chronic, vague, or mysterious illnesses. Both approaches produce an ascending scale of healing, i.e., excellent relief and progressively longer times between visits.

Case 2: T, a 57-year-old man, comes in for his regular monthly treatment for chronic low back pain. Through our long-standing relationship, he has become familiar with shamanic healing, including soul retrieval, and he has agreed to my performing osteopathic manipulation and/or shamanic healing as the need arises during any treatment session. Today's osteopathic examination shows a large chronic strain extending from cervical vertebra 1 to sacral vertebra 5, which has also created a tear down the middle of his luminous body. With the help of my shamanic Upper World teacher and one of my power animals, we release the strain, but an energy hole remains in the patient's luminous body. I then call the spirit of a plant specific for soul retrieval to go with my teacher to retrieve the soul part most timely and beneficial to return to him today.[31,33] My teacher completely heals the returned soul part, and then the carrier plant returns it through my hands to the patient. I release a number of additional restrictions in the patient's body to help him further integrate this healing. At the end of treatment, I share with him what has happened, what my teacher told me about his soul loss and soul part, and a simple integration ritual to do before our next appointment. I also instruct him to get extra nourishment and rest for the next 48 hours.[31]

I have found that soul retrieval becomes easier to perform during an osteopathic treatment when plant spirit allies work with a teacher to retrieve the part, heal it, and help return it. The osteopathic release of restrictions also works well to help the soul part settle in properly.

At T's return several months later, I notice a generalized stiffness throughout his muscles, tendons and joints both at the beginning and the end of an osteopathic treatment. With him fully relaxed, I use my hands as divining tools and ask simple yes/no questions of his higher self to determine the source of this stiffness. I receive a vibratory "yes" answer to the query of gluten sensitivity as the cause of the stiffness. My power animal confirms this by nodding her head and showing me the image of a bagel! When the treatment is finished, I recommend to the patient that he gradually substitute rice and quinoa for gluten. He is able to do this over six months time, and his generalized body stiffness disappears.

Shamanic divination is quite accurate when osteopathic manipulation has released all of the current strains and the patient's body is relaxed and centered, providing a clear divining field. In this case, a power animal confirmed the diagnosis in a humorous and to-the-point way.

Case 3: S, a 46-year-old woman, makes an appointment for shamanic healing. During the session, she undergoes extraction of multiple spiritual intrusions near her throat and chest and receives a soul retrieval. Several days later, she develops moderate acute headaches that persist and returns for an osteopathic manipulative treatment. At that time, no new intrusions are detected, but several chronic restrictions between cervical vertebra 3 and thoracic vertebra 4 and 6 are released by me, giving her substantial relief and allowing the soul piece that she received in the previous shamanic session to expand more fully throughout her body.

Conclusion

In my clinical practice of combining osteopathic manipulative treatment and shamanic interventions, I have noticed several important results: (1) some body restrictions are difficult to release until shamanic healing occurs; (2) the release of these restrictions can help shamanic work integrate more deeply; (3) some patients who experience body pain after shamanic healing have had body restrictions surface that were then released by OMT; and (4) some patients clearly benefit from the simultaneous experience of both approaches in a combined session with faster healing and increased relief of symptoms, suggesting that the power of both healing approaches combined is greater than either one alone or in sequence.

Overall, my experience using both approaches is that many patients follow an ascending scale of healing, with an increasingly fewer number of follow-up appointments and an increasing time period between appointments. There have also been a significant number of patients who report that they have had partial or complete relief of chronic symptoms that resisted conventional or other alternative healing methods.

Dr. Still believed that osteopathic medicine was a divinely inspired and authentic field of medicine meant to develop further over time. This encouraged his student, Dr. William Sutherland, to develop the inherent motion of the cranium, sacrum, and nervous system into the field of Cranial Osteopathy that exists today.

Similarly, I believe that the combination of shamanic healing and OMT represents both a potent healing combination and a deeper development of the spiritual foundations of osteopathic medicine that is true to Dr. Still's original vision and that holds much promise in the relief of human suffering.

References

[1] Eliade M. *Shamanism: Archaic Techniques of Ecstasy*. Princeton, NJ: Bollingen Books; 1964; 33-36.

[2] Field J. Personal communication, 1999.

[3] American Academy of Osteopathy, Osteopathic Medicine: A Distinctive Branch of Mainstream Medical Care. 3500 Depauw Boulevard, Indianapolis, IN, 46268.

[4] Magoun HI, Jr. *Structured Healing*. Vail, Colorado: Privately published; 2001; 80-82.

[5] Still AT. *Osteopathy, Research and Practice*. Reprint. Seattle, WA: Eastland Press; 1992; 6. (Available as an eBook through www.interlinea.org)

[6] Still AT. *Autobiography of Andrew T. Still*. Reprint. American Academy of Osteopathy; 1905. (Available as an eBook through www.interlinea.org)

[7] Still AT, *Autobiography of Andrew T. Still.* 19.

[8] Hagopian BS. "On Becoming an Osteopath." *Alternative Therapies* 2001; 7: 6: 85-91.

[9] Sutherland WG. *Teachings in the Science of Osteopathy*. Rudra Press; 1990;

3:13-14, 34-35, 169.

[10] Mehl-Madrona L. Personal communication, November 2002 and October 2005.

[11] Harner M. *The Way of the Shaman*. HarperSanFrancisco; 1990; 40.

[12] Truhlar R, Doctor AT. *Still in the Living*. Cleveland, Ohio: Privately published; 1950; 86. (all quotes from this source are from Dr. Andrew T. Still)

[13] Ingerman S. *Medicine for the Earth: How to Transform Personal and Environmental Toxins*. New York: Three Rivers Press; 2000; 131.

[14] Truhlar R.; 132.

[15] Sutherland, WG.

[16] Fulford RC. *Dr. Fulford's Touch of life. The Healing Power of the Natural Life Force*. New York, NY: Pocket Books, Simon and Schuster; 1996; 14.

[17] Ingerman S. *Shamanic Journeying: A Beginner's Guide*. Boulder, Colorado: Sounds True; 2004; 9-10.

[18] Harner S. "Shamanic Journeying and the Immune Response: Hypothesis Testing." *Shamanism* 2003; 16: 2: 13.

[19] The Four Winds Society. Healing the Light Body Curriculum 1997-1999.

[20] Truhlar R.; 99.

[21] Becker RE. "Be Still and Know. A Dedication to William G. Sutherland, DO." *Cranial Academy Newsletter* 1965; 5-8.

[22] Harner M.; xiii.

[23] Ingerman S. *Shamanic Journeying: A Beginner's Guide*; 7.

[24] Truhlar R.; 84.

[25] Hagopian.; 85-91.

[26] Harner M.; 46.

[27] Truhlar R.; 111.

[28] Miro-Quesada O. Personal communication, November 2001.

[29] Sharon D. *Wizard of the Four winds: A Shaman's Story*. New York, NY: Macmillan Publishing; 1978; 14-15

[30] Becker RE.

[31] Cowan E. Plant Spirit Medicine Curriculum, 1999.

[32] Broz G. Personal communication, November 2003.

[33] Rysdyk E, and Knowlton A. "Spirit Passages" curriculum; 2000.

[34] Harner M.; 69.

About the author

Dr. Michael R. Verrilli, DO, MS, is a board-certified osteopathic physician who maintains a practice of osteopathic manipulative medicine and shamanic healing in Northampton, Massachusetts. He trained at Botsford Hospital, the Cleveland Clinic Foundation and Hartford Hospital. Dr. Verrilli has been initiated into Peruvian shamanism by Q'ero elder Don Manuel Quispe. He studied with C. Allie Knowlton and Evelyn Rysdyk and is a graduate of their Spirit Passages Two-Year Advanced Training Program. He is also a graduate of the Four Winds Society Medicine Wheel, Light Body and Mastery Programs, and a graduate of Eliot Cowan's Plant Spirit Medicine Program.

XI

Shamanic Naturopathy: An Integrative Approach

Melissa M. Dawahare, NMD

A twenty-eight-year-old female patient complained of stress, anxiety, trouble falling asleep, difficulty in relationships, sadness, crying spells, rage, and anger problems. These issues started in her teenage years and were never diagnosed or treated by a healthcare professional. The young woman self medicated with alcohol, which initially relieved the complaints, but soon only made matters worse.

Searching for answers and a way to heal, she consulted a naturopathic medical doctor who diagnosed her medical conditions. She decided to use naturopathic medicine – diet changes, herbal remedies, homeopathy, counseling, and other modalities – to treat these problems instead of conventional medications and treatment. The naturopathic doctor prescribed a constitutional homeopathic remedy and other naturopathic therapies for her.

Within one month of starting the naturopathic protocol, her excessive rage and anger disappeared. She would still get angry, but her response was appropriate instead of blown out of proportion. Her sadness and crying spells also resolved. Feeling calm and able to relax, she overcame her sleep difficulties three months into her treatment. She continued her alternative medical treatments for five years. During that time she consulted with a shamanic healer and added several sessions of shamanic healing to her health program.

Today she is a completely different person. She changed careers from a registered nurse in Western medicine to a naturopathic medical doctor and shamanic healer in alternative medicine. She sleeps well, no longer drinks alcohol, and is more emotionally stable.

The person you have been reading about is me. I am living proof of the effectiveness of combining naturopathic medicine with core shamanism to treat the whole person: body, mind, and spirit. I found naturopathic medicine by 'accident' when looking in the yellow pages for something else. On seeing the local naturopathic medical school in the phone book, a chill came over me and I knew I was destined to attend their institution. I rediscovered shamanism when a memory of reading the word 'shaman' in a book at age 11 returned to me during meditation. Acting on this memory, I immediately investigated shamanism and began studying it formally that very weekend.

I feel gratitude for this synchronistic guidance. Both naturopathic medicine and shamanism have become invaluable tools in my personal life and professional healing practice. This chapter introduces the scope of both modalities and shows, through case studies, the impact of combining them in clinical work.

Naturopathic medicine

Naturopathic medicine, or naturopathy, is an art, science, and philosophy as well as a form of prevention, diagnosis, and treatment of sickness and disease. It was founded on six basic ethical principles: do no harm, use the healing power of nature, identify and treat the root cause of illness, treat the whole person, the physician is a teacher, and prevention is always the best cure.

Naturopathic medical doctors (NMDs) are trained as primary-care physicians and typically practice in offices, clinics, and wellness centers. Some naturopathic doctors also have hospital privileges, but this is the exception rather than the rule. They use standard mainstream biomedical diagnostic techniques such as physical exams, labs, ultrasounds, and x-rays to help diagnose disease. While naturopathic doctors have prescriptive authorities in some states, they typically use a combination of clinical nutrition, botanical medicine, homeopathic medicine, physical medicine, lifestyle counseling, oriental medicine, and other forms of complementary and alternative medicine (CAM) to treat illness instead of prescription drugs.

The formal study of naturopathic medicine requires a minimum of eight years: a four-year undergraduate degree and a four-year doctorate degree in naturopathic medicine. Although the law does not require traditional residency programs after graduation from naturopathic medical school, many naturopathic physicians choose to complete a residency program.

Licensing laws for naturopathic medical doctors currently exist in fourteen of the fifty states, the District of Columbia, the US territories of Puerto Rico, and the US Virgin Islands. The scope of naturopathic medical practice varies in each state, territory, or island, but in all locations, naturopathic medical doctors are required to graduate from a four-year residential naturopathic medical school and pass extensive postdoctoral board exams in order to receive a medical license.

Core shamanism

The shamanic training I bring to my work is from the Foundation for Shamanic Studies, created by anthropologist Michael Harner in 1979. From various indigenous traditions of shamanism, he developed an experiential healing methodology he termed "core shamanism" which includes the following key techniques (see Introduction): power animal retrieval, soul retrieval, extraction, psychopomp, and divination.

My training with the Foundation for Shamanic Studies has been and continues to be quite thorough and challenging. High-quality training and mentoring is imperative for any student of shamanism to bring true spirit and healing to their shamanic work.

Case studies integrating shamanism and naturopathy

As a naturopathic physician, I work in a private office setting with several other physicians. I set up my treatment space with the aide of my spirit helpers whom I consulted through divination for colors, room arrangement, and even what to hang on the walls. Creating my healing room took time, but the results were worth it. Now visitors who walk into the treatment area experience a noticeable difference and often comment on how peaceful and serene the room feels.

To comply with the naturopathic medical licensing laws in my state, I keep my practice of naturopathic medicine and shamanism separate. By this I mean naturopathic patients visit for naturopathic medical treatment while shamanic clients visit for shamanic healing sessions. Despite this distinct separation, I have found the integration of these two modalities occurring naturally when I work with people and my experience in naturopathy and shamanism deepens.

There is a great deal of crossover as the spirits work with my patients/clients in both ordinary and non-ordinary realities. For instance, when I journey shamanically for clients, my spirit helpers frequently use my knowledge of naturopathic medicine. In the journey, they may suggest a naturopathic modality or two especially suited for that particular client in addition to the shamanic interventions. It works in the reverse way as well: when I see a patient for naturopathic medicine, my spirit helpers guide me to ask certain questions in the medical history intake. If I am debating between several diagnoses, the spirits may guide me toward one diagnosis (based on facts) over the other, or perhaps even suggest a physician to refer to for proper diagnosis. Once I have a diagnosis, the spirits help me choose naturopathic modalities that will help the patient heal best. It has become a very fluid process.

Multiple sclerosis

A forty-three-year-old man diagnosed with multiple sclerosis (MS) visited my office. He suffered from bladder dysfunction and urinary incontinence, neck vein clots, tremors, depression, and chronic low back pain. He also had multiple viral infections in the past and ate a diet high in animal fats and dairy products. Other symptoms he was experiencing were decreased mental clarity, lack of balance, and dizziness.

His medications were amantadine, azathioprine, tolterodine, docusate sodium, famotidine, levetiracetam, and warfarin. The mental and emotional strain from his multiple illnesses contributed to a divorce from his wife and separation from his daughter. Previously he enjoyed sports—racket ball, swimming, and running—but now he was confined to a wheelchair. He was not able to feed or bathe himself and was living in a nursing home. He wore diapers for urinary incontinence and had been declared medically incompetent to handle his finances. This once family-oriented athletic male was debilitated by his illnesses.

A friend of his, who knew about naturopathic medicine, brought him into my office in 2005. I treated him for a period of three months before he moved out of state and his medical care was transferred to another physician. Although he originally came for naturopathic medical treatment, once he learned about my shamanic practice, he asked for shamanic healing to be included in his treatment plan.

The naturopathic medical treatments I prescribed included numerous dietary changes (including a raw foods diet), vitamin B12 injections, multiple supplements (including ginkgo biloba extract), and exercise which have all proven to be effective in the treatment of MS.[1] Twice a week acupuncture treatments were effective in alleviating symptoms and slowing down the MS disease progression.[2]

His shamanic treatments included a power animal retrieval, soul retrieval, divination, and several extractions. Power animal retrievals are useful in cases of depression, soul retrieval is valuable in cases of physical, mental, or emotional trauma, and extractions can bring relief from chronic localized pain.[3] The divination information my spirit teachers gave me suggested that the client's depression was anger turned inward. When I shared this information with him, he broke into tears and said that he was indeed angry at himself for not having a better relationship with his daughter but hoped to fix that soon.

With the help of his regular medical doctors, he was slowly weaned off some of his allopathic medications. On follow-up, his tremors had significantly decreased, his bowels began to function in a normal manner, his depression lifted, he regained control of his bladder, and his low-back pain almost completely disappeared. More impressively, he went from a wheelchair to a walker and then to walking slowly unassisted after a few months of treatment.

On final follow-up with the patient, he reported continued adherence to the dietary changes and supplement regimen. His mental function improved and he was allowed to take control of his finances. After three months, a repeat of the deep venous ultrasound showed no evidence of blood clots in the neck veins. By the end of his treatment, although he had not resolved all of the issues with his daughter, he was communicating with her on a weekly basis.

Menopause symptoms, smoking cessation, and wrist pain

A fifty-year-old woman came into the office for help with her menopausal symptoms, smoking cessation, and wrist pain. After unsuccessfully trying conventional medicine for these, she decided to try naturopathic medical treatments and shamanism instead. During our initial interview, she reported having occasional mood swings, feelings of anxiety, hot flashes, and chronic pain in the left wrist after a yoga injury. She smoked half a pack of cigarettes per day for the past thirty years.

The naturopathic medical treatments I prescribed included intramuscular injections of vitamin B12 (which have been shown to help improve joint issues[4]), Chinese and Western herbal formulas, and mind-body medicine. Acupuncture treatments were administered three times per week for wrist pain[5] and as well as for the symptoms of menopause and smoking cessation.

Her shamanic sessions included extraction and soul retrieval. The shamanic extraction work removed the spiritual intrusions that were contributing to her problems, and the shamanic soul retrieval (known to help in physical illnesses and addiction[6]) restored lost soul essence to her, which assisted the client in being able to break free of her thirty-year smoking habit.

After a few months of naturopathic and shamanic treatments, her wrist pain completely resolved. During this same time period, she weaned herself completely off the cigarettes. Her menopausal symptoms of hot flashes, mood swings, and anxiety were greatly reduced. At her most recent follow-up visit, she was still free of wrist pain, not smoking, and having only an occasional hot flash.

Stress, migraine headaches, and shoulder pain

A forty-five-year-old woman who came to my office reported a dull aching pain in her neck and left shoulder. She was experiencing chronic stress, tension, depression, and felt trapped by her life choices. She was unhappy with her living and working situations and felt unable to make changes for herself. She also reported an addiction to coffee and caffeine, and suffered from debilitating migraine headaches and frequent urinary tract infections. While she originally came for naturopathic treatment, once trust was established and I informed her of the potential benefits of shamanism, she asked for shamanic healing to be included in her treatment as well.

I conducted naturopathic medical treatment and shamanic healing for about six months with her. The naturopathic treatments consisted of lifestyle counseling, clinical nutrition, and oriental medicine, including acupuncture. Lifestyle counseling and clinical nutrition focused on diet changes to avoid foods high in dietary amines, which have been found to induce migraine headaches.[7] Yoga classes three times a week were added to address her chronic stress and tension. I added acupuncture because it generally produces excellent results in decreasing or eliminating shoulder pain.[8]

Soul retrieval and power animal retrieval were the shamanic treatments I used over this six-month course of treatment. The practice of power animal retrieval makes a person power-filled,[9] which gave this patient strength to make more fulfilling life choices regarding her work and home-life.

During the final appointment, the patient reported a complete resolution of her shoulder pain and migraine headaches, and clearing of her depression. She bought a new home and found a new job two months after the soul retrieval and reported that being in touch with her lost soul essence helped her to gain clarity about her life to make these changes. She stopped drinking coffee, learned healthier eating habits, and continued her practice of yoga.

Allergies and asthma

A thirty-eight-year-old woman had chronic allergies, asthma, and frequent attacks of bronchitis and pneumonia. Other symptoms included shortness of breath, coughing, thick nasal discharge, itchy eyes and nose, and constipation. Her medications included fluticasone/salmeterol and montelukast. She initially came to see me for soul retrieval and other shamanic healing. Once she learned about naturopathy and the other therapies I offered, she requested her treatment plan be expanded to include naturopathic medicine. Her plan varied over a course of six months: clinical nutrition, homeopathic medicine, and immune-system support were the main naturopathic treatments.

She received soul retrieval, useful for chronic medical conditions such as hers,[10] and I also taught her how to journey. The use of the shamanic journey to increase immune-system response has been documented and may explain her exceptional results.[11,12,13] For asthma and allergies, clinical nutrition requires the elimination of food allergens and food additives from the diet.[14] I added omega-3 fatty acids and antioxidants to her nutritional program to help support her body's inflammatory response. The homeopathic medicine I used was Kali Bichromicum, which is indicated in cases where mucous membranes are affected and nasal discharge is thick.[15]

At the follow-up appointment, she was symptom-free of both allergies and asthma. She continues her dietary changes and limits her exposure to known allergens. Her homeopathic medicine did not need to be repeated, and she reported using shamanic journeying as part of her spiritual practice. She later reported she felt the soul retrieval was the most important part of the healing plan.

Rhinitis, itchy nose and eyes, and headaches

A forty-one-year-old male came to my clinic with chronic allergies and headaches. His symptoms included rhinitis, itchy nose and eyes, and headaches. Aside from these concerns, he had no other significant past medical problems. He exercised four times a week and ate a diet which included a large amount of breads and pastas. Occasionally he took diphenhydramine to relieve his symptoms.

Initially he sought my help for soul retrieval. After a divination journey to consult with my power animals and teachers, I performed soul retrieval for him after which he reported an increased sense of wellbeing. After discussing the options available, he asked to have naturopathic medical treatments as well. These started with the homeopathic medicine Allium Cepa, which is indicated for his type of allergic symptoms[16] and included milk thistle, an herbal remedy that improves liver function. He also changed his diet to reduced dietary wheat products, as high gluten grains including wheat, barley, rye, and oats are involved in immune system dysregulation.[17]

During his final visit, he reported a 75% reduction in allergy symptoms. The dietary changes were more difficult than he expected, but he was able to comply with them. He no longer takes medications for his allergies and uses the homeopathic medicine, Allium Cepa, whenever he has an acute allergic attack. He continues to connect with his returned soul essence and reports feeling closer to his youngest son.

Unexplained weight gain and chronic fatigue

A thirty-nine-year-old female came to my office with concerns of unexplained weight gain, chronic fatigue, and excessive stress. She had some insomnia, anxiety, and seasonal allergies. Frustrated by her lack of response to traditional medical treatments, she wanted to see if naturopathic medicine and shamanism would work to improve these troubles.

After a thorough medical history and physical exam, food sensitivity and neurotransmitter testing was ordered. Her lab results confirmed a diagnosis of food allergies and adrenal fatigue. Her naturopathic treatment protocol included nutritional supplements, a rotation diet, and avoidance of food allergens. Persistence and dedication to the plan paid off; the patient was able to safely lose 12 pounds within a month, which motivated her to keep going. Her stress and anxiety dropped by half, and she started sleeping better. Her improvement stalled after three months of treatment and she decided a shamanic healing session would be helpful.

Her shamanic healing session included an extraction and a powerful soul retrieval. The soul essence returned to her was lost at the time of her father's death, at age eleven. The spirits confirmed through divination that this soul loss was a part of her present day medical problems.

At follow up several months later, she had achieved her ideal weight and even added an exercise regimen on her own to her wellness program. Her insomnia and anxiety were gone in spite of some ongoing stress in her life. She continued to process her feelings over the loss of her father while integrating the returned soul essence and felt good about the progress she had made.

Conclusions

While research supporting allopathic medicine is immense, research supporting naturopathic medicine is beginning to catch up. The literature documenting the effectiveness of shamanism as a form of healing is much smaller, but growing, with studies currently underway supported by the National Institute of Health (NIH).[18]

Combining naturopathic medicine with shamanism provides a treatment approach that addresses the whole patient: body, mind, and spirit. In my experience, combining the two has proven to be quite effective. I feel my job is to go between the worlds of the science of naturopathic medicine and the 'science' of spirits, helping clients achieve optimal health.

Learning core shamanic healing practices, naturopathic medicine modalities, and when to use each of them takes a great deal of dedication and patience. They are lifelong studies in which one never graduates, and something new is learned with each patient or client.

References

[1] Murray M. and Pizzorno J. *Encyclopedia of Natural Medicine Revised 2nded.* Rocklin, CA: Prima Health; 1998; 666-76.

[2] Maciocia G. *The Practice of Chinese Medicine: The Treatment of Disease with Acupuncture and Chinese Herbs.* Philadelphia: Churchill Livingstone; 1994; 701-707.

[3] Harner M. and Harner S. "Core Practices in the Shamanic Treatment of Illness." *Shamanism* 2000; 13: 19-30.

[4] Murray M. and Pizzorno J.; 807.

[5] O'Connor J. and Bensky D. *Acupuncture: A Comprehensive Text.* Seattle, WA: Eastland Press; 1981; 662-63.

[6] Ingerman S. *Soul Retrieval: Mending the Fragmented Self.* New York: HarperCollins; 1991; 14-23.

[7] Murray M. and Pizzorno J.; 648-65.

[8] Maciocia G.; 591.

[9] Harner M. *The Way of the Shaman.* New York: Harper Collins;1980; 76.

[10] Ingerman S.; 14.

[11] Harner S. "Shamanic Journeying and Immune Response." *Shamanism* 2003; 16: 2: 9-13.

[12] Harner S. and Tryon W. "Effects of Shamanic Drumming on Salivary Immunoglobulin A, Salivary Immunoglobulin M, Anxiety, and Well-Being." In: Pentikainen J. and Hoppal M. eds. *Proceedings of the International Association of Historians or Religion.* Helsinki: Finnish Literature Society 1992; 196-204.

[13] Harner S. and Tryon W. "Psychological and Immunological Responses to Shamanic Journeying with Drumming." *Shaman* 1996; 4; 1-2: 89-97.

[14] Murray M. and Pizzorno J.; 260-272.

[15] Boericke W. *Pocket Manual of Homeopathic Materia Medica and Repertory.* New Delhi: B. Jain; 1997; 361-64.

[16] Allen HC. *Allen's Key Notes.* New Delhi: B. Jain; 1997; 22-23.

[17] Helms S. "Celiac Disease and Gluten-Associated Disease." *Alternative Medicine Review* 2005; 10: 172-192.

[18] ClinicalTrials.gov, http://clinicaltrials.gov/ct2/show/NCT00071474. Retrieved April 24, 2012.

About the Author

Melissa M. Dawahare, NMD, is a naturopathic medical doctor, a registered nurse, and a shamanic practitioner with over fifteen years of clinical experience in mainstream and alternative healthcare. Dr. Dawahare trained with and is a faculty member of the Foundation for Shamanic Studies. She is also a member of the Arizona Naturopathic Medical Association, the Society for Shamanic Practitioners, and the Circle of the Foundation for Shamanic Studies.

XII

Shamanic Intervention in a Cardiac Rehabilitation Program

Sandra Ingerman, MA

People who have suffered heart attacks are understandably worried, anxious, and depressed that another might occur. Ironically, these emotions can actually raise the risk of a second or third ischemic incident. Depression in particular has been shown to be associated with increased risk of cardiovascular morbidity and mortality. While numerous conventional and complementary therapies may successfully address depression and lower its impact, few therapies involving spirituality have been tested. In 2003 Dr. Sara Warber, Associate Professor of Family Medicine at the University of Michigan's Integrative Medicine Department, asked me to partner with her to create a pilot research study on the effects of spiritual work on patients who had suffered a heart attack. Specifically, we were interested in what effects shamanism would have using the healing protocol that I developed in my shamanic practice called "Medicine for the Earth."

My passion in studying shamanism has always been to discover how we could use indigenous healing ceremonies and practices to deal with modern day issues. Could we bridge these ancient practices into a Western culture? I believed the answer to this question was yes, and devoted my shamanic practice and teaching to bringing shamanism into the West to address the physical and emotional illnesses that are so prevalent today.

In *Soul Retrieval: Mending the Fragmented Self*[1] published in 1990, I wrote about how shamans heal trauma using a ceremony called soul retrieval. This became the focus of my work, and I found that soul retrieval successfully helped heal clients who had suffered traumas such as emotional and physical abuse, automobile accidents, difficult recovery from surgery, war-time stress, and lingering grief. I traveled throughout the United States and Europe teaching this healing method to practitioners of shamanism, with very positive healing results.

As I continued to teach, I realized the importance of showing clients themselves how to identify changes they needed to make in order to lead a more harmonious life. This typically required them to create a vision of a positive present and future for themselves that was different from the challenges they were faced with in the past. Furthermore, many clients needed to learn how to create a new life filled with passion and meaning. This type of 'aftercare work' was necessary to create long-term effects from shamanic healing and to prevent the positive results of soul retrieval from wearing off like some type of 'spiritual aspirin.' Only by creating a healthy lifestyle could clients maintain the positive effects of shamanic healing, and teaching this became central to what I called 'life after healing.'

The evolution of Medicine for the Earth

As I continued to explore how to help people create a healthy way of life, I began to wonder at what point do we begin to focus our individual healing process not just on ourselves but on the needs of the earth. How can we care for and heal the planet? So my work moved from a focus on the individual to looking at environmental problems. And out of this exploration I wrote *Medicine for the Earth: How to Transform Personal and Environmental Toxins*,[2] which became the basis for the cardiac rehabilitation study with the University of Michigan.

One of the most important messages I received over twenty years of shamanic journeying was that it is *who we become* that changes the world and our environment, *not what we do*. The true work is learning how to change thoughts, attitudes, and belief systems. This is actually performing 'alchemy of the soul' to change our inner environment so that our inner state of being is reflected out into the world. The literal definition of alchemy is "working within and through the dense darkness inside." This is big work and involves a commitment to engage in spiritual practices daily and throughout the day.

Stories that come from many spiritual and religious traditions attest that miracles were once an everyday occurrence. I researched different traditions to find clues as to how miracles were performed by shamans, mystics, and saints. As I read, a formula that seemed to be part of all miracles started to emerge. Each element of the formula could not be taken separately, but when combined, created the transmutation or 'miracle.' In this context, transmutation can be understood as the ability to change the nature of a substance; in particular, this means that the work of effecting environmental change is to change toxic substances into neutral substances.

Eventually I stated the formula as *intention + union + love + harmony + concentration + focus + imagination = transmutation*. For miracles to occur, we must hold a strong intention of what we want to see happen. All spiritual practices teach about the power of intention, which inevitably leads to action.

Furthermore, miracles involve union with a divine force, which spiritual teachers tell us is the source of love. Love is a great transformer and an essential ingredient in all miracles. Where there is an open heart filled with love, there is miraculous energy to bring through. Being in the presence of people who imbue the power of love can produce healing in and of itself. These people often do not use methods or techniques; they lift up everyone around them into a higher consciousness.

Spiritual traditions also teach that to be healthy we must live a harmonious life. Harmony within creates harmony without. Most tell us, too, that a key to the success of a spiritual practice is the ability to concentrate. In other words, we must maintain a strong focus on both our short term and long-term goals.

Imagination is another key in performing the miracle of transmutation. We must be able to envision an environment that is pure and clean and which supports all of life. With the power of imagination, we have the ability to sculpt the world we live in with each thought we have. We all use our imaginations, of course, though sadly it is often not in a mindful manner.

Many shamans say we are dreaming the wrong dream. We live with the illusion that we are separate from nature, separate from the spiritual realms, and that we are victims of our life and environment. These illusions are seeds that grow into plants of fear, anger, hate, despair, and darkness. We need a new dream to create a new earth.

A widespread spiritual practice to change our dreams involves engaging all the senses. We must be able to see the sights and colors of the world we want to live in and feel the sensations of what it would be like to live in such a world. We must be able to hear the sounds of life around us, smell the fragrances, and taste the tastes. We must be able to engage these senses to call our dream into being as if it is already here now, rather than imagining our creations as being in the future. Starting now, we can live in gratitude and appreciation for the beauty that we can see in all things.

I began writing *Medicine for the Earth* before my first trip to Egypt in 1998 and finished it after my second trip the following year. During this time I had a powerful dream in which the Egyptian god Anubis appeared to me and told me that the missing piece of my work in reversing environmental pollution is transfiguration. I had heard stories from shamanic traditions about shamans shapeshifting into animals such as wolves and ravens. But I could not connect that action to reversing environmental pollution. An important insight about this came from one of my clients who was dying of liver cancer. When I told her about my dream, she became very animated and started to share her passion for Gospel stories about Jesus. Being a fundamentalist Christian she knew quite well how Jesus transfigured into a brighter light than had ever been seen, and while in this transfigured state of divine light worked miraculous healings.

Now I understood Anubis' message to me: light heals and transmutes. And my research into various spiritual books showed countless references to healers and spiritual masters from all traditions transfiguring into divine light in performing miraculous healings. Since we are spiritual light and connected to all, spirit is who we are beyond our skin. When we drop all that separates us from our divine light, everything around mirrors back to us a state of divinity, light, and perfection.

For years I worked with groups of people on an experiment to see if as a community we could transmute pollution in the environment from toxicity to a neutral substance. We took de-ionized (pure) water and polluted it with ammonium hydroxide, which is a common pollutant in the environment, and is a strong base. It is easy to check its presence with the use of pH strips to check alkalinity. Our ceremony involved letting go of what keeps us separate from our own divinity, and feeling ourselves as the power of the universe, divine, the source of light. The water reflects back to us that place of complete harmony, and in that place, we radiate spiritual light that affects everything around us. I have presented this work to many groups, and every time the pH of the water has dropped 1-3 points toward neutral. The actual ceremony lasts about 20 minutes, and the pH changes within this time frame. From a scientific point of view this would be seen as impossible.

Since these initial experiments, I started using a gas discharge visualization (GDV) camera that allows one to capture the physical, emotional, mental, and spiritual energies emanating to and from an individual, plant, liquid, powder, or inanimate object and translates those energies into a computerized model. This diagnostic camera measures and evaluates the energy of the auric field and integrates that information into a computer-generated report with pictures. The camera enabled us to document the change in energy of the substances present in our circle. To change the variables in the experiment, we also put food (a peach and crackers) and soil in our circle, along with the water, and the GDV camera was able to capture the change of energy of those items as well as the water.

Another interesting thing occurred during these experiments. Not only did the water, soil and food show changes, but people present at the ceremonies reported experiencing profound emotional and/or physical healing. On reflection, it seemed to me that since our bodies are composed mostly of water, we too would be affected by being in a circle where water is being detoxified. So we started to invite people to lie in the middle of the circle along with the water or other substances during our ceremonies, and found that participants felt the alleviation of many different symptoms. One woman, who had been struggling with lupus and needed a service dog to help her walk, started hiking the day after she was in the middle of our circle. The ceremony was years ago, and she has been hiking ever since.[3] Some people reported problems of depression and anxiety clearing up, as well as the disappearance of a variety of ailments. I have found that long-term changes occur with the people who have kept up the practice of transfiguration on a regular basis.

It is important to note that in our ceremonies we have not tried to manipulate the environment. We do not focus on the substances on the altar of our circle. We change *ourselves* by transfiguring into divine light, perfection, and oneness with the understanding that our outer world will reflect back to us the inner changes that we make.

When working in this way we perceive everyone and everything in the room in its divinity. Although on a physical level there might be illness being reported, on a spiritual level we recognize the divine perfection of all of life. In this way we stimulate the radiance of each being to shine forth. As we begin to change our consciousness and get in touch with the light inside us, we can effect great changes in our outer world. It is who we *become* that changes the world.

Healing the Heart study

In the study at the University of Michigan, published in *Explore: The Journal of Science and Healing* in July/August 2011,[4] we were able to show that a non-denominational spiritual retreat can help patients with severe heart trouble feel less depressed and more hopeful about the future. The core of the study was a four-day Medicine for the Earth retreat, assisted by Kate Durda, that included techniques such as meditation, guided imagery, drumming, journal writing, and outdoor activities. Heart patients who participated saw immediate improvement in tests measuring depression and hopefulness. Those improvements persisted at three- and six-month follow-up measurements. Obviously this gave the participants tremendous hope. Previous research has shown that hope and its opposite, hopelessness, have an impact on how patients face uncertain futures. Our study was the first randomized clinical trial to demonstrate an intervention that raises hope in patients with acute coronary syndrome, a condition that includes chest pain and heart attack.

"The study shows that a spiritual retreat like the Medicine for the Earth program can jumpstart and help to maintain a return to psycho-spiritual wellbeing," says Sara Warber, MD, one of the study authors. "These types of interventions may be of particular interest to patients who do not want to take antidepressants for depression symptoms that often accompany coronary heart disease and heart attack."

The Medicine for the Earth group was compared to two other groups: one that received standard cardiac care and the other that participated in a lifestyle change retreat run by the University of Michigan Cardiovascular Center focusing on nutrition, physical exercise, and stress management. The study used a number of standard mental and physical benchmarks to assess the success of the program. The Medicine for the Earth group went from a baseline score of 12 on the Beck Depression Inventory, indicating mild to moderate depression, to an improved score of 6 immediately afterward: a 50-percent reduction. Their scores remained at that level 6 months later. The lifestyle group saw their scores drop from 11 to 7 and remain there. The control group's score started at 8 and went down to 6.

Participants also showed marked improvement in their scores on a test measuring hope. Scores on the State Hope Scale can range from 6 to 48, with higher scores indicating greater hope. All three study groups started with average scores between 34 and 36. After the Medicine for the Earth retreat, participants' average scores rose and stayed at 40 or above, while the other two groups' averages remained significantly lower, ranging from 35 to 38 at three and six months later.

The conclusion of the study was that a spiritual retreat such as Medicine for the Earth could be used to increase hope while reducing depression in persons with acute coronary syndrome. "Our work adds an important spiritual voice to the current discussion of psychological wellbeing for patients facing serious medical issues, such as acute coronary artery disease," Warber says.

Most of the participants in the Michigan retreat were Christian and would not be open to working with helping spirits or shamanic practices. I adapted my vocabulary to match a vocabulary that they could understand and work with, and they reported that the practices were very powerful for them. This was a strong reminder to me of how we often get very attached to using particular words when teaching spiritual practices and need to be flexible in our descriptions to reach a broader audience with the work.

Some of the principles and practices we worked with during the retreat were:

1. The transmutation formula of intention + union + love + harmony + concentration + focus + imagination = transformation.

2. Our perception creates our reality. If we believe we can create a life filled with good health, then we will and can. As we learn how to appreciate the beauty of life, our life reflects back that beauty.

3. We can perceive a person as healthy or ill. When we perceive a person in perfect health, we help to lift them into a state of perfection.

4. Everything in our physical world starts in the invisible realms. This means our train of thought and the words we use to express our thoughts affect our health on all levels.

5. If we use meditation to breathe through our hearts and to learn how to observe our thoughts and state of being, we can learn to dis-identify from our emotional triggers.

6. We used guided imagery to meditate on our life as a garden. We reflected on the thoughts and words that we use to seed our garden, looking for thought-seeds of hope, inspiration, and love.

7. Journaling was used to write our thoughts, words, and decrees that we wished to focus on throughout the day that would lead to our desired outcome.

8. We worked with creating a state of wellbeing by using our imagination, engaging all of our senses to see, hear, feel, taste, and smell the happy and healthy life we wished to create. We also performed a ceremony in which our group helped to empower and support each participant's heart's desire.

9. We connected with nature as a powerful healing force that can give us a sense of wellbeing. Each person sat with a tree as a way to relax and feel a connection with the heartbeat of the earth. We took short walks while appreciating all that the earth, water, air, and the sun give us so that we may thrive.

10. Before going to bed at night, each participant set his or her intention for a healing dream during sleep.

11. Guided imagery was also used to help participants discover their own story of creation so that they could understand the principle of 'union with the divine.'

12. Once participants experienced their creation story, they used the practice of transfiguring into divine light. Then we did a simple ceremony to imagine ourselves traveling deep into our bodies until we experienced our inner spiritual light. When we had experienced the flow of our spiritual light, we radiated it out to the other members of our circle. In this way we experienced everyone in his or her divine perfection, feeding the health of each participant in our circle.

After the four-day workshop, participants were encouraged to work with all the practices that were learned during our time together. They were asked to continue the practice of transfiguration and also to continue to perceive everyone who was in our group in their divine light. Each person was encouraged to feel the love of the circle throughout every day and to 'take in' all the elements as light by breathing in air, drinking water, eating food, and taking in the sun as love and light. This practice allows our cells to absorb love and light throughout the day so that radiance shines through us, creating a state of health and wellbeing.

Everyone was also asked to create sacred space in his or her home or office: bringing in special objects, posting decrees or words of health or inspirational images in these environments, and placing flowers, candles, stones, etc. to remind them of their divinity.

Participants were also encouraged to continue to transform their problematic thoughts, attitudes, and belief systems with the methods learned during the workshop. And lastly, practices in working with gratitude were part of the continued daily work, as well as continuing to use one's imagination to focus on their life dream.

Each person in our circle was amazed at the depth of the growth and healing that came from the practices they were taught during this four-day workshop. But they were also very deeply touched by the love and support of the circle; this was a new and life-changing experience for them.

When we continued our follow up, there were many personal stories and endorsements of how the Medicine for the Earth retreat touched each person during and after the workshop. Almost all were in tears of joy over the success of their experiences. Many commented on the love that they felt in the circle. One person would recommend the retreat to other heart patients "because it changes the view on life and lifts the burden of stress to let your heart be free and shine to heal itself." One participant simply stated, "There is hope!"

Later, follow up phone calls kept participants sharing the positive impact of the work. One year after the retreat, we scheduled a reunion at a retreat center in Michigan for those who could attend. Not everyone could make it, but most of the group did come and brought their families because they wanted their own loved ones to meet others in the group and get a taste of the work we did together.

Implications for research

From a study such as this, a question arises naturally as to whether statistics are more important than the qualitative reports of how the shamanic work impacted participants.

All students, practitioners, and teachers of shamanism hear a wealth of stories about physical and emotional healings that come from shamanic practice, whether from indigenous healers or Western shamanic practitioners. Often these results cannot be explained by science: malignant tumors disappear, chronic illness is cured, and emotional illnesses lift. Doctors shake their heads and say there is no explanation for these results. Obviously this does not happen for everyone, but the numbers of people who do receive healing from the work are significant.

For the most part, Western society does not recognize the power of the invisible realms. Westerners want to experience everything on a tangible level where scientific proof can show the efficacy of the work. But do we really need scientific, quantitative data when we can see obvious improvement? In many ways, I feel empiric research may distract practitioners from moving forward with spiritual work so needed right now. As we watch bacteria and viruses mutate and evolve faster and faster, do we have the time to write grants and take years to plan research studies to prove the power of shamanism and other alternative forms of healing?

In order for us to pass on the healing power of shamanism during this rapid time of change on the planet, it is important that we embrace the mystery and not try to over-rationalize it or try to control the work. Healing comes in the energy brought through from the world of spirit, not through specific methods.

What I have written is my own personal bias based on my spiritual work. In spite of this caveat, it is clear that scientific studies and allopathic medicine have provided all of us with modern day discoveries of new medicines and treatments to prevent and cure many illnesses we are plagued with. Although as a shamanic practitioner and teacher I am naturally excited about forging ahead with the spiritual work, I also have a deep respect for science and research.

I believe it is time to bridge the important research that comes from empiric science with spiritual practices that are time tested. Our culture needs proof and evidence in order to be open and to feel hope that alternative treatments do work. And as we showed with the Healing the Heart study, hope is an important aspect in creating true and long lasting results in all healing. So I deeply support continuing research that will allow the Western mind to embrace what spiritual practitioners have to offer.

The power of shamanism is the unlimited love and light that can be brought through from the spirits and the power of the universe. And when we experience that we are spirit, too, and allow our own divine light to shine through, we bring back radiance to all of life and this great earth.

References

[1] Ingerman S. *Soul Retrieval: Mending the Fragmented Self.* HarperSanFrancisco; 1991.

[2] Ingerman S. *Medicine for the Earth: How to Transform Personal and Environmental Toxins.* New York: Three Rivers Press; 2000.

[3] Horrigan B. "Medicine for the Earth, Medicine for the People." Interview. *Alternative Therapies in Health and Medicine* Nov/Dec 2003; 9: 6; 76-84.

[4] Warber S., Ingerman S. et al. "Healing the Heart: A Randomized Pilot Study of a Spiritual Retreat for Depression in Acute Coronary Syndrome Patients." *Explore: The Journal of Science and Healing* 2011; 7: 4: 222-233.

About the author

Sandra Ingerman, MA, is a licensed marriage and family therapist and mental health counselor. She teaches workshops internationally on shamanic journeying, healing, and reversing environmental pollution using spiritual methods. Sandra has trained and founded an international alliance of Medicine for the Earth Teachers and shamanic teachers and is the author of eight books including *Soul Retrieval, Medicine for the Earth, Shamanic Journeying: A Beginner's Guide, How to Heal Toxic Thoughts, How to Thrive in Changing Times,* and *Awakening to the Spirit World: The Shamanic Path of Direct Revelation.*

XIII

Shamanic and Psychotherapeutic Healing of Trauma

Daniel Foor, PhD, MFT

The healing of trauma is an essential aspect of contemporary psychotherapeutic practice; this form of human suffering is also transformed and healed through the rich traditions of indigenous wisdom and shamanism that typically fall outside the domain of psychotherapy. These indigenous traditions are increasingly challenging and enriching mainstream psychology, and the utilization of shamanic healing methods by mental health professionals is but one way in which this is occurring. As the number of licensed counselors and psychotherapists using shamanic healing methods increases, there is a critical need for dialogue on how these two bodies of knowledge and practice understand and heal trauma.

Healing trauma from a psychotherapeutic perspective

There is considerable debate within the field of psychology about trauma and the degree to which traumatic experience underlies different types of psychological suffering.[1] Trauma specialist Judith Herman says that post-traumatic stress disorder (PTSD) describes a specific cluster of symptoms that include anxiety, depression, and certain personality disorders that are caused by traumatic experience.[2] In popular usage, even among mental health professionals, trauma typically refers to continued suffering from hardships such as childhood abuse and neglect, domestic violence, war, sudden and overwhelming loss, and profound lack of love and understanding among one's closest relationships.

Herman outlines three main stages of recovery from PTSD: (1) establishing safety, (2) remembrance and mourning, and (3) reconnecting with ordinary life.[3] 'Establishing safety' involves tending to both physical and emotional safety, minimizing the possibility of ongoing retraumatization, and building a therapeutic alliance or other healing connection to support the recovery process. In the second stage of 'remembrance and mourning,' the practitioner invites the client to fully express past traumas, accept these traumas for what they are, and incorporate them in a transformed way into their life stories. The third stage of 'reconnecting with ordinary life' is a journey from isolation into increasingly healthy and vital relationships with self and others. In this stage, one learns to improve interpersonal relationships by establishing healthy boundaries, feeling empowered in decision-making, and giving voice to one's desires and emotions. As helplessness and isolation are the core experiences of psychological trauma, so empowerment and reconnection are core experiences in recovery.[4]

Treatment of trauma tends to be most effective when it addresses both the client's ability to relate to others as well as the physical or neurological levels of trauma.[5] Physical trauma can include that which we experience as babies before we acquire language, as well as trauma that imprints on us at any age.[6] In practice, treatments that address the physical level of trauma may occur with therapists trained in somatic therapies or with healers using yoga, chi gong, or martial arts. Today two popular modalities of trauma treatment used in clinical mental health settings that directly emphasize the physical body and nervous system are Eye Movement Desensitization and Reprocessing (EMDR) and Somatic Experiencing. As Judith Herman notes, "There is no single, efficacious 'magic bullet' for the traumatic syndromes."[7]

Healing trauma from a shamanic perspective

Contemporary shamanism is a highly diverse and complex tapestry of varied beliefs, traditions, and practices. A distinction is often drawn between various forms of indigenous shamanism and neoshamanism, a late-twentieth-century revival movement. Neoshamanism draws inspiration from traditional indigenous shamanism as well as from European earth spirituality, Western esoteric traditions, and aspects of the New Age movement. Many senior practitioners of neoshamanic healing have also trained, sometimes extensively, with indigenous healers. And, due to the ease of travel today, many indigenous teachers go to all parts of the world, and so it is possible to do in-depth training in Asian, South American, and African shamanism without ancestral ties to these regions and without leaving North America. Regardless of whether a practitioner received his or her training from indigenous shamans or neoshamanic teachers (or a blend of the two), most shamanic practitioners serving as healers in modern, industrialized

Western cultures will inevitably encounter clients who suffer from serious trauma symptoms. In fact, post-traumatic stress clients are giving shamanic healers an opportunity to engage in dialogue with psychologists and clinical mental health providers. Such dialogue should result in the best possible care for those suffering from post-traumatic stress.

Shamanic healers use several metaphors to conceptualize sickness and healing that are analogous to what is called 'complex trauma' in psychology. Perhaps the most recurrent concept is that of 'soul loss.' In its appendix of culture-bound syndromes, the DSM-IV, a standard diagnostic text of psychiatric disorders, acknowledges that, "soul loss may be related to Major Depressive Disorder, Posttraumatic Stress Disorder, and Somatoform Disorders." It further states that the practices and symptoms described as soul loss throughout Latin American cultures "are found in many parts of the world."[8] Neoshamanic practitioners, as well as many indigenous shamans, view soul loss as occurring "whenever we experience trauma (and) a part of our vital essence separates from us in order to survive the experience by escaping the full impact of the pain."[9] Among some shamanic healers, soul loss is understood to be moderately common, while others perceive soul loss to be rare and serious. In the traditions where soul loss is understood to be less common, often the symptoms of chronic psychological distress are thought to be caused by intrusive foreign spirit entities. For example, in Buryat Mongol shamanism a person may experience varying degrees of interference from intrusions, or even full-blown possession by a foreign spirit, without suffering soul loss.[10]

Once a shamanic healer has diagnosed some combination of intrusive energies and/or soul loss, the next step is to respectfully remove the intrusions, then locate and return any lost or fragmented soul parts to the client. These processes are led by the shamanic healer and are completed in one or several sessions. Some shamanic healers observe that occasionally the intrusive spirits return after the healing, and sometimes the returned soul part refuses to stay with the client.

Assuming neither of these complications arises, traditions differ widely in how the healing process proceeds. At the first meeting of the Society for Shamanic Practitioners, Lucy Nesbeda characterized soul retrieval as the technical fix preceding the more long-term challenge for the client to change or transform his or her lifestyle.[11] In contrast to traditional psychotherapy settings, usually regular ongoing sessions with shamanic healers following soul retrieval are not required. This may be because shamans have historically relied heavily on the family and extended community to support the client in reconnecting and relating after the initial shamanic intervention. There is also the tradition of actively involving family, loved ones, or even the extended community in the shamanic healing ceremony itself.

Identifying common ground

Both psychotherapeutic and shamanic healers agree that the symptoms of trauma almost always arise in response to an external cause or a combination of causes, most of which are clearly identifiable and severe in nature. Nearly all other mental-health disorders separate the question of causation from diagnosis, but the DSM-IV diagnostic criteria for both Posttraumatic Stress Disorder (PTSD) and Acute Stress Disorder (ASD) require that the person be exposed to a traumatic event. Similarly, shamanic soul loss implies an external cause. Contemporary shamanic literature contains long lists of symptoms and causes of soul loss including incest, physical abuse, war, accidents, rape, major illness, surgery, and death of a loved one. Even when the cause of psychological distress is an intrusive spirit, such a spirit is typically described as having appeared at a time when the person was in a weakened emotional and physical state.

Mental health professionals and shamanic healers alike acknowledge varying degrees of severity with trauma or soul loss. In psychological terms, some of the variables that tend to create severe PTSD or other symptoms include sexual victimization, intentional acts of violence, the degree of unpredictability or uncontrollability of the trauma, the extent of combat exposure, and the grotesqueness of death. Herman suggests that a new diagnosis of complex PTSD be included in the DSM-IV in order to address the fact that the severity and expression of trauma can vary so widely.[12] Various shamanic traditions recognize degrees and types of soul fragmentation or soul loss. Buryat Mongol shaman Sarangerel Odigan observes that in her tradition there are several different types of soul energies that play different roles in the human psyche; "lost *ami* souls can be coped with for long periods, even years, but a lost *suns* soul will eventually result in severe mental illness and rapid physical decline."[13] Tibetan Bon shaman Tenzin Wangyal Rinpoche writes that soul loss "can happen all at once—as in the case of a single devastating incident—or over time when there's a traumatizing or dehumanizing environment."[14] Celtic shamanic healer Caitlin Matthews asserts that "with minor soul-fragmentation, people can still function to some degree, but with serious soul-fragmentation people have great difficulty looking after themselves."[15]

Both shamanic and psychotherapeutic healers distinguish between healing interventions that aim to relieve symptoms and those intended to empower and transform clients so that they can return to their communities. In psychological terms, a therapist's intervention to merely reduce symptoms (possibly using prescription medicines) never replaces the long-term goal of reconnecting with the world through healthy relationships and self-love. Helping a client to learn relational skills is central to psychotherapy. Some of this learning occurs in the relationship between client and therapist. However, as the length of average treatment in psychotherapy today continues to diminish for various reasons, it leaves us with the question of how long the lengthy process of relational healing can continue. It could be that psychotherapy in North American may be headed toward an indigenous approach of increasing reliance on the family and extended community to create the setting in which relational healing takes place. Shamanic healer Alberto Villoldo affirms that "there is a difference between curing and healing. Curing is remedial and involves fixing whatever outer problem arises. Healing is broader, more global, and more complete. Healing transforms one's life and often, though not always, produces a physical cure."[16] Sandra Ingerman devotes an entire book to the process of psychological growth and empowerment following the so-called technical fix or one-time cure of a soul retrieval ceremony.[17]

Psychotherapists and shamanic healers also agree that healing trauma in individuals is inseparable from healing the sources of trauma in the larger, broader culture. In the words of Judith Herman:

> Only after 1980, when the effects of combat on veterans had legitimized the concept of post-traumatic stress disorder, did it become clear that the psychological syndrome seen in survivors of rape, domestic battery, and incest was essentially the same as the syndrome seen in survivors of war. The implications of this insight are as horrifying in the present as they were a century ago: the subordinate condition of women is maintained and enforced by the hidden violence of men. There is war between the sexes. Rape victims, battered women, and sexually abused children are its casualties.[18]

Of course the most important intervention of all is to prevent abuse in the first place and create an environment where all people can thrive without fear of injury from other human beings.[19] Indigenous or shamanic wisdom consistently asserts that our relationships with the extended community of nature and nonphysical beings, as well as with other humans, are direct reflections of our internal, psychological wellbeing. "Ill-health is often understood as a result of inadequate interaction with other persons, both human and other-than-human," and shamans are specialists in the art of making ritual repairs when our ethical behavior toward others breaks down.[20]

Treatment considerations

There are a small but increasing number of individuals who are both licensed mental health professionals and practitioners of shamanic healing. These clinicians are integrating indigenous and shamanic healing with more established orientations such as Jungian psychology (e.g., Bernstein[21], Duran[22], Sandner[23], Smith[24]), object relations and attachment theory (Drake[25], Gagan[26]), somatic psychology (Mindell[27]), energy psychology (Brockman[28]), and eco-psychology (Gray[29]). Some have private psychotherapy or shamanic healing practices, some are employed at mental health or government agencies, and some are ceremonial leaders of group healing rituals or retreats.

My personal training in shamanic soul retrieval methods has been with both neoshamanic and traditional indigenous teachers, and I have also worked as a psychotherapist at a community mental health center serving English and Spanish-speaking individuals, couples, families, and youth, some of whom clearly qualified for a diagnosis of PTSD. The following case study of soul retrieval from my personal experience at this community mental health agency highlights several of the core issues faced by shamanic-oriented psychotherapists who attempt to harmonize these two approaches to healing trauma.

Carmen

Carmen is a 34-year-old Peruvian woman suffering from anxiety attacks, moderate depression, irregular eating habits, unhappy intimate relationships, and the chronic stress of being legally undocumented and physically separated from her family in Peru. She is the single mother of a six-year-old boy who struggles with moderate hyperactivity and defiant behaviors both at school and home, and she is engaged in a tense, ongoing custody battle with her ex-husband. Carmen has a strong, positive connection to her cultural roots in Peru, including Catholicism, as well as an openness to direct relationship with benevolent forces or guides such as Jesus Christ, the saints, and her beloved dead or ancestors.

Carmen is self-reflective, consistently attends sessions, and is actively engaged in the therapeutic process. After ten to fifteen sessions that included several family therapy sessions, interactions with her son have improved and her eating and exercise habits are better. Therapy then turns to a discussion of early childhood abuse from extended family members and reflection on these as the possible roots of her anxiety and depression. She describes a persistent feeling of emptiness and of emotional disconnection from aspects of her past, and this leads to a discussion of traditional forms of healing such as soul retrieval. She is receptive to this, and one session involves a modified soul retrieval. The therapy continues for another five to seven sessions, gradually transitioning to every two weeks, then once a month until her final formal session. At this session, Carmen said the soul retrieval work was a turning point in a positive and healing experience with psychotherapy.

Cultural appropriateness of soul retrieval work

In the case of Carmen, her Catholic background and her close connection to her indigenous roots provided a cultural foundation for her to accept the possibility that aspects of her soul (or self) may be lost and in need of recovery. Had I explained the process in the traditional terms of shamanism rather than in language more culturally familiar to her, it is possible that she would have been less receptive and the work would not have proceeded. It's also possible that fifteen sessions into a therapeutic relationship, Carmen may have felt unwilling to express discomfort with or decline a suggestion for soul retrieval that might compromise that relationship. If so, her consent for the soul retrieval and even the efficacy of it would have been compromised. Even if all other clinical indicators point toward soul retrieval, if the client does not have a basic understanding of soul retrieval and does not give genuine consent for the work, soul retrieval by any name would not be appropriate.

Clinical appropriateness of soul retrieval work

In this case, I viewed the client's description of feeling empty and out of touch with an earlier aspect of her life as a trigger that some form of soul retrieval work may be helpful. If her symptoms had been resolved without such an intervention or had she not trusted me sufficiently from previous sessions, I would not have suggested it. What is clinically appropriate after ten sessions may be misplaced if it is brought up too early in the therapeutic relationship. Other situations that might suggest that soul retrieval work is not appropriate for a client include active or recent psychosis, untreated addictions, a still tenuous therapeutic connection with the therapist, and any other thought or personality disorder that the magical or otherworldly aspects of shamanic healing might trigger. Soul retrieval work may also be both clinically and culturally impossible when psychotherapy is being billed to insurance or when the mental health setting is not conducive to it or when the healer works under the clinical license of a supervising therapist.

Clinical approach to soul retrieval work

With Carmen I did not sing or use a drum or rattle, I did not burn any sage or other sacred smoke, I wore no ceremonial garb, I did no invocation or audible prayer, and I did not enter into a deep trance or leave my body at any point. These classic aspects of soul retrieval work seemed unnecessary and likely to disrupt psychotherapy in a community mental health agency. Furthermore, by walking Carmen through the process herself, the efficacy of the healing was enhanced. Knowing this would require a full fifty-minute session, we planned in advance for the work.

When we began, I invited her first to attune to her helpful guides, and Christ and a deceased and much loved uncle appeared. These guides helped her when I next asked her to locate the younger disconnected aspect of herself and to begin to dialogue with it. Lastly, I encouraged her to welcome this aspect of herself back into her physical body and her present-day life.

Another advantage of guiding Carmen through the process directly is that I at no point made any claims to be accessing otherworldly or intuitive knowledge on her behalf. By avoiding the overt role of shamanic healer, I reduced the risks that my client might idealize me in an unhelpful way. Had she done so, it may have strained our relationship in terms of power and authority, which are already unequal in relationships between clients and therapists. Guiding her through the work also affirmed her own ability to relate directly with the unseen worlds in healing and transformative ways.

Need for ongoing relational healing

Psychotherapists often need to form positive attachments with their clients to facilitate healing the client's ability to relate to others. This type of learning may play out over months or even years of therapy. In these cases, the psychotherapist provides the client with an 'emotionally corrective experience' that would ideally be filled by loving family, friends, mentors, and extended community. After some integration from the soul retrieval session, Carmen's therapy focused on areas of everyday life that needed more attention before ending therapy. Reflecting on her comments in our closing session, the single most useful aspect of therapy for Carmen was the positive experience of the therapeutic relationship itself rather than any given intervention, including the soul retrieval. I would not say that this rules out the benefits of brief psychotherapy or stand-alone shamanic soul retrieval sessions. Rather it underscores the importance of some form of ongoing interpersonal intimacy and support needed in the lives of individuals healing from trauma, especially when the source of the trauma is relational in nature.

Conclusions

Until recently there has been a relative lack of writing and research on how contemporary shamanic healers in psychotherapeutic settings employ shamanism in healing and transforming trauma; however, for shamanism to be more widely accepted more studies are needed that clearly show the benefits of shamanic healing. Research has recently documented the tangible effects of prayer and meditation, and shamanic healing also is now being studied empirically without devaluing its non-tangible and creative aspects. For example, studies have surveyed the use of shamanic methods in the field as a whole (e.g., Bock[30], Foor[31], Sifers[32]), the neurological and physiological effects of shamanic practice (e.g., Winkelman[33], Wright[34]), and the clinical benefits of the repetitive drumming often utilized in shamanic practice (e.g., Bittman[35], Winkelman[36]). My hope is that shamanic healers will influence psychological theory, but for that to happen, there needs to be shared terminology and clinical models as well as reliable research upon which to base integrative models for shamanic-oriented psychotherapy. Mental health practitioners already using shamanic methods in their work, including those who have contributed to this book, provide an excellent starting point for this important dialogue.

References

[1] Briere J. *Psychological Assessment of Adult Post-Traumatic States.* Washington, DC: American PsychologicalAssociation; 2004; 62-63.

[2] Herman J. *Trauma and Recovery.* New York, NY: Basic Books; 1992; 21.

[3] Herman J.; 197.

[4] Briere J. *Child Abuse Trauma.* Newbury Park, CA: Sage; 1992; 41.

[5] Van der Kolk BA. "The Complexity of Adaptation to Trauma: Self-Regulation, Stimulus Discrimination, and Characterological Development." In: Van der Kolk BA., McFarlane AC., Weisaeth L., eds. *Traumatic Stress: The Effects of Overwhelming Experience on Mind, Body and Society.* New York, NY: Guilford Press; 1996; 184.

[6] Herman J.; 156.

[7] Herman J.

[8] *Diagnostic and Statistical Manual of Mental Disorders, 4th Ed.* Washington, DC: American Psychiatric Association; 1994; 849.

[9] Ingerman S. *Soul Retrieval: Mending the Fragmented Self.* HarperSanFrancisco; 1991;11.

[10] Odigan S. *Chosen by the Spirits.* Rochester, VT: Destiny Books; 2001; 101.

[11] Nesbeda L. "Shaman as Leader, Leader as Shaman." Unpublished manuscript; 2005; 2.

[12] Herman J. *Trauma and Recovery.* New York, NY: Basic Books; 1992; 121.

[13] Odigan S.; 108.

[14] Wangyal T. *Healing with Form, Energy and Light.* Ithaca, NY: Snow Lion; 2002; 58.

[15] Matthews C. *Singing the Soul Back Home.* Boston: Connections; 2002; 226.

[16] Villoldo A. *Shaman, Healer, Sage.* New York, NY: Harmony Books; 2000; 20.

[17] Ingerman S. *Welcome Home: Following Your Soul's Journey Home.* San Francisco: Harper; 1994.

[18] Herman J.; 32.

[19] Briere J.; 164.

[20] Harvey G. *Animism: Respecting the Living World.* New York, NY: Columbia University Press; 2006; 149.

[21] Bernstein J. *Living in the Borderland: The Evolution of Consciousness and the Challenge of Healing Trauma.* New York, NY: Routledge; 2005.

[22] Duran, E. *Healing the Soul Wound: Counseling with American Indians and Other Native Peoples.* New York, NY: Teachers College Press, Columbia University; 2006.

[23] Sandner D. and Wong S., eds. *The Sacred Heritage: The Influence of Shamanism on Analytical Psychology.* New York, NY: Routledge; 1997.

[24] Smith C. *Jung and Shamanism in Dialogue: Retrieving the Soul/Retrieving the Sacred.* New York, NY: Paulist Press; 1997.

[25] Drake A. *Healing of the Soul: Shamanism and Psyche.* Ithaca, NY: Busca; 2003.

[26] Gagan J. *Journeying: Where Shamanism and Psychology Meet.* Santa Fe, NM: Rio Chama; 1998.

[27] Mindell A. *The Shaman's Body: A New Shamanism for Transforming Health, Relationships, and the Community.* San Francisco: HarperSanFrancisco; 1993.

[28] Brockman H. *Dynamic Energetic Healing.* Salem, OR: Columbia Press; 2006.

[29] Gray L. "Shamanic Counseling and Ecopsychology." In: Gomes M., Kanner A., Roszak T., eds. *Ecopsychology: Restoring the Earth, Healing the Mind.* San Francisco: Sierra Club Books; 1995; 172-182.

[30] Bock N. "Shamanic Techniques: Their Use and Effectiveness in the Practice of Psychotherapy." Unpublished master's thesis. University of Wisconsin, Madison; 2005.

[31] Foor D. *An Interview-Based Inquiry Into Challenges Faced by Licensed Mental Health Professionals Who Utilize Shamanic Healing Methods.* Unpublished Doctoral Dissertation. San Francisco: Saybrook University, San Francisco; 2009.

[32] Sifers S. *The Use of Shamanic Counseling by Counselors and Clients: An Exploration of a Spiritual Movement.* Unpublished doctoral dissertation, University of Utah, Salt Lake City; 1998.

[33] Winkelman M. "Physiological and Therapeutic Aspects of Shamanic Healing." *Subtle Energies* 1990; 1: 3: 1-18.

[34] Wright P. "The Interconnectivity of Mind, Brain, and Behavior in Altered States of Consciousness: Focus on Shamanism." *Alternative Therapies in Health and Medicine* 1995; 1: 3: 50-56.

[35] Bittman B., Berk L., Felten D., Westengard J. et al. "Composite Effects of Group Drumming Music Therapy on Modulation of Neuroendocrine-Immune Parameters in Normal Subjects." *Alternative Therapies* 2001; 7: 1: 38-47.

[36] Winkelman M. "Complementary Therapy for Addiction: Drumming Out Drugs." *American Journal of Public Health* 2003; 93: 4: 647-651.

About the Author

Daniel Foor, PhD, is a psychologist and marriage and family therapist whose doctoral research focused on the use of shamanic healing methods in a clinical mental health setting. He offers trainings, community ceremonies, and individual healing and mentorship sessions in the San Francisco Bay Area focusing on ancestor work, earth medicine ritual, and wilderness questing. He is also the founder and executive director of the Earth Medicine Alliance, an interfaith non-profit organization helping to repair our relationships with the rest of the natural world.

XIV
A Shamanic Presence In Hospice Care

Leslie S. Bryan, MA

The word hospice (from the same root word as 'hospitality') originated in the Middle Ages and referred to a lodging place for the weary or ill traveler.[1] The term reappeared in the 1960's when Dr. Cicely Saunders first introduced the concept of specialized care for the dying at Yale University. She gave lectures to medical students, nurses, social workers, and chaplains about hospice as a new concept of holistic care for the terminally ill whose main features were symptom control and improved quality of life. These lectures catalyzed the movement in health care that we know today as hospice care.[2]

In 1967 Dr. Saunders founded a healthcare program that provided specialized care not only to patients who had just a short time to live, but care that also extended to their families. The first actual hospice in the U.S. was Connecticut Hospice, opened in 1974.

When Elizabeth Kubler-Ross's best-selling book *On Death and Dying* was published in 1969, it brought the topic of death out of the shadows.[3] Her interviews with five hundred terminally ill patients resulted in her outlining the five stages of emotions preceding death and greatly helped to promote the hospice movement. By 1983, the United States Congress had established a trial Medicare Hospice Benefit that provided such strong evidence of high quality care and cost effectiveness that hospice was made a permanent part of the Medicare/Medicaid system. This Medicare Hospice Benefit was the first third-party provision for the emotional and spiritual support of patients and their families.[4] Throughout the 1970's and 1980's, rapid growth of the hospice concept led to the establishment of the National Hospice Organization in 1988.[5]

The current use of the term hospice refers to compassionate and holistic care that may take place in a patient's home, hospital, freestanding in-patient facility, care center, or nursing home. Care is provided by an interdisciplinary team of professionals whose goal is to provide as much quality-of-life as possible to both patient and family by managing symptoms, relieving pain, and providing support as all parties come to terms with the end of life.[6]

Today there are more than 3,200 hospices in the U.S., and in the year 2000 about one in every four Americans who died received hospice care, or roughly 600,000 people.[7]

Death and dying from a shamanic perspective

Working with the dying and helping the soul pass on to the spirit world is an essential practice of shamanism.[8] For shamans, death is a rite of passage and transition, not 'the end' and not a failure. The soul of the dying person moves out of the body and into the other world of spirit. In most traditions the spirit world has three levels: an upper world and a lower world that encase the middle world in which we live. These worlds exist parallel and concurrent to our reality, with only a thin 'veil' separating the two. Each soul has a distinct journey through the act of dying – from the physical realm, through the veil, into the spirit world. Some souls simply rest in the spirit world after their illness or accident, while others still need to be healed. Some souls, however, go right to the work that they are meant to do with the spirits, which sometimes includes acting as guides or spiritual teachers for people still living in the physical world.

A 'good death' in the world of shamanism occurs when the body dies and the soul moves on to the upper or lower world, according to that soul's cultural belief. A traumatic death is one in which an accident, heavy medication, or high levels of pain cause the soul to get stuck in the middle world. In such an instance, the soul might stay in the place where it died, or return to its home, or possess a person who is either conveniently close at hand or with whom it resonates energetically. In the case of possession, a shamanic practitioner may be called upon to perform a rite of depossession to dislodge a spirit from a place or person to move it on to upper or lower world. This assisting of souls to move on from middle world after death is called psychopomp (from the Greek word *psychopompus* meaning 'leader of souls').[9]

During a psychopomp ceremony a shaman calls on helping spirits and fills him- or herself with their power before meeting the spirit that is stuck in the middle world. She then helps the spirit realize that the body is dead, tells the spirit that it is time to move on from this world, and provides the spirit with assistance to proceed to the other world. In my practice, I help the spirit to 'go into the light' by filling myself with my own divine light and connecting it to the light of the upper and lower spirit worlds. This creates an illuminated pathway for the soul to travel easily into the next world.[10]

Troublesome deaths can occur even in the protected world of hospice, as I learned early in my work at the in-patient unit. One day a nurse told me that two patients in two different rooms were very agitated, demanding that the nurse remove all the people from their rooms. The nurse and I verified that no one except the patients were actually in either room. I gathered my ceremonial supplies, and returned to perform a psychopomp ceremony on the entire hospice unit. I journeyed, gathering all the souls stuck there and sending them into the light. Then I cleansed the unit with burning sage and holy water. The results were dramatic: both patients' agitation disappeared, and they each died peacefully the following day.

I have repeated this ceremony and others to cleanse a unit of spirits and keep it clear. One method for doing this it to empower a crystal and ask any spirits stuck in the hospice unit to come to the stone and peacefully wait there until I perform the psychopomp ceremony.[11] The results are usually very positive, and the staff reports no further disturbances.

Diverse views of death and dying

Traditional cultures have diverse views of death, dying, and rebirth. For example, in Vedic India there is nothing resembling spirit guides for the dead. The dying person is simply told the road to follow and she finds her own way to Yama, the King of the Dead, and the Ancestors. This is very similar to Indonesian and Polynesian belief systems as well as ideology found in the Tibetan Book of the Dead.[12] In contrast, the Saami people of Lapland believe that families have a clan spirit, which is passed down from generation to generation. This spirit acts as a guardian who helps a person during illness, and at the time of death steps aside to allow the individual's spirits to take over the actual transition to the other world.[13]

As death is seen diversely, so is the shaman's role diverse, and culturally specific. The Altaians, Goldi, and Yurak peoples of Central and North Asia call on the shaman to lead the dead to the beyond only after funeral rites are complete. The Tungus of Siberia only ask the shaman for psychopomp if the dead continue to haunt the living beyond the usual period of mourning.[14]

The soul's destination also differs vastly from culture to culture. The Saami believe souls return to an underworld, *Jabmeaimo*, where they receive a new body and continue to live a type of parallel life. A Celtic belief is that spirits go to the otherworld and await rebirth. The Hopi believe the soul or breath-body returns to the underworld via the original hole through which their ancestors first came up to earth.[15] An old Druidic belief is that the soul continues to reincarnate through the circles of existence until it reaches the White Life.[16]

Personal beginnings in hospice

My introduction to working with the dying was treating D.B.

When D. B. walked into my New York City office for shamanic healing in the spring of 2000 I had no idea that my life would change and that I would be called to hospice care. D. B., a retired professor at a New York City university and internationally renowned in her field, had just been diagnosed with pancreatic cancer. The prognosis was poor – she was given just three months to live. After researching the standard medical treatments for pancreatic cancer and finding that success rates were low with limited quality of life, she initially chose not to go that route. D.B. wanted to have the best quality of life for as long as possible. She organized her own program of alternative therapies, including a shamanic practitioner in up-state New York, a prayer circle in Florida, Reiki, and me. For three months we met every Wednesday in my office, and when she was no longer able to make the trip, I saw her in her Manhattan apartment. Our sessions focused on caring for and strengthening her body as well as ceremonies that inspired her spirit.

While pancreatic cancer usually causes a great deal of pain and debilitating nausea, D.B. was able to continue many normal activities and lived pain-free. She also held a very positive attitude about her illness. Unfortunately her blood count showed her body was not fighting the disease, so she elected to do an experimental medical program. A radiation seed was implanted at the tumor site, and she was put on a low dose of continuously administered chemotherapy. However, the radiation seed slipped, harming her liver, and the chemotherapy gave her oral lesions. We continued working together throughout these treatments. Though she became physically weaker due to a combination of advancing disease, liver damage, and bouts of severe diarrhea, she was able to maintain a good quality of life. She remained moderately active, enjoying friends and food. Amazingly, the only pain she experienced was from the oral lesions.

Nine months after her initial diagnosis, D. B. collapsed and became bed-ridden. She was actively dying; her body systems were shutting down. Several family members came to visit her, and one of them called to inform me of the swift decline in her condition. Because she was surrounded by loved ones, I decided not to go to her bedside immediately. I chose instead to do healing work on her from a distance at my home in New Jersey, recognizing that shamanic healing occurs initially on the spiritual plane where time and distance do not have linear boundaries.

In the shamanic journey I performed after receiving the call from D.B.'s relatives, I went to the spirit realm and asked what healing methods the spirits would prescribe. I was told to fill her, the room, and all the people in it with healing light, thus creating a circle of light. Even after the journey I continued to hold this circle in my consciousness. Later one of the family members told me she felt a warmth and sense of peace come into the room at the time I was journeying.

The following day D.B.'s relatives left, and I went to her bedside. For the next week I sat vigil with her and her partner, C.L. During that time I 'watched' the energy as it departed D.B.'s body and continued to hold the circle of healing light to ease the transition for her and her partner. C.L. told me stories about D.B. and about their life together. We laughed and cried and talked about life without D.B. During our conversations C.L. told me that D.B. was a very private person who did not trust people easily but that she had trusted me right from the beginning and that our sessions and our time together were very important to her. I was pleased because she was very special to me and surprised because she never told me how she felt.

During two days of our vigil, D.B. physically interacted with the spirit world. She reached out and spoke to people in the room that only she could see. Late one night she became lucid and told C.L. that she had seen the door to the other world but that she couldn't get it open. Immediately afterward she slept deeply for two days. Very near the end and in a coma, D.B. moved her arms in an odd way, and we realized she was trying to open the door. It was a sliding door and she was trying to push it aside.

D.B. died very peacefully in the middle of the night. I told C.L. not to be surprised if her spirit stayed around to make sure that C.L. was all right, and explained that oftentimes spirits like to manipulate electronic or electrical devices. Several days after D.B. died, C.L. called me laughing, and said she could not keep enough light bulbs in the house. As she changed the bulb in one lamp, another would blow. D.B.!

After a few days D.B. moved on to the spirit world. Occasionally I could feel her presence with me. Even after working with D.B. for nine months, I did not immediately realize the impact she had on my life or what she had taught me. Our time together redirected my shamanic practice. I decided to sign up to volunteer on an in-patient hospice unit, and I set my visiting day for Wednesday, unaware at the moment that it was the same day of the week that I had my usual appointment with D.B.

Many people are overwhelmed by the idea of death and are paralyzed by the actuality of helping someone to die. I began to notice that few people are called to hospice work, but I also recognized that I was very comfortable with death and dying and had been very effective with D.B. I began to see my calling was to hospice care.

Our shamanic work together gave D.B. a good quality of life through her illness and enhanced her peaceful transition. Only several months later did I realize that for me this experience had erased the boundaries between traditional shamanic healing and modern Western hospice care. I learned that the two culturally divergent healing modalities could in fact coexist and that I could function in both. This prompted me to join a hospice staff where I regularly blended the two approaches to offer solace to those in need. And I am regularly surprised by the degree to which the hospice staff has come to accept shamanic practices as a viable component of end of life care.

In March 2001, I began volunteering on the in-patient hospice unit of a major private hospital in New York City, a short term facility where patients come for crisis management, monitoring of a change in health status, respite care (so the caregiver may have some time to rest and recover), or end of life care. I had no prior connection to this institution, and from the beginning I presented myself to the staff as a shamanic healer. I described to them the work I wanted to do, which was a range of shamanic healing for both the patients and their families. While the staff never reacted with overt skepticism or resistance to my work, for my first two years they watched from a distance with curiosity. As our time together and experiences on the unit evolved, they became increasingly supportive. Now they eagerly send me into patients' rooms to "do that healing thing you do."

Setting and initial contact

A large portion of my work is with the 'actively dying,' that is, when body systems are shutting down. These patients are usually no longer eating or taking in fluids by mouth or intravenously (a dying body does not need nutrition), and they are often unresponsive in a coma or a very deep sleep. Sometimes they move around in the bed so actively that the family may perceive them to be struggling.

Very often the dying process is difficult for patients who don't want to let go of this life or the people in it. They may be in great anxiety or severe pain; they may be frightened of dying or confused about what is happening, or simply, they may not know what they are 'supposed to do.' Pain, anxiety, fear, and confusion can hold a person's soul in their body and prevent it from moving on. Sometimes these emotions reveal unresolved issues the patient must work through before being able to let go of life. Pain medications may be administered, but they treat the body and do not address the discomfort of the spirit. Even heavily sedated patients may have difficulty completing their death.

Upon entering a patient's room, the most important thing I can do is be in my heart and be fully present in the moment and ready to help in any way I can. The dying process is different for each patient and for each family member. I cannot change the process to make it more convenient for the family or for the medical staff or for myself, but I can be present as it is happening and facilitate it by being in an egoless place. I cry with both patients and family; I laugh with them; I let them know they are not alone. Shamanically I transfigure, fill with divine light,[17] and call in my helping spirits. I also call in the angels who help the dying. Then I fill the room with divine light to promote healing for everyone who enters. Sometimes I sing quietly.

When I entered the room of B.B., a man in his late 60's with throat cancer, three of his children were present. The nurse, who asked me to treat both patient and family, told me that B.B. had just admitted to himself that he was dying. He was in a semi-conscious state: he knew what was going on around him but was not very communicative. His children were quite frustrated because every time they tried to do something to comfort him, he would shoo them away. They felt totally helpless. When I asked them about their father, they told me stories about their childhood. B.B. was a political activist and had brought them up to be 'doers,' so sitting quietly and watching their father was a difficult experience for them.

I connected with B.B.'s spirit and saw that he was a great teacher, especially for his children. When I asked them about this they confirmed that their father had always been their best teacher. I told them that he had not yet finished teaching them and that he was now giving them his last lesson. He didn't need or want them to do anything for him; he just needed them to be there. When I said this, B.B. smiled and winked at me. The children were confused about what he needed or they should do. I explained to them about being present and being still. Several days later one of the daughters told me that after our conversation, the energy in the room completely shifted, as did their experience of being with their father. They were able to be there, still and peaceful, and enjoy the last days of their father's life.

Flexibility and variety

Working shamanically on a hospice unit requires flexibility due to the variety of forms the dying process takes and the wide range of belief systems that exist in our culture.

When I sit with dying patients, I often do not know what their belief system says about where souls go after death. In my shamanic terms, I expect souls to go either to the upper world or to the lower world, but I work simply to assist the soul to make a safe transition to either place. In order to do this, the transfigured state I become is not culturally specific, but a divine light that is connected to the divine light of the patient. Then I open that light to both the upper and the lower worlds so the soul may depart to either. By holding the light of both worlds, I form an energetic triangle to illuminate the pathway for the departing soul so that it accommodates patients whose cultural and religious belief systems are unknown to me. I believe it also aids those souls who are confused about where they are supposed to go.

Whenever I am asked to see a patient, I work within whatever belief system he or she presents to me. When I tell patients or family members that I do shamanic healing, they are usually curious and ask me questions, which I try to answer, but generally I do not talk about journeying to the other worlds or about shamanism as a spiritual practice. It is not an appropriate time in their lives for me to introduce new ideas or belief systems to patients or families. For example, if the family has been saying prayers, or the patient is holding a rosary, or a Buddhist altar is on the windowsill, I change the language I use to describe what I do appropriately. This helps them feel more comfortable with my work.

When I was working with L.B., an older woman with lung cancer who was unconscious and very close to dying with a blood pressure of 60/54 and body temperature of 93, her daughter and nephew were present. The daughter in particular was having a difficult time dealing with her mother's pending death. She had always taken care of her mother and her feelings swung wildly between grief and guilt. The atmosphere in the room was so tense that I decided to tell them only that I had been asked by the nurse to come in and do healing work. I sensed that L.B.'s soul was confused, not only about what was happening, but also where it would go. I transfigured, connected to her light, opened the light of the upper and lower world and held them for her. I made a small gesture with my hands, to hold the light, which the nephew noticed and asked if it was something religious. I said that wasn't the word I would use, but that I would call it spiritual. The daughter asked me what I was doing, and I said I was helping her mother see where to go when she leaves this world. The nephew and the daughter were visibly pleased and calmed, knowing L.B. was being guided through the dying process.

Then they asked me how they could help her. Since religion had been brought up previously I surmised the family held strong religious beliefs, so I asked them to recite L.B.'s favorite prayers or sing her favorite hymns. So they read from the Bible and prayed. L.B. settled down calmly, and within an hour the pattern of her breathing had changed to apnea, a suspension of breath for several minutes followed by a gasping breath, a sign that the body systems are shutting down. Later I learned that she died very peacefully two hours after I left her room.

Sometimes I am called upon to help patients who are in great pain or agitation and for whom medication seems to have no effect. An example is C.S., a woman in her early 60's with stomach cancer. She was in enormous pain and on a regimen of large doses of morphine that were only moderately effective. When I asked her if she would like me to lightly massage her feet, she asked me if I could please rub her abdomen instead. I transfigured, connected to her divine light, and began to gently rub her abdomen with peppermint oil. She was delighted with the smell and immediately unclenched the muscles in her entire body that had been held in pain. As I worked with her for approximately half an hour, she relaxed, telling me that the pain had completely subsided. A family member later told me that she did not need to take the next two injections of pain medication and was sent home shortly thereafter. She died before I could see her again.

Another method I find very helpful for calming pain and agitation is Tuvan drumming. The Tuvan shamans of Siberia believe their drums are filled with healing powers that can be released into a person. I ask my helping spirits to fill my drum with energy, then I drum softly over the patient. E.L., a woman in her 80's with severe Alzheimer's, was very agitated, trying to get up and walk even though she was no longer strong enough to support herself. I was asked to sit with her and calm her. After using Tuvan drumming for twenty minutes she was able to relax and sit quietly in her chair for an hour.

Creating a safe container

In order for people to talk about their own death it is imperative to create a 'safe container,' something I always do when I enter a room and call in my helping spirits. D.W., a woman in her 40's with end-stage lung cancer, accepted that she was near death; however, she continued to be cheerful, talkative, and even curious. She was estranged from her family and seemingly had few friends, so I visited her frequently during her hospital stay. I sensed that we had created a safe environment in which to explore the reality of dying. In the course of one of our conversations, I asked her what she thought the pathway to death looked like. She closed her eyes and went on a journey, describing to me in minute detail the course of a babbling brook. Afterwards we sat quietly; the image gave her great peace. Suddenly we both burst into laughter. Her oxygen pump was making the same babbling brook sound that she saw in her journey! The machine brought death in to her room, and she was able to laugh at it.

Transition point

Sometimes the circumstance requires that I take a more active role when a patient is frightened or doesn't understand what is happening. T.F. was a woman in her late 40's with breast cancer that had metastasized to her lungs, bone, and eventually her brain. Through our conversations, I discovered that she had very strong religious beliefs and would not be open to my doing healing work with her. Instead I made sure that I always connected with her spirit while we talked about whatever she wanted: art, current events, and the troubles she was having with her treatment. She was well loved by the entire hospice staff, as she was very kind and thoughtful.

During her final admission she was very weak and confused, a completely different person from who she had been during other stays. When she became so agitated that she tried to get out of bed, I was asked to sit with her. She was in a great deal of pain and very restless, even though she was being heavily medicated for both pain and anxiety. The nurses told me that she kept asking to go home, but they didn't know how this could be arranged as she lived alone with no family or friends. When I heard her asking to go home, I realized that 'home' was not the physical place she lived, and when she asked me if I would help her go there, I said yes. So I began by asking her if she would like to go somewhere peaceful. "Yes," she said. Then I asked her to close her eyes and follow my guided visualization. We went to a place where there was no pain and no fear, a place in which she was at peace. When we were finished she opened her eyes and said, "I know this place."

A little while later T.F. sat up in bed and asked, "How would you get out of the hospital?" I told her I would go with the angels. She had a strong connection with angels and was comforted when I told her I could see her room was filled with them, all of whom were there to help her. I encouraged her to see them too. She grew calm and lay quietly for a few minutes, but suddenly she popped back up, struggling to get out of bed, and said she was afraid. When I asked her what she was afraid of she said, "They are going to hurt me when I leave." I talked her back into bed and assured her that she was going to a place where she would be loved and well cared for, and then I asked, "Would you like that?" She smiled.

"Where do I go?" was her next concern. I asked her if she would like to see the pathway. She did. I asked her to lie quietly, close her eyes and follow my voice during another visualization. We went along a road looking for a door or doorway. Afterward she reported that she had enjoyed the walk but thought she had not actually found the door. But now she knew where to look for it. She was very calm and was able to fall asleep. I sat with her for several hours while she slept and read to her from *The Little Prince*, a book that was by her bed. When I left that night she was sleeping soundly.

Unhappily, I had to go out of town and was unable to continue my work with her. That was the last time that I saw her. Later a nurse told me that T.F. awoke from that sleep in an agitated state and continued to struggle for several days before she was able to let go and pass on. The medical director was reported to have lamented, "Sometimes you can medicate the body but that does not help the spirit." We'd all hoped for a more peaceful death for T.F.

Aftercare

I am rarely with a patient at the time of death, but when someone dies, the body is left in the room until the family comes or other arrangements are made so I often have an opportunity to sit with them until then. While there, I call in helping spirits and angels to guide the soul's journey to the other world. For some souls it is a peaceful time; for others it is not.

As I began my shift one day I was told that M.A. had just died. I did not know this man or anything about him, but I went in to sit with the body and wish the soul a good journey. When I walked into the room, I was met by a powerful force so strong that it shoved me against the wall. No one was in the room but the body and me. Once I regained my balance, I realized that M.A.'s soul was still present, and not happy, and did not want to leave the room. I gathered all my helping spirits and called on the angels to come and fill the room and M.A.'s soul with light. I talked with him and explained that the body had died and that it was time to move on. Slowly his soul filled with light and his anger subsided until he was able to depart this world. I sat holding the light until I no longer felt his presence. Afterward I asked the nurse about M.A. and she said he had been a very angry, difficult patient.

J.M. had an easier departure. He and I built a friendship during the many times he was a patient on the hospice unit. J.M. was a man in his 50's, a Viet Nam war veteran who had AIDS, hepatitis C, diabetes, and end-stage liver cancer. He had no remaining liver function, and the medical director couldn't understand how he was still alive. Even his diabetes was unusual in that his blood sugar counts were always best at night after he had eaten a sweet dessert. Though J.M. was very sick and in a great deal of pain, he was a consummate gentleman. I spent a lot of time with him as he only had few family members and didn't care to see them. He was not a religious or spiritual man, so I never talked about shamanic healing. I merely offered to do things that he would find relaxing, such as talking and gently rubbing his feet with lavender oil, which helped him to relax.

On his final admission, he was in so much pain that he couldn't sleep and was always very restless. He told the doctor that he could not stand the pain any longer and asked her to increase his medication so he could sleep. She obliged and also offered him an increased dose during the day to which he consented. I sat with him while the doctor gave him the injection. I talked with him until he fell asleep.

A few days later in the early morning hours he died peacefully. I was called and went in to sit with his body. I placed lavender flowers around him and around the room. I sang to his soul, and bid it farewell. I felt J.M. thank me for caring about him and his soul left. The chaplain came and we said prayers. J.M. had a good death.

Conclusion

One of the reasons I love working with the dying and their families is that they have so much to teach us. For most of them, life and its meaning are immediate and clear. There are no games. You see who they are; there are no more masks to hide behind. They have taught me about love and caring, about facing fear or guilt, about the fragility of life, about being of this world, about living and dying.

Perhaps one of my greatest lessons about being present and holding the light was given to me by a very dear friend, O.H., who was very ill with multiple sclerosis for eight years and ultimately died on the hospice unit. During the many years of her illness, she never asked me nor gave me permission to do healing work with her. It was very frustrating for me to sit by and watch someone I loved become progressively sicker and not be able to use my healing skills. Only after she was admitted onto the hospice unit did I understand that my presence, my light, was the only thing she needed from me—that my being in the room with her made a difference in her healing process.

I have seen the benefits that shamanic healing brings to terminally ill patients and their families, and I am fortunate to be with people physically and spiritually in a way that helps them depart from this world. It has been a great gift to be able to touch people, help people, and heal people on a level that Western medicine does not address.

References

[1] Perlow J. *Hospice Volunteer Training Manual.* New York, NY: Beth Israel Hospital; March 2001; 1-6.

[2] National Hospice and Palliative Care Organization Website. About NHPCO. Retrieved October 18, 2005. www.nhpco.org.

[3] Hospice of Michigan website. Brief history of hospice movement. Retrieved October 18, 2005. www.hom.org.

[4] Hospice of Michigan website.

[5] Hospice of Michigan website.

[6] Perlow J.;1-6.

[7] Hospice of Michigan website.

[8] Kalweit H. *Shamans, Healers, and Medicine Men.* Boston, MA: Shambhala; 1987; 137.

[9] Ingerman S. Teacher training notes on death and dying, 2005.

[10] The method of filling with divine light and connecting to the light of the upper and lower worlds is not a traditional psychopomp shamanic practice. It is a synthesis of trainings I received from Sandra Ingerman's "Medicine for the Earth" and "Healing with Spiritual Light," as well as Betsy Bergstrom's "Shamanic Depossession."

[11] Bergstrom B. Training notes on shamanic depossession, 2005.

[12] Eliade M. *Shamanism: Archaic Techniques of Ecstasy.* Princeton, NJ: Princeton University Press 1964; 418.

[13] Madden K. *Shamanic Guide to Death and Dying, 1st ed.* St. Paul, MN: Llewellyn Publications 1999; 139.

[14] Mercea E.; 209.

[15] Madden K.; 146.

[16] Madden K.; 186.

[17] Ingerman S. *Medicine for the Earth: How to Transform Personal and Environmental Toxins.* New York, NY: Three Rivers Press; 2000; 189-199.

About the author

Leslie S. Bryan, MA, has a shamanic healing practice in New York City with a specialization in healing through the end of life. She provides healing services at the Jacob Perlow Hospice at Beth Israel Hospital in New York City. After September 11, 2001, she worked in the Integrated Stress Clinic at St. Vincent's Hospital in New York City, and later with CRREW, a network of healers that serves search and rescue teams as well as the community at large. From a background career in the performing arts as dancer, choreographer, producer, university professor and arts administrator, she trained in esoteric healing, cranial sacral biodyamics, shamanic healing, and shamanic depossession.

Traditional Forms of Shamanic Care

XV

South African Indigenous Healing: How It Works

David Cumes, MD

Sangomas or inyangas are shamans, healers, priests and prophets who have been the backbone of Bantu communities of Southern Africa for eons. However, with rapid Westernization and the increasing allure of the commodity market, the old ways are rapidly eroding. Indigenous knowledge has always been transmitted orally, and there is little written down about the secret traditions of initiation. Hence, the bibliography listed at the end of this chapter is scant. This information is a result of personal experience gleaned during my own initiation into the world of sangoma and my subsequent experiences with these healing realms. The knowledge has been gained experientially and not by the scientific method. Some of it is secret and cannot be revealed. Methods may differ somewhat from healer to healer but the general principles are the same. I will describe the traditions that I encountered during my initiation and subsequent practice. There are others.

Since sangoma wisdom is an oral tradition, the individual's initiation depends on the mentor and the spirit guides involved. The ancestors find the most efficient way to impart the information so that the healer can do the work. The way in which they transmit the knowledge will be unique to that person's receptivity and talents.

After my own initiation as a sangoma, I began walking in two worlds: the material world of my surgical practice as an allopathic urologist in Santa Barbara, California, and the spiritual world of a South African traditonal healer. Today I use biomedicine for standard health concerns like infections and cancer where the diving bones are no substitute for a CT scan or an MRI. However, since Western medicine is sadly lacking in the psycho-spiritual dimension, many patients who are cured by Western medical technology often remain unhealed and go on to develop another malady. Hence, I also use traditional sangoma medicine, where appropriate. I have a Ndumba, or sacred-healing hut (in the form of a yurt), in my backyard where I practice divination with bones, dispense plant medicines, and conduct rituals for psycho-spiritual ailments. I prefer to think of the work I do in my medical office and the operating room as 'curing,' whereas the ministering I do in the Ndumba as 'healing.' Many of my patients now come to me for psycho-spiritual help before or once the physical complaint has been eradicated by Western technology. In addition to helping uncover the deeper causes of the illness, the bones sometimes reveal an undiscovered problem that as yet has no accompanying symptoms, the consequent diagnosis and treatment of which could be life-saving.

Introduction to sangoma healing

The sangoma, inyanga, traditional or indigenous healer uses altered states of consciousness, spirit possession, and sometimes out of body spirit flight to gain knowledge about any problem at hand. This ability may be hereditarily transmitted, arise out of a dream or vision bestowed by the spirit world, or occur because of selection by the tribe. Sometimes the calling arises out of a deformity, disability, illness, or even a psychosis. The ability to go inward facilitates access to alternative realities — the hallmark of the shaman. The fact that the healer has suffered usually gives her greater empathy and compassion for the feelings and emotions of others. When sangomas commit to *Thwasa*, the initiation process, they understand that they have been chosen to work with the spirits in order to heal others. Some sangomas are self-chosen, but those that are 'called' wield much greater power. Without guiding ancestral spirits, the sangoma is relatively impotent. The initiation is about creating a relationship with the student and the spirits who wish to work through him or her. In South Africa, traditional healers can be either women or men. There is no practical difference between a sangoma and an inyanga—both are 'possessed' and derive their power from the ancestors. Classically, the sangoma works in a trance state by channeling the ancestors from the spirit world. Inyangas more commonly translate messages from the cosmic realm by reading divination bones and work with plant medicines. Both work with dreams, and there are highly specialized sangomas who practice *femba*, which can be likened to psycho-spiritual surgery that rids the patient of intruding spirits. Normally, a sangoma will channel her own ancestors but sangomas who specialize in femba are also able to channel the client's ancestors for information or intrusive spirits in order to exorcise them.

All the healers have special gifts. They can divine the future, diagnose illness, find lost objects or people, and establish direct contact with the ancestors and the supernatural. But to become a sangoma requires arduous and difficult training. Not just anyone is called and, though sometimes burdensome, the calling is regarded as a gift and great honor. The goal of an ancestor who channels healing through a living relative is to help and to heal. When a sangoma abuses the gift, the ancestors may withdraw their support and the healer will lose this power. Hence most traditional healers practice with great humility and acknowledge that the source of their talent is the ancestors.

The theory of reincarnation is germane to the African mindset and has a profound effect on the thinking and behavior of many Africans. Reincarnation links them to their ancestors who may reincarnate back into the same family. Healing between kin therefore continues beyond the grave.

There are white people in South Africa who mistakenly believe that black people worship their ancestors. This is untrue. No godly power is attributed to these entities. Rather, they are thought of in the same way as guardian angels who act as intermediaries between God and humankind. Black South Africans believe that illness and misfortunes may result from a lack of relationship with the ancestors. The ancestors have the power to support and protect their descendants. They can improve relationships, health, wealth, and other conditions. In some dysfunctional families, where the sins of an ancestor have not been dealt with ritually and neutralized (forgiveness is key), that ancestor may intrude and inhibit the flow of energy to the living and, in this way, cause harm. If the afflicted one makes a sacrifice to the ancestor, this will heal him, please him, and dissipate the malevolent energy. Ancestors therefore become scapegoats when problems are encountered in life, and they are praised when events run smoothly.

There are three diagnostic methods of the sangoma: spirit possession (spirit mediumship or trance-channeling), the divination bones, and dreams. In the Bantu tradition, the ancestral spirit of the sangoma or inyanga comes 'down' from the cosmic 'field' and possesses the healer. The spirit occupies the sangoma's body while the ego or persona steps aside. In this way healers can access information that is not localized in space and time and not readily available to those not trained as sangomas. The sangoma's ancestors are able to speak directly through the medium of the healer to the patient, and the information is highly specific to that individual.

The practice of throwing divining bones probably developed over time because healers found spirit mediumship too exhausting. Becoming possessed is hard work, and it would be impossible to treat many patients if possession were the only method. Possession requires drumming, chanting and dancing that are demanding of time and energy. The divination bones are an alternative way of allowing the ancestral spirits to have a conversation with the patient through the healer. Reading the bones is a little like unraveling the metaphor of a dream. The healer becomes an interpreter and messenger for the ancestral spirit, who sets up an information 'field' accessible to the sangoma through the bones. When the bones are thrown by the sangoma, they do not fall in a random fashion but in a way that the ancestral spirit controls. A meaningful and usually highly accurate interpretation can be made.

Another way the ancestors communicate with the inyanga is through dreams. Interpretation of dreams is a vital tool of the sangoma. Healers often dream plant remedies for their patients, information that comes as a vision of a particular plant. Other psychic information can be sent through dreams to assist the sangoma in caring for the client.

Energetic mechanisms of healing

In Zulu, *Umbilini* means 'the place of the two,' that mystical place where body and soul unite and become one powerful thing. Umbilini is a manifestation of primal feminine force that may vibrate and ascend up the body with clapping, chanting, singing, drumming and dancing. This vibration or shaking can be witnessed when the sangoma goes into trance and becomes possessed. All indigenous Southern African people believe that the primal feminine serpent or snake residing in the lower belly is vital for fertility and for channeling the ancestors. The Bushmen of the Kalahari call this energy *Num*.

The Umbilini enables the sangoma to cross the veil and enter the cosmic field where the ancestors dwell. The field is non-local, and within it is the universal mind or universal consciousness. Carl Jung would have called this the collective unconscious. From a Jungian point of view the sangoma or inyanga has the ability to access an archetypal world where healer encounters the guiding spirits.

If one were to visit a sangoma who, without knowing you, could diagnose your health situation in the past, present or future, you would be receiving information not localized in time. If he were to tell you about the health of your children living in another country, this would be information not localized in space. These kind of shamans are now called 'medical intuitives' in the West. The diagnostic information they provide with the help of the ancestral spirits can be uncannily accurate. This technology has been available to all peoples in South Africa through sangomas for eons.

The universal healing energy that is channeled through the sangomas and any true healer is just love in disguise — in order to heal one must open the heart, must go beyond the constraints of ego. There is a veil between the worlds between matter and spirit, between this and that, and the key to opening up this veil is love. Entheogens or mind-altering plants can also open up the heart and allow one to go beyond ego. But unlike the Americas where many reasonably safe plants with these properties abound, in South Africa these types of plants have a very narrow margin between mind-altering effects and death; hence they are rarely used.

The Ancestors and foreign spirit guides – 'possession'

There are several Bantu groups in Southern Africa. The Nguni, who are the majority, comprise the Zulu, Swazi, and Xhosa and share similar languages. The others comprise the Sotho and Tswana (similar language), Venda, and Shangaan. The shamans of both groups are called sangomas and inyangas.

A sangoma is able to communicate with the cosmic, the terrestrial, and the water spirits as well as the ancestors. The ancestors are honored and revered but not worshipped as one would pray to God. All tribes believe in a single Great Spirit, or God (*Umkulunkulu* in Zulu, *Modimo* in Sotho), who is seen as remote and inaccessible. The ancestral spirits are there to mediate between the living and God. Since the spirits are linked to the cosmos, the land, and the water (hence shells are often present in the healer's repertoire of bones) they can provide information that is not confined to the space-time continuum.

Sangomas use drumming and dancing to help channel the ancestors. Possession or spirit mediumship among the Nguni peoples is usually overt and extroverted, whereas amongst the other tribes it is more often implicit rather than explicit. However, there is much overlap among the different tribes: drumming and possession by ancestral spirits are common to all groups, and all tribes channel information from the ancestors through dreams and divining bones.

The word *sangoma* comes from the Zulu word for drum, and it is the sound of the drum that brings forth the spirit. The drumming is accompanied by special songs and chants. When the spirit enters the body, the sangoma's voice may change as he or she becomes the channel for the ancestor. Sometimes the sagoma will speak in tongues and often with a different accent. The ancestor who presents can be quite fastidious and demand a certain cloth or garment. Sangomas usually have an array of these and will wear a specific cloth depending on which spirit is addressing the group. Since most of the spirits are African, they request traditional attire, but a foreign spirit can make a special request which then must be honored. Many sangomas will dance to work themselves into a trance or will be 'danced' at the will of their ancestor once she or he enters their body. The tremendous energy and skill necessary to dance in this way can be remarkable and many times the channel would seem incapable of performing in this fashion unless he or she was, in fact, 'possessed.'

In Nguni tradition, in addition to ancestral spirits there are terrestrial (or bush) spirits, cosmic spirits *(ndzau),* and water spirits *(nzunzu)* who are very powerful. Foreign spirits unrelated to the family also exist and may be friendly or not. Sometimes they were people who knew the grandparents while alive and now are 'hanging about' in the ethers with them. Some foreign spirits, on the other hand, are up to no good and these intruders may cause mischief or get in the way of the energy flow of the living. Malicious foreign spirits may also be present because someone's dead relative killed them long ago. These bad spirits, who are capable of causing significant harm, can be exorcised by femba, a form of psychic diagnosis and psycho-spiritual surgery or exorcism.

Role of reincarnation

Reincarnation plays an important role in African philosophy, and family members may reincarnate into their own 'blood line.' Because of this, black Africans, whose traditions are intact, believe in a Biblical sense that "the sins of the fathers are visited upon the children." Psychology may attribute this to hereditary biochemical derangements or unskillful parenting which lead to hurtful influences and bad conditioning of the child. African philosophy goes further than this, believing that not only can unhappy and dysfunctional spirits affect their progeny from the beyond, but also that a dysfunctional spirit can reincarnate into the family and recreate the same dysfunction in a future generation. As an example, an alcoholic grandfather who has passed on reincarnates into the family line, perpetuating the alcoholic syndrome. All ancient wisdoms believe in karma or the law of cause and effect. We come back in order to perfect what we did not do in our previous life time, and many times we come back into the same family to do so.

Since ancestral spirits may reincarnate into the same family, it is crucial to heal the sins that may have occurred in the past such as murder, theft, abuse, and so on. By reaching out, forgiving, and healing the spirit who perpetrated the crime, everyone is healed, and another cycle of karmic dysfunction in the family is averted or lessened. Forgiveness and acceptance are critical here. It is best achieved while everyone is alive, but in African tradition, forgiveness and healing can occur even when the spirit has passed on.

Spirits sometimes feel the need to complete the healing work they never finished as a sentient being and will choose a suitable person who is alive to act as a channel for their mission. Spirits need the living to complete their work and improve their karma. By allowing them to help us they, in a sense, can come 'alive' again.

Some of the Bantu's healing concepts may appear Biblical because they are in touch with 'original truths' that go back millennia. This could also be a result of the missionary influence or in the northern regions of South Africa because of contact with a tribe of black Jews called the Lemba.

The commandment of "honor your mother and father . . ." is germane to African thinking and the respect goes all the way back to the grandparents, great grandparents and beyond. An interesting Harvard study performed on medical students in the 1950's, and still ongoing, demonstrated that the single most important factor mitigating in favor of good health was a good relationship with the parents. It is noteworthy that of all ten commandments this is the only one that says; ". . .so that your days will be long upon the earth." Sangomas would endorse the fact that anyone who gives this respect will be protected in life and in health.

Thwasa

Thwasa, which comes from the word for moon, is the process of self-discovery and recognizing one's spiritual links and destiny. Metaphorically, the Thwasa student begins as a new moon and matures into a full moon to become an inyanga, the one who doctors. The person who is called becomes 'possessed' by the ancestors who draw attention to their needs by making the elected one ill. The symptoms can take many forms: psychosis, severe headaches, abdominal pain, shoulder and neck complaints, among others. The patient may go to a Western-trained doctor who will be unable to find anything wrong. He or she may then see a traditional healer for treatment. The sangoma will divine and say that the patient is 'possessed' and that the only recourse is to become a sangoma. The 'sangoma sickness' mysteriously disappears after initiation has begun. The process of being called and then initiated is called Thwasa. Failure to respond to the calling will often lead to more illness until the person concedes and goes to be trained. Alternatively, the potential Thwasa students can work through a sangoma to enter into a dialogue with the spirits, explaining why they cannot undergo training at this time. Ancestors are reasonable, and if respectfully approached and told why this calling might not be possible, they may relent.

Medicine or Muti

The medicine or *muti* that is used is based on plants and, sometimes, different animals. The muti may have pharmacological properties, but one cannot isolate the power of the remedy from the strength of the healer or that of the ancestors. The more powerful the ancestors, the more masterful the healer, the more effective the muti will be. This phenomenon is an example of the combination of placebo and distant healing. Pharmacological companies are frequently disappointed when research of these plants of power proves them no better than placebo, whereas they may be very effective if given by the sangoma. From the sangoma's standpoint, the vital ingredient missing would be the power of the ancestral spirits assigned to the plant to do distant healing or the relationship with the spirit or the energy of the plant itself.

Sangomas are also able to manipulate the power of belief and faith, or placebo. In Western medicine, randomized, controlled, double-blinded studies are conducted to test the true pharmacalogical action of a drug, unimpeded by the placebo effect, or the patient's belief that the drug will work. We know that the patient's 'inner healer' is able to cure many maladies if there is a strong belief in the treatment being administered. In various trials, the placebo or dummy medicine often leads to at least 30% of the patients showing a response. While Western doctors are focused on eliminating the placebo effect, sangomas are masters at enhancing it, using their powerful rituals and their own charisma. Placebo is augmented with ceremonies and plant medicines which act as 'containers' for the healing. The muti is always prescribed with a heavy application of attention, intention, action and affirmation, which have now become part of the modern, integrative or holistic approach.

Distant diagnosis and distant healing have been used by sangomas for thousands of years. Indigenous healers can enter the cosmic field and invoke the help of the spirits for healing. Whereas placebo works directly on the inner healer through the power of belief to effect healing, distant healing works via the field to cause healing without the benefit of faith.

Mutis also often have powerful symbolism; for instance, lion fat may be used to promote courage. Each time the muti is used, it may be accompanied by a ritual that confirms the intention and acts as a powerful affirmation to the inner healer, and as a prayer to the ancestral spirits. In the West we know that distant healing and prayer work even if the patient is unaware he or she is being healed or prayed for. There are an increasing number of studies showing that distant healing or prayer is statistically significant in improving the outcomes of patients afflicted with certain diseases.

The effect of muti may be a sophisticated version of distant healing if the sangoma's prayers and ancestor's intentions accompany the treatment. The muti can also be regarded as a password or special request to the ancestor for a particular healing. Since the ancestors have access to universal healing energy, they have the ability to cure almost anything. Each muti carries a different message about what is needed for that specific problem. There is a mutual understanding between healer and ancestor based on tradition, dreams, and empiricism as to what plant to use for that problem. Different healers may use the same plant for different complaints and that implies that the ancestral spirit and placebo rather than pharmacological effect are doing the healing. For instance, one healer may use a plant for constipation and another healer the same plant for diarrhea. The plant is a 'prescription' to the spirit world to invoke the healing.

The homeopathic 'Law of Similars' states that if things resemble each other they are linked and can affect one another. In other words, like affects like. For this reason, reeds that shake in the water may be employed for tremor, snake venom may be used against snake bite, black smoke adopted to bring rain, and bark or roots that are red can be utilized to treat blood or menstrual disorders. Hence the principles of muti are somewhat similar to those of homeopathy. The muti is like a request to the ancestor for a particular healing much in the way one would get a written Rx from a doctor to take to the pharmacist. Since placebo alone is therapeutic in at least 30% of cases, just filling the prescription may heal the problem. The sangoma with his skillful intuitive diagnosis, spectacular dancing and powerful rituals may enhance the placebo effect significantly.

The problem may not be related to physical health, and if there is marital disharmony causing 'dis-ease' it will be reflected in the bones and remedies will be given. Sangomas do not distinguish between disease and 'dis-ease.' Since one will eventually lead to the other, sangomas go to the source of the problem and correct it.

Medicines can be administered in various ways: bathing, steaming, or inhaling. They can be taken by mouth or by enema, rubbed on the body as a salve, and, in special circumstances inoculated or rubbed into an incision. There are medicines for every eventuality: physical illness, mental illness, social disharmony and spiritual difficulties. There are also love potions, medicines for dreams and luck, among others.

Rituals

Reverence for the ancestors is very much part of the Thwasa's training and will continue throughout the healer's life. When entering the *ndumba* or healing hut where the ancestors reside, one takes off ones shoes, bows down on entering, and claps twice as a greeting. *Pahla,* or praying, is done kneeling down, and each sentence is punctuated by a clapping of hands. In some traditions there is no walking in the ndumba; instead the healer will hobble forward on her knees. Snuff, preferably made of home-grown tobacco, is a frequent offering used in rituals. The plant *mphepho* (Helichrysum) is burned to attract the attention of the ancestors. Since the ancestors cannot communicate with the living in the normal way, special techniques to 'bridge the cosmic field' are required. Sangomas will drink foam or bubbles made of water mixed with special muti, which is soul food for the spirits. By feeding the spirits, one draws the ancestors near. The ancestors are always fed when there is a ritual involving food or sacrifice. Sorghum beer or regular beer or wine may be offered as well.

Many tribes have an amaryllis plant in the homestead where the ancestors reside, and offerings will be made to this plant while holding conversation with the spirits. Members of the village will check in with the plant on arriving or leaving to ask the ancestors for favors and safety along the way. Depending on the tradition, a tree, a forked branch planted in the ground, or even river stones may be used in the same way.

Femba, the African equivalent of psychic diagnosis and surgery, is a way of exorcising malevolent or intruding spirits that are getting in the way of a person's progress in life. Houses, dwellings, farms, garments, belongings, cars and businesses all can be spiritually cleansed by femba. Femba not only involves exorcism of malevolent spirits but can also be a reconditioning of the spirit body to eliminate illness, imbalance, or a block in energy flow.

To the sangoma, each helper spirit has a role to play. One may assist the sangoma in reading the bones, another may help with plant remedies, and yet a third may want to come and dance. Others may be there to manage financial and business affairs. Depending on the talent of the spirit, the knowledge of the sangoma will vary. Some have more powerful ancestors than others. Usually the ancestor assists the channel with the expertise he or she had while alive. For instance the ancestor who helps read the bones may have been a sangoma, another an herbalist, and yet another a business person. Each will offer expertise in their particular field.

Causes of illness

Illness can be thought to arise from the following factors:

From God or the ancestors

On rare occasions it is felt that the Great Spirit can cause sickness. Sometimes the ancestors will want a living soul to join them on the other side and this may account for illness or death. When a grandparent is about to die and leave the planet, the newborn is about to enter it – hence both are close to the spirit realm. The grandparents in life and in death are the spirit guides to the child while the parents attend to his or her material needs. A loving, deceased grandparent may visit a spirit who may have just incarnated on the earth plane in the dream time and accidentally lure it away back to spirit world. This may account for the mystery of crib death, and it is interesting that there are many rituals to protect a newborn child during the vulnerable first few months of its life.

Ancestors may also cause illness by omission rather than by commission by turning away and not affording protection to their progeny.

Intrusive spirits

The role of intrusive or earth bound spirits has already been partly discussed. These may show up as 'shades' in the bones. Earth bound spirits may not pass over to the other side due to confusion, and they may get lost between the worlds. This can occur due to traumatic death from suicide, murder, war, drugs, alcohol, accidents, etc. The Zulus have a remedy for those who die away from home whose spirits may get lost. When they transport the body back home, usually by train, they will reserve a seat for the spirit and put the branch of a buffalo thorn tree on the seat. The buffalo thorn is unique in having both straight and hooked thorns. The straight thorn is symbolic of the spirit going up to heaven and the hooked thorn signifies the body that will be returned to the earth. When the spirit sees this it will understand it is dead and accompany the body back home to be with the ancestors.

It is important to realize that war veterans who are haunted in their dreams may in fact be visited by vengeful spirits they had killed in combat. A sangoma might disagree with the psychological treatment of war veterans with post-traumatic stress disorder and say that their nightmares were due to intrusive spirits. Zulu warriors in battle would disembowel their victims to release the spirit and also apologize to them and say that it was nothing personal. Further, on returning from war, warriors were ritually cleansed by sangomas to exorcise any ghosts that may have attached.

Pollution

Pollution occurs as a result of contact with some occurrence or phenomenon that is impure and is recognized by the Zulu as 'dirt' or 'dirty.' Causes of pollution include miscarriages, abortions, birth (especially of twins), illness, crime, death (especially murder), burial, menses, pregnancy, sex, a journey, eating the meat of an animal that died of disease, and pork. A husband is polluted for one year after the death of his wife or child, and a wife for a year after the death of her husband. Cleansing rituals are dispensed that usually involve bathing with muti.

Witchcraft and sorcery

Although sangomas usually work on the light and not the dark side, they are frequently called to consult about problems that are related to witchcraft. They have to know how to counteract hexes and also how to protect themselves and their homesteads from witches' antics, which sometimes can even involve attempts at poisoning. Sangomas have remedies for their patients and themselves if they are concerned about witchcraft.

While a healer can heal someone far away, a sorcerer can create disease and even death from a distance with a hex. White and black magic have been known for millennia and are now being validated by science. These malevolent effects can be local or non-local. Non-local influences work through the field without the knowledge of those who are affected. Local effects work directly with the knowledge of the victim through the nocebo effect (opposite of placebo). The key to nocebo and placebo is the belief system of the patient, the absence or presence of hope, belief, trust, and faith. Sangomas are masters of the placebo effect; sorcerers work with nocebo. It is worthwhile stressing the fact that witchcraft can harm someone even if that person does not believe in it. Just as distant healing can be effective, so too can distant harming through sorcery.

Malevolent ancestors, and especially vindictive foreign spirits who may have been wronged, can also cause illness, misfortune, accidents, and even the death of those who have wronged them. Problems can be countered by prayers, rituals, muti and sacrifices. Ancestors who have turned away can be encouraged to return and defend their descendants against malicious or intruding spirits. Illness is therefore frequently connected to human relationships between the living and the dead. However, if these relationships are perfectly functional and healthy, the sangoma will look to witchcraft or sorcery and pollution for the cause of the problem. Diagnoses are made with the help of femba, trance-channeling, dreams, and the divining bones. There is usually a remedy for any dilemma.

Witchcraft and sorcery arise from a heart of envy. Therefore anyone can be a witch or a sorcerer — for instance, a wife who is jealous of her husband or a businessman or politician seeking to eliminate the competition. Witches and sorcerers work on the dark side with the help of evil spirits. They have real power and are able to manipulate the field, which is non-denominational or spiritually neutral. Evil messages go through the field just as effectively as do healing ones. But most of those who work in the field, work on the light side for the sake of good and not bad.

Sorcerers use herbs, poisons and body exuviae of their victims (hair, nails, urine, and so on). The 'Law of Contagion' states that once two things are in contact they can affect one another. The hair or nail from the victim can be used with harmful muti to hurt or harm.

Witches also use 'familiars' which they ride or send to perform their treacherous deeds. Familiars include spotted hyenas, baboons, polecats, weasels, genets, wildcats, snakes, owls, and bats.

The commandment, "thou shall not covet…" is really an edict against witchcraft since at the source of all witchcraft is the principle of envy. Witchcraft is universal and not only confined to indigenous societies. The witch or sorcerer is 'the traitor within the gates.' Their power resides in their not being known to be malevolent so that they can continue to work unimpeded. Any hex can be countered, but only if one is aware that it exists.

Totems or power animals

The dead can communicate with the living not only by means of spirit mediumship, dreams, and divining bones, but also by using animals. Among the Zulu, snakes feature prominently, especially mambas and pythons. The python is usually a favorable message from the beyond, the mamba a warning. Some diviners have communication with the ancestors through a spirit animal (*intyala*), which can come in the form of a lion, leopard, or elephant and to which due respect must be accorded. The energy implicit in different animals is given great importance when it comes to the divining bones.

Divining bones

The divining bones are not strictly all bones but comprise shells, money, seeds, dice, domino-like objects or even dominos themselves, and other objects that have been appointed by the sangoma and the spirit to represent certain polarities (for instance a miniature car to represent a journey). Animal bones from lions, hyenas, anteaters, baboons, crocodiles, wild pigs, goats, antelopes and others form the large majority of the objects in the sangoma's bag, and there are bones for all psycho-socio-spiritual events. The bones represent all of the forces that affect any human condition, anywhere, whatever their culture. The primal energies and attributes the animals represent hold enormous power. For example, the hyena represents the thief who comes in the night, and a hyena bone is often used to locate a stolen or lost object. The anteater is the animal that 'digs the grave' and an anteater bone may be used where death is concerned, or it may represent a deceased person or his spirit.

There is a protocol for consultation with any sangoma or inyanga. The consultation takes place in the ndumba. The client places a fee under the mat on which the bones are to be thrown. Sometimes the healer will burn *mphepho* or light candles. Before throwing the bones, the healer invokes the ancestors by giving snuff or tobacco, kneeling, clapping, rattling and chanting a song. The purpose of all these rituals is to call the ancestors into sacred space to help the client. The healer's bones are contained in a skin bag. The healer asks the patient to pick up the bones and put them into the bag. The client shakes the bag of bones, places a pinch of snuff in the bag as an offering, blows into the opening of the bag, states his or her name, and empties the bones on the mat. Traditions vary depending on the healer's training or on prior instructions given by the spirit who is 'throwing the bones' for the healer. Sometimes more than one sangoma is present, and the others will chorus the reading of the main healer by chanting the word *siyavuma'* (we agree) after each interpretation. First, a general reading is given and then specific questions are answered. Each question requires a separate throw of the bones.

The first throw is general in scope and defines any problems the patient may have — work, money, home, spouse, children, sorcery, ancestors, and other specific situations. There is a bone for just about every polarity of the patient's psycho-socio-spiritual state of being.

Different traditions assign different meanings to the bones or objects, and each particular teacher will have her own method, which she passes on to the student. The Thwasa student will need to stay with this particular system because an agreement is made with the ancestor, the mentor, and the student so that all three of them understand how each bone is assigned. Although there is an intellectual component to divining – the healer has to read the message that is laid out — the reading is also highly intuitive. The sangoma is 'possessed' by the guiding spirit who passes on intuitive messages to help the healer to 'see' the problem at hand. The information forthcoming hence often extends beyond what the bones reveal. The bones also function as a way of getting the rational left brain out of the way so that the right brain can do its intuitive work. The ego is put aside since it is the ancestor, and not the healer, who is providing the information. This also allows the sangoma to reveal information that would be unheard of in psychotherapeutic circles; for instance, "your husband is no good and things will not go right for you until you send him away."

There is an understanding between the healer and the spirit as to the meaning of the bones and how they line up in relationship to each other. In fact, when the bones are thrown, they do not fall in a random pattern but rather in a distinct arrangement which can be read by the sangoma whose training has taught him to diagnose past and present ailments and predict future occurrences with extraordinary accuracy. It seems that a mini-field of attention, intention, and coherence is set up between the healer, the patient and the ancestor that allow the bones to lie in an intelligent pattern.

The reading is usually concerned with what is happening at that moment in the patient's life. Since the healer is reading a metaphor, she may get the wrong image and have to change direction. Divining is like interpreting someone's dream, and only the owner of the dream will know if the meaning rings true. The information is given humbly and democratically. The healer will ask the client if she agrees and, if so, will continue along the same line of exploration. If the client disagrees, the healer will look at the same polarity in a different way and reinterpret. For instance, money and energy are interchangeable. The bones may reveal that the client has no money when in fact the problem relates to a lack of energy or vitality or being 'burnt out.' Usually the patient is well aware of what is going on in his life. The bones will highlight or focus on a problem that requires attention and that may have been ignored or denied.

The healer is attentive to the fact that there is always free will and that anything can be changed. For instance, if the ancestors advise against taking a certain person for a spouse, and the partner is adamant, then muti can be dispensed to make the potential partner more acceptable. Rituals can be offered to the ancestral spirits to remove any black shadows that might be darkening the future of the relationship.

Bone readings are usually concerned with helping people deal with their current dilemmas – intrusive spirits, witchcraft, health or 'dis-ease,' money and business, bad luck children, spouse, life path, spirit, heart, ancestors and so on. But the bones can also warn a person not to take an upcoming journey or highlight a past event that has bearing on the present. The future can always change because of free will. Therefore far-reaching and accurate prophecy is sometimes difficult since free will is ever-present to shift the variables and alter the future.

If one were to ask a sangoma how dowsing works, she would say that the ancestor was moving the dowsing stick in the direction of water. Similarly, sangomas will sometimes use special devices that 'point,' or indicate direction, to help them glean information from the ancestor. For instance, the healer may place different mutis around the mat and see which the pointer indicates is the most suitable for the client.

The bones are the psychospiritual CT scan of the sangoma and speak to the cosmology of the human condition; Western medicine has sophisticated technology to diagnose the physical but nothing like the bones that can diagnose the psycho-spiritual. Even psychotherapy falls short in many instances and does not even acknowledge that some of these forces exist. Some churches used to do exorcisms for involuntary possession but now send the afflicted person for psychotherapy. Dreams can also help us with the psycho-spiritual but unlike the bones, dreams cannot be 'called.' We may ask for a dream but not get one. The power of the bones is that they can be called when information is needed.

Dreams

For most of us, the easiest form of access to the cosmic infinity and realms not localized in space and time is the dream world. According to the sangomas and other ancient wisdom, our dream state is every bit as real as the waking state, and all we have to do is decipher the cosmic conversation. We have to understand the metaphors and the passwords. These may be highly individual, and it is up to each one of us to find our own individual 'Morse code.'

Sangoma say that there are basically two types of dreams: instructional and non-instructional. Carl Jung called the instructional dreams 'big dreams.' These important dreams often have a different quality; they may be numinous or luminous, in technicolor, or have a heightened intensity. On occasions we will see our spirit guides in our dreams. Such events may be visitations rather than dreams.

Sangomas are specialists at interpreting dreams. They dream about patients coming to them and about specific plant remedies for those patients. Even though they may never have seen that plant before, they will go into the bush, find it, and then dispense it. Sangomas appreciate that these spirit dream messages usually occur in the early hours of the morning. They say this is when the ancestors are active.

Because of free will, dreams (like the bones) tell us 'what to see and not what to be.' They open us up to a non-local, space time continuum which can give us information to make our lives easier. We are perfectly entitled to ignore the advice and accept the consequences.

All dreams are liable to pollution from trickster spirits. The field, like the internet, is impartial to messages, light or dark, and both have free access. Just as there are viruses, Trojan horses, pornographic pop-ups, etc. on the web, so there are dark energies in the spirit world that want to corrupt the sangoma's dream files. These dark forces are part of the interplay of light and dark and part of the design of the polarity balance set in place by the Great Spirit. The advantage of the bones over dreams is that they are far less vulnerable to sabotage since they are protected by the sacred space or 'fire wall' of the ndumba.

Cases

I once threw the bones for a relationship. The question from the woman (whose partner was not present) was, "Should my boyfriend move in with me, and how does it look for our future together?" The bone representing him fell directly on top of her bone and the two were balanced perfectly. The meaning was obvious even to her; they were meant to be together. He eventually did move in with her, and their relationship flourished.

On a separate occasion I was consulting a woman who had been betrayed by her closest friend in a love triangle. Forgiveness is a given in African traditions, but the question she had for the bones was, "Should I renew the friendship or not?" When I threw the bones the one that had been assigned to her friend flew across the room, hitting against the door of the yurt. The answer was made violently clear: the betrayer should not remain within the sphere of my client's life, metaphorically delineated by the borders of the mat on which the bones are thrown.

The bones are reading the waking dream that is the client's life, and similar information can be transmitted to the sangoma visually or metaphorically in dreams. I recently dreamed that someone I knew in South Africa was ill. I had him tested, and he proved to be HIV positive. Had I thrown the bones, the display would have shown the bone designated for him misaligned and in proximity to the crocodile bones (which indicate disease), oriented in a negative polarity. This would have given me the same information as the dream and an identical outcome.

Sometimes patients in California come to me for treatment decisions and second opinions. I see them first in the office with their medical records to find out what has been done and where they are in the process. I want to clarify as many of the facts as possible by eliminating many of the variables that could take hours to work out through the bones: the more the variables, the more the questions, and each question may require a separate throw. It is much better to parse all the questions and distill them before going to the bones and much less confusing for the spirit guide who throws the bones.

I frequently have people who come with a dismal prognosis from another physician, but the bones disagree and say they will be well. One woman was diagnosed with pancreatic cancer, one of the worst of cancers. The bones said to have the surgery and that she would be cured. Several years later she was doing well, without evidence of recurrence.

Another patient had a radical prostatectomy for prostate cancer and soon after the PSA marker, which should have been zero, started to climb. He refused radiation and hormonal therapy, and instead came to me for a bone divination. The bones agreed with him. Now he is on a macrobiotic diet with phytochemical supplements, and he is feeling energetic and doing well, which would not have been the case if he had been on hormone therapy. Many patients with organic disease want to know which way they should go. The bones can help where there are several good choices but only one best choice for that patient's particular spirit and life path.

The bones always seem to offer hope. When patients come to me, we do healing rituals and use plant medicines to connect them to the Source and to the ancestors, both theirs and mine. They are getting medicine not localized in space and time that treats the whole of who they are.

Conclusion

Ancestral reverence and the different healing techniques described in this chapter are highly valued in African society and have been in force for eons. Sangomas are able to communicate with the dead. This phenomenon is quite alien to Western thinking, and is easily dismissed and even ridiculed. Yet dead spirits may play a much bigger role in our health, wealth, and happiness than we may think.

Our Western education has brought us many technological marvels, but we should not doubt that we have paid a huge price for them. In the West we are victims as well as beneficiaries of our religion, education, culture, and conditioning. Africa, on the other hand, has aboriginal psycho-spiritual technology that we are only now beginning to appreciate. We need to recognize how much we have forfeited and how much we can learn from native peoples who are still in touch with their original energies and can access these realms with such ease. We invent fancy names for mystical phenomena, such as coherence, physiological arousal, cathartic conversion experience, congruence, medical intuitive, and distant mental influence on biological systems. African healers have known these principles for eons. In fact, theirs is the original medicine. We should call our standard allopathic techniques complementary and alternative. We are going back to what we once knew.

Recommended reading

Hammond-Tooke D. *Rituals and Medicine.* Johannesburg: Paper Books; 1989.

Hammond-Tooke D. *The Roots of Black Africa.* Johannesburg: Jonathan Ball Publishers; 1993.

Byrd RC. "Positive Therapeutic Effects of Intercessory Prayer in a Coronary Care Unit Population." *Southern Medical Journal* 1988; 81:7: 826-829.

Targ E. "Distant Healing." *Noetic Science Review*, (Aug-Nov 1999): 49.

Radin D. "Moving Mind. Moving Matter (extract from The Conscious Universe)." *Noetic Sciences Review*, 46 (Summer 1998).

Thomas CB., Duszynski K. et al. "Family Attitudes Reported in Youth as Potential Predictors of Cancer." *Psychosomatic Medicine* 1979; 41:4: 287-302.

Cumes D. *Africa In My Bones. A Surgeon's Odyssey into the Spirit World of African Healing.* New Cape Town: Africa Books; 2004.

Cumes D. *Inner Passages Outer Journeys.* St. Paul, MN: Llewellyn Publications; 1998.

Cumes D. *The Spirit of Healing.* St. Paul, MN: Llewellyn Publications; 1999.

About the author

David Cumes, MD, received his surgical training in Johannesburg, South Africa, and has taught at Stanford Medical Center. After extensive travel which included time with the Bushmen and shamans in Peru and South Africa, Dave was initiated as a sangoma or medicine man in South Africa in 2002. He is the author of five books: *Inner Passages Outer Journeys*; *The Spirit of Healing*; *Africa in my Bones*; *Healing Trees and Plants of the Lowveld;* and *Messages from the Ancestors —Wisdom for the Way*. His roots are in Africa and his quest is to bring the primal essence of these methods back to the West.

XVI
Soul Retrieval in Central and South America

Alberto Villoldo, PhD

One day a middle-aged man came to see my shamanic teacher Eduardo Calderon complaining of intestinal pain and blood in his stool. During the healing ceremony, Calderon, one of Peru's most renowned healers, inquired about the man's marriage. He replied that he believed his wife was cheating on him, which she had denied. At that moment, Calderon exclaimed loudly that this was the cause of the man's illness; his broken heart was causing the bleeding, and his intestinal pain was because he was unable to swallow and digest his grief. During the subsequent soul retrieval ceremony, Eduardo summoned the young man that his client once was, so that his strength, confidence, and vitality might return. Then he blew the youthful spirit into the top of his head and recommended that he go on a bland diet of rice and greens for two weeks. Within a few days the bleeding stopped and the intestinal pain ceased, the man felt stronger, more youthful, and imagined that he was recovering his wife's attention. Four-and-one-half-years later the symptoms reappeared and the man went to the local public health clinic where they were unable to find a cause for his bleeding, and he died within six months. Today, his family tells people "his wife made him sick, and then the doctors killed him."

Like biomedical practitioners, the folk healers known as curanderos in Hispanic communities recognize that externally visible conditions such as skin lesions, wounds, snakebite, infections, and fungus respond well to herbal and pharmacological treatment. The inside of the body, on the other hand, is invisible, and diseases that afflict the inner organs frequently have their origins in the invisible world. These origins are mysterious or magical in nature, and belong to the domain of the soul.[1] For such conditions curanderos focus their attention on the metaphysical disease origins in the invisible world.

It is difficult to appreciate the healing practices of the curandero when we do not recognize the invisible world in which he is a mediator. Science has spent nearly one hundred years debunking the metaphysical interpretations of disease. When researchers first discovered that diseases responded to specific pharmacological treatments, they came to the understanding that all illness had its origin in the visible (microscopic) world. This was reaffirmed with the discovery of wonder drugs that target pathogens invisible to the naked eye and allow the physician to 'diagnose by treatment.' Through the pioneering work of Pasteur, Koch, and Lister the metaphysical origins of disease were replaced with a science that only studied the role of physical infectious disease agents. As a result, the plagues and epidemics that decimated Europe and the Americas were largely eradicated, and much superstition was eliminated from the practice of medicine.[2] The identification of physical agents of disease and their corresponding treatment became the dominant pursuit of biomedicine. Today physicians treat the body and psychotherapists treat the soul.

In Central and South America, as well as in Hispanic communities in the United States, the physical and metaphysical dimensions of healing remain powerfully intertwined. Popular belief assumes that you cannot heal the body unless you also attend to the soul: for it is the condition of your soul that determines the condition of your health. The roots of this thinking lie in a pre-Columbian Native American medical paradigm that suggests illness results when you are out of balance with nature and your own inner nature. In Latin America this belief became interwoven with the dogma of the Roman Catholic Church that emphasized salvation of the soul above all else. As a result, the healing process entails primarily the healing of the soul, and only secondarily the administration of medications.[3] Soul loss variously referred to in Spanish as *Susto, Espanto, Mal de ojo, Mal del aire* is a frequent affliction.[4] A growing body of evidence indicates that procedures such as soul retrieval are effective in treating illnesses with a psychological basis.[5] The curandero argues that all ailments have a psychological basis and that the body and the soul cannot be treated separately. If you do so the disease will inevitably return.

The jaguar and the microbe

While the Roman Catholic roots of the healing systems of Hispanic America are consistent throughout the region, the Native American heritage varies from mountain to valley to coast, and between nations like the Maya, Toltec, and Inka. There are more than 600 distinct Native language groups in Central and South America alone, yet the Native peoples of the Americas share many common beliefs.[6] Anthropologists have identified universal themes and practices among folk healers and indigenous practitioners. As a medical anthropologist, I have focused my studies on the Inka, the largest remaining indigenous group in the Americas with more than forty million members. They have been the least influenced by modern civilization with its homogenizing influence of radio, television, and education. Most of the references I make to Native American healing beliefs are from my research with Inka curanderos or shamans.[7]

For shamanic healers there is no difference between being killed by a jaguar or by a microbe. To educated persons from the west, however, one is an unfortunate accident while the other is a disease. For indigenous people it is important to be on good terms (in balance) with both jaguars and microbes; when you are out of balance with either, the ordinarily benign relationship with nature becomes predatory and opportunistic. To the scientist this may seem quaint and animistic; yet if we can put aside for a moment the arrogance of Western thinking, we can find common ground between the perspective of the curandero and the scientist. Take host-pathogen interactions, for example. Research in immunology indicates that disease is as much a function of host resistance as it is of the pathogen or invasive agent. The same viral or bacterial pathogen will affect two people differently. While the indigenous person believes that you become sick or not (and even how sick you become) depending on how in balance you are with nature, the scientist believes that how sick you become is a function of how resistant your immune system is. To the scientist, nature is always predatory and opportunistic. To the indigenous curandero this seems like an unnecessarily hostile and violent attitude, not unlike the conquistador himself. In the indigenous view nature is benign and collaborative, turning hostile and predatory only when one is out of balance.

Until recently, people in the west thought that the mind was located within the brain. Today research in psychoneuroimmunology and neuropeptides demonstrates that the mind is in the body, in-between and within each and every cell. Until recently it was difficult for us to accept that a person's reaction to a pathogen is conditioned by their emotions and levels of stress. It is also very difficult for us to understand the curandero's belief that the condition of our souls also determines how successfully we survive encounters with jaguars and other 'accidents.' In the curandero's world the mind extends beyond the body into all of nature. When you return to balance, life ceases being predatory and becomes benign and supportive once again. Thus, the condition of your world reflects the condition of your soul. Change the condition of your soul and your entire world changes.

The curandero paradigm

Every healing system is based upon a set of givens, assumptions about the nature of reality that make up that system's paradigm. The curandero system works on a paradigm that is complementary to that of biomedicine. It is founded on the existence of a healing system that we do not yet recognize: a meta-system that has both visible physical components, such as blood, white blood cells, T-lymphocytes and invisible information components such as the soul.[8] The nonphysical component responds to stress, emotional states, suggestion, imagery, symbols, and the elemental forces of nature. Curanderos rely on imagery, symbols, suggestions, and a dialogue with the forces of nature to unlock and accelerate the body's natural healing processes. The notion of a healing system has also been entertained by Western researchers and over the years medical science has identified the primary systems of the human body as the circulatory system, digestive system, endocrine system, autonomic nervous system, parasympathetic nervous system, and the immune system. However, two other systems are also central to the proper functioning of a human being: the healing system and the belief system. The two work together. The healing system is the way the body mobilizes all its resources to combat disease while the belief system is the activator of the healing system.[9]

There are many pharmacological tools available to curanderos, yet these are considered limited when used alone. The healing system must be engaged and activated, and this is accomplished by identifying the healing needs of the soul, and then addressing them. The curandero not only diagnoses the cause of the disease, but the cause of the soul loss, and identifies the steps that must be taken to recover the soul parts that will bring wholeness and healing. These healers are masters of psychosomatic health in which the body and soul are not divorced.

Key principles of their healing paradigm include a number of assertions such as that all living beings are interconnected by information keeping us in dialogue with nature. That there are two kinds of time: ordinary time and sacred time. Ordinary time is monochronic, that is, it 'flies like an arrow.' The past happened and is behind us, the present is now, and the future is ahead of us. This kind of time is causal, it allows for predictability and repeatability, essential to scientific thinking. Sacred time is polychronic; it 'turns like a wheel.' You can influence events that have occurred in the past and even alter destiny. The nature of this time is non-causal. In ordinary time, the cause of an illness might be dietary and the missing nutrients can be detected through laboratory analysis. In sacred time, the cause of the same condition can be traced to the patient's failure to perform a ritual two years earlier, to *Susto* or 'fright,' or even to the anticipation of a terrible fate that might occur in the near future. These explanations are not seen as contradictory.

Through the practice of shamanic journeying, a healer is able to enter sacred time to find the metaphysical cause of an illness. Additionally, in sacred time the healer is able to assist the client in selecting the desired future healed state and determine the steps necessary to reach it. This future state can then begin to guide and inform the client in their healing process as it activates the body's healing system. The curandero believes that the body can be informed not only by the past, but also by the future. Once the healed state is selected, it can guide the client to it.[10]

The healer is able to retrieve parts of the client's soul that have been lost or compromised. The soul is associated with the inside of the earth, a shadowy and dangerous realm populated by beings that represent unknown and often repressed elements of our individual and collective psyches, as well as by aspects of ourselves that we disown.[11] The Inkas refer to this domain as the Lowerworld (*Uhu pacha*), inhabited by beings and forces that predate the birth of humanity. On the positive side, the domains inside the earth are also the source of fertility and creativity, where we germinate the seeds of our future. It is the task of the healer to help clients recover those parts of themselves that they have disowned and to serve as midwives to new healed selves. By journeying, the healer is able to penetrate the most intimate domains of the soul. They can also observe events that occurred in the past that caused the sickness. They can also negotiate with beings, or elements of the psyche, that may be in disharmony, and retrieve elements of the soul that bring life-changing instructions necessary for healing.

The soul is an essential, tangible, and knowable element of the self. It exists outside ordinary time, yet manifests in time, carrying biological and psycho-spiritual information that organizes the body and influences physical reality. This information is contained within a luminous field surrounding the physical body, organizing it in the way magnets organize iron filings on a piece of glass.[12] Healers who read the messages of the soul perceive this luminous field and upgrade the quality of information within it, bringing about health in the physical body. A physical intervention such as surgery, performed without re-informing the soul, results only in the elimination of symptoms, not in healing the patient. In time, the ailing soul begins to re-inform the physical body and the disease reappears. The healing process eliminates the toxic imprints for disease and re-informs the soul, triggering the body's natural healing response.

Soul retrieval journey

"Before the coming of the missionaries," the old man said, "everyone knew the way to the realms of the soul, back to the belly of the Earth. When the missionaries came they taught us that we had been kicked out of the Garden of Eden, just as they had. The people then began to forget. Today, only the shaman remembers the way." This man was an Inka healer that I had the opportunity to study with for more than twenty years. He explained to me that like the heart, we have a four-chambered soul. "Each of these chambers is a room that can be entered to bring balance and healing to a patient." You follow an underground river that takes you to the shores of a great cavern deep in the earth. This is a spirit journey accompanied by rhythmic drumming. Once in the belly of the earth you secure permission from the keeper of the Lowerworld who allows safe passage through the chambers of your client's soul. If a healer attempts to enter the soul without permission, he may loose his own soul, receive a disease, and even perish.

The four soul chambers are like archives that contain scenes from a person's past that continue playing themselves out as if they were happening now. The first soul chamber contains the story of a person's pain, grief, and loss. Next is the chamber of promises, which holds spiritual contracts a person entered into during their lifetime, and in some instances, even before they were born. These are soul-debts, analogous to sins, that the curandero is able to renegotiate on the client's behalf. Some of these were dreadful promises, such as to avenge the death of a loved one. Buried inside this chamber are the guiding life visions that souls brought with them into this world. It is the task of healers to uncover such visions and help clients to align their destiny with the vision they had chosen. The third chamber holds the life force. The healer must discover, elicit, and reawaken this force. The fourth chamber contains treasures—gold or precious gems buried deep in the soul—which is the healer's task to discover and bring to the surface. The expression of these treasures is associated with the result of the healing process.

The curandero can heal, renegotiate events from the past, and bring closure to events he witnesses in each of the chambers. He is able to retrieve a soul fragment, for example, representing the client at age six when his mother and father had to flee their village and he was lost in the jungle for two days. The healer retrieves elements from each of the four chambers of the soul and breathes them back into his client, with instructions the client needs to regain his health. These instructions are as important as the journey itself. The beings the curandero battles and negotiates with, and the situations he encounters, are representative of the illness and point to steps the client can take to begin the healing journey.

Three main themes predominate in these instructions. The first is personal responsibility: clients must recognize their illnesses and take responsibility for the lessons inherent in them as well as self-healing possibilities. Second is personal empowerment: clients are empowered to correct what is out of balance through prayer, offerings to persons or spirits, and they are given symbolic tools. And third is lifestyle change: healing requires modifying one's relationship to nature; abstaining from alcohol; caring for children, loved ones, and the village; as well as undertaking dietary or ceremonial changes.

If clients recognize and assume responsibility for the lessons in their illness, the healing system is triggered. When they not only know why did this happen, but what they must do to learn from this condition, they are empowered to correct that which is out of balance. If clients are willing to undergo the lifestyle changes associated with the healing process, the self-regenerative element will be triggered.

Conclusions

Research into the healing practices of curanderos suggests that they are most effective in treating conditions with psychological components, and that the success of these practices may be explained in part in terms of hypnotic or placebo processes.[13,14] The healing rituals may contain waking suggestions that trigger physiological responses to symbolic processes. The practice of soul retrieval continues to flourish under many names throughout the Americas, and Hispanics continue to look to the health of the soul as an essential condition to the health of the body. Medical systems that ignore the soul will continue to underserve Hispanic and other indigenous communities.

References and endnotes

[1] This distinction is not very clear-cut, as illnesses of the skin and others can also be the result of spiritual maladies.

[2] While during the Renaissance the medical arts were flourishing in the Americas (the Spanish are known to have written to the King to send no doctors to the New World), in Europe medicine was entering another dark age. During this period, numerous disgusting remedies and therapies became common, such as the powder of sympathy, a mixture of copper salts that was applied to the patient's blood-stained garment rather than to the patient (to his good fortune)

[3] This is a sweeping generalization that other researchers may find objectionable.

For example, the notion of the 'soul' exists only among populations influenced by Christianity, and not among the (very few) isolated indigenous communities remaining in Central and South America.

[4] There are many categories of sickness not considered 'real' pathophysiological categories by modern medicine that are often considered culture-bound syndromes. Many of these syndromes are universally found among all cultures.

[5] Finkler K. *Spiritualist Healers in Mexico: Successes and Failures of Alternative Therapeutics*. New York: Bergin and Garvey Publishers; 1985.

[6] Bourguignon E. "The Effectiveness of Religious Healing Movements: A Review of the Literature." *Transcultural Psychiatry Res. Rev* 1973; 13:5-21.

[7] The Inka *curanderos* are shaman-healers known as *pacos*.

[8] This healing system appears to have three sub-systems: an auto-diagnostics system, a self-repair system, and a regenerative system. Any of theses three components can be out of balance and malfunction: the body may fail to recognize the presence of disease (i.e. cancer); the self-repair system may fail to engage (i.e. autoimmune disorders); or the regenerative may fail (i.e. bone regeneration).

[9] O'Regan B. and Hirshberg C. *Spontaneous Remission: An Annotated Bibliography*. Institute of Noetic Sciences; 1993.

[10] This conceptualization of time is not unique to *curanderos* in the Americas. Stanner's (Stanner WEH. "The Dreaming." in Lessa W. and Vogt EZ., ed., *Reader in Comparative Religion*, Evanston: Row Peterson; 1958, 513-23) account of the "Dreaming" illustrates the folded sense of time of the Australian Aboringenes, where an individual can 'influence' the past that shapes his 'present.' Other studies by Van Gennep and Durkheim illustrate how the conception of time is a consequence of culture and not inherent in humans.

[11] There is a striking similarity between these domains of the soul and the 'shadow' of Jungian psychology. To the church, this description seemed very close to that of the Christian hell, and many healers, particularly women, were classified as witches and to this day persecuted and discriminated against.

[12] This energy field is known to the Inkas as the *popo*, or energy body.

[13] Sammons R. "Parallels Between Magico-Religious Healing and Clinical Hypnosis in Therapy." in Kirkland J., Mathews HF. et al, ed., *Herbal and Magical Medicine: Traditional Healing Today*. Durham, NC: Duke University Press; 1992; 53-57.

[14] Schumaker JF. *The Corruption of Reality: A Unified Theory of Religion, Hypnosis,*

and Psychotherapy. Amherst, NY: Prometheus Books; 1995.

About the author

Alberto Villoldo, PhD., is a psychologist and medical anthropologist who has studied the healing practices of the Amazon and Andean shamans for more than 30 years. Dr. Villoldo founded of The Four Winds Society, an international organization that trains individuals in the practice of energy medicine and soul retrieval, and is the author of *Shaman, Healer, Sage*; *The Four Insights*; *Mending the Past and Healing the Future with Soul Retrieval*; and *Illumination*.

XVII
Reviving the Tradition of Faery Doctoring

Tom Cowan, PhD

The faery faith in Celtic countries has had a curious history: in almost every century it was assumed that belief in faeries was disappearing. Irish folklorists around 1900 were told that only the old people still believed in faeries. The Reverend Robert Kirk in the late-seventeenth century found that the belief in faeries in Scotland was not thought to be as strong as in earlier times. Around 1400 the English poet Chaucer commented on the same phenomenon. In the twelfth-century Giraldus Cambrensis of Wales reported that the belief in faeries was waning. And Irish monks in the so-called Dark Ages declared that belief in the old spirits was definitely dying out. As one modern researcher has put it, belief in faeries seems to always be going, going, going—but never gone.[1]

In fact, interest in the faery world is enjoying a resurgence in our times due to the widespread revival of all things Celtic and undoubtedly also due to the resurgence of shamanism. The number of people today with shamanic skills and beliefs, and sensitive to encounters with invisible beings, might be greater than ever before. Even in the early 1970s when the current shamanic revival was just beginning, historian Keith Thomas concluded his massive study of "religion and the decline of magic" with a caveat that the connection between the modern world and the disappearance of magic is "only approximate" and that "the role of magic in modern society may be more extensive than we yet appreciate."[2]

Who are the faeries and what is faery doctoring?

A major feature of the faery faith is that some illnesses, misfortunes, and natural disasters are caused by, or directly involve, the faery world or the Sidhe (pronounced 'shee'), and that men and women called 'faery doctors' can help in healing these conditions. Faery doctoring, then, comes from the primal Irish tradition of the Sidhe, a term that refers both to a realm of the Otherworld and to the spirits that dwell there. Over the centuries other names for the Sidhe have arisen: Faerie, Land of Youth, Realm of the Shining Ones, the Land of Heart's Desire, Summerland, Elfhame, and many more. In this article the terms faeries and the Sidhe will be used interchangeably.

Anthropologists and folklorists agree that most indigenous cultures conceive of a realm peopled by invisible spirits similar to the Sidhe. The Sidhe, therefore, has existed from time immemorial and extends to all corners of the world. The Celtic view has always been that other spirits besides the faeries live in the Sidhe (such as some of the ancestors, the old gods and goddesses, and nature spirits like the Green Man and the Ladies of the Lake) and the Sidhe can be contacted from many places around the world.

To be clear, however, faery doctoring is not part of the 'English garden variety of fairies.' Victorian artists and illustrators created such beguiling, whimsical images of this tradition that many people assume these accurately reflect the Irish faery tradition of the Sidhe. They do not. A more serious view of faeries is the poet William Butler Yeats's description. They are "conscious beings who are not of heaven but of the earth, who have no inherent form but change according to their whim, or the mind that sees them. Do not think the fairies are always little. Everything is capricious about them, even their size."[3] Spelling faery with an 'e' helps to remind of us of this.

Over the last century faery doctoring has been in decline and discredited in many Celtic places due to the same developments that have discredited shamanic healing. For example, the advancement of Western medicine into rural areas has offered an alternative to faery doctoring and other folk healing remedies. As rural people become better educated, along with their urban counterparts, folk practices of all types begin to look like superstition, and there is an understandable desire on the part of marginalized nations and regions to want to be considered modern. Lastly, disapproval by Christian authorities has always made faery doctoring somewhat suspect and, like shamanism in many places, an air of secrecy has surrounded the practice. And yet faery doctoring, like the faery faith itself, has never died out, and along with the resurgence in shamanism over the last thirty or forty years, it too may actually be on the rise.

The times call for a revitalization of the faery doctoring tradition for a number of reasons. Many illnesses and conditions today exhibit symptoms that are associated with traditional faery illnesses. These include lethargy, tiredness, lack of energy, depression, low enthusiasm for life, and a rundown feeling often accompanied by unexplained aches and pains. Some of the modern illnesses associated with these symptoms are chronic fatigue syndrome, Lyme's disease, HIV virus, chronic insomnia, lupus, seasonal affective disorder, fibromyalgia, and various types of clinical depression.

The medical profession seems unable to explain the causes or cures of many of these diseases. In some cases the medical profession is uncertain whether or not to even designate some of them as diseases at all. The ambiguity suggests to me that we need to address more than just the physical condition of these syndromes. We need to explore the spiritual dimensions of illness as well, the way healers in Celtic lands looked to the faerie folk as critical participants in most illnesses.

In traditional terms a person suffering from a faery illness is thought to have been 'taken' by the faeries, or is 'away' in the Sidhe. Sometimes people will say that 'something else'—like a 'stick' or 'stock of wood' or an 'old faery'—has been left in that person's place. All of these expressions are ways to say quite simply that the person is not him or her self. What is common to these symptoms is a lack of energy—the person's vitality and zest for life is missing. To put it in more traditional terms, when the faeries have 'stolen' the person's vitality, energy, or life force, he or she exhibits the symptoms mentioned above.

Attributing illness and misfortune to spirits is a common view among indigenous peoples, a view often derided by Westerners who think of themselves as more enlightened. But, as Angela Bourke points out in her study of faery doctoring in Ireland in the 1890s, *The Burning of Bridget Cleary*, believing spirits to be the cause of illness is not due to ignorance and superstition, or to a lack of intelligence and information, but is a question of "idiom and worldview."[4] Speaking of spirits as involved in a person's illness was a way of explaining real phenomena and offering solutions that could produce real results. Bourke reminds us that intelligent people can entertain more than one ideology, and one's lifestyle can accommodate multiple theories and practices. Michael Newton in *A Handbook of the Scottish Gaelic World* agrees that, "human beings have a wonderful capacity for being able to hold mutually conflicting beliefs with equal conviction."[5] Native American medical doctors, for example, prescribe traditional prayers and ceremonies, such as the sweat lodge, in addition to surgery and medications. Faery doctoring treatments can work alongside Western medicine.

Faery doctoring as holistic healing

Faery doctoring is about alleviating the symptoms that reflect a loss of energy and vitality. Like other shamanic approaches, it seeks to heal the spiritual aspects of illnesses, not necessarily cure the illness itself, and when successful, the patient feels more whole, more connected to life. Alleviating these symptoms can bring about a renewed sense of wellbeing in the client, even when the illness itself persists.

Shamanic healers hope to bring a client into a more holistic relationship with his or her life, family, friends, social environment, and the natural world. This has always been the goal of faery doctors and other folk healers. The view that a patient needs a holistic plan of recovery is very ancient. Karen Louse Jolly writes in *Popular Religion in Late Saxon England: Elf Charms in Context* that medieval healers, whether they were trained in the universities or learned their methods from popular folk healers, viewed human beings as "multifaceted creatures with a complex interaction of body and soul, a mixture of matter and spirit" that connected them with "the entire cosmos, so that they are affected by it and capable of interacting with the spiritual forces inhabiting it."[6] Anglo-Saxon medical manuscripts attest to a worldview in which shamanic remedies such as charms, rituals, power objects, and extraction procedures were seen as methods to invoke the spiritual forces needed "to counteract ailments involving the mind or soul." This medieval worldview is similar to that of indigenous people everywhere and has persisted in the folk and faery healing traditions despite the advancements in Western medicine that focus almost exclusively on the physical.

The faery doctor recognizes the presence of the fay folk (another common expression for faeries) in the wellbeing of the community. Independent spirits dwelling in the rocks, springs, forests, waterfalls, and 'invisible places'—some exhibiting good will, others ill will—affect the human communities along with their crops and livestock. They were never banished from the landscape by Christian propaganda that sought to demonize them and instill fear of them as evil spirits. Alexander Carmichael, who collected prayers, charms, and healing rituals from the Scottish Highlanders and Islanders in the late nineteenth century, wrote that a holistic view of physical and spiritual phenomena characterized rural life. He writes, "Religion, pagan or Christian, or both combined, permeated everything—blending and shading into one another like the iridescent colors of the rainbow."[7] He noticed that Highland people were "sympathetic and synthetic, unable to see and careless to know where the secular began and the religious ended." The nineteenth-century faery healer, like many Christianized indigenous shamans today, called upon the saints, angels, and Holy Trinity as well as the spirits of animals, the elements, and the Sidhe for healing. In other words, they were perfectly capable of holding two opposing ideologies in the mind at the same time and working with both for a desired outcome.

This raises a fundamental question: Why would the Sidhe take our energy?

Preserving the balance

From a shamanic point of view, there is a critical balance between ordinary and nonordinary realities. There is a constant and reciprocal exchange of life and energy between the worlds. In fact, it is a shaman's responsibility to help maintain this balance and harmony between the spirit world and ours. When the balance is upset, disasters occur—sometimes in the environment, sometimes in the tribe, sometimes in an individual person's wellbeing.

According to Irish folktales and legends, the faeries—the Otherworld forces—need energy from the world of mortals for activities which might include performing odd jobs for them, playing music at their feasts, fighting in their battles, helping a team in their games, being their lovers which might include producing faery children, and midwiving or nursing babies of the Sidhe. Sometimes a cow is taken for its milk. A tool or work implement may go missing and later be returned. In the old tales, all of these situations point to a basic fact: the Otherworld needs our input, energy, and cooperation, our love and affection. Patrick Harpur suggests that the "mere presence of humans seems to be a source of strength" that lets spirits like the Sidhe "draw on our psychic energy to give themselves substance." They "need and take—or exchange—our food, blood, power of procreation and our offspring. In other words, they need what is most substantial and vital to us. They need our life."[8] When we don't give willingly, or in sufficient amounts, the Otherworld takes it.

One might think that living in such close and cooperative proximity to the spirit world would be a source of comfort. But since the Otherworld operates from a moral code quite different from our own, taking our vitality can seem like stealing, and we understandably react with fear and suspicion. But in reality this exchange of energies might be simply the basic mechanism that keeps our universe functioning and capable of sustaining life. It is going on all the time, whether or not we attribute it to the faeries. The old tales also talk about the faeries helping us in return: in our gardens, farms, kitchens, workplaces, games, music, and art—and even our battles. In the classic work, *The Fairy Faith in Celtic Countries*, Evans-Wentz recounts an Irish man asserting that the faeries "always stand for right and justice" and that they favored the Boers during the Boer War in Africa and the Japanese in the Russo-Japanese War "because the Russians are tyrants."[9] But political sympathies aside, the faeries are willing to teach us how to heal illnesses, even the ones they themselves create.

We live in a world of reciprocal responsibilities and exchanges. Gearoid O' Crualaoich, in *The Book of the Cailleach: Stories of the Wise-Woman Healer*, notes that this reciprocal worldview is fundamental for a society that "recognizes the dependence of its continued wellbeing on the maintenance of harmonious relationships with ancestral Otherworld forces. Breaches of cosmological harmony bring afflictive retribution in the form of, allegedly mysterious, loss of wellbeing."[10] Obviously today, fewer and fewer people acknowledge a spirit world that requires reciprocal exchanges with our own. In fact, the Western lifestyle is built on continuous consumption with very little sense that something must be given in exchange. This can be seen most glaringly in the physical realm where humans exploit resources, consume material things in large quantities, waste great amounts of energy and resources, and pollute the environment in the process. World population is also greater than ever before and therefore so is the demand on the physical world. From a shamanic point of view, however, appropriating the physical world has ramifications in the spirit world because the two are intimately connected.

The reason increasing numbers of people are suffering from faery symptoms, almost epidemic in scope, seems clear. To rectify this alarming imbalance between the worlds, the Sidhe must take back energy in some sense proportionately to what we consume. They take what they need. My personal belief, based on my own reading and study and on instruction from spirit teachers in nonordinary reality, is that two of the primary concerns of spirits like the Sidhe are sustainability and renewability. Their role is to help maintain the physical-spiritual balance between the worlds so that Earth can continue to support life. So it's possible that by sustaining their realm, they in effect sustain and strengthen ours.

Faery involvement

Modern illnesses with traditional faery symptoms are not always faery related. Just as not every trauma involves soul loss, not every illness that manifests as energy depletion indicates faery theft. Careful diagnosis is required. Similarly, not everyone who suffers from a faery-related illness has been targeted by the faeries out of malice, mischief, or retaliation for some slight or injury. This interpretation agrees with what the old tales say: While sometimes the faeries do seek revenge for some slight or harm done to them, quite often their impulse is random, or we might say amoral.

The faeries can be involved in illness in several ways. At times it's possible they do cause illness. But our style and pace of life can cause illness on its own. Even when they are not the cause, however, the Sidhe can still use the illness as an opportunity to acquire energy. Illness is like a window through which they can reach and grab energy.

In many of the old tales, the person 'taken' must be rescued, and the stories depict this in various dramatic ways. We need to distinguish, however, between the literal plot devices of storytelling and the metaphorical activities that are conducive to spiritual healing. The key element here is the rescue. Similarly, soul retrieval is a rescue of someone's soul by a shaman who journeys into nonordinary reality, finds the lost soul, and then returns with it.[11]

Rescue from Faery

The rescue from Faerie, however, is not exactly the same as the rescue involved in soul retrieval. The primary difference is that the shaman or faery doctor cannot journey into the Sidhe, find the vitality, and steal it back. The faery world or the Sidhe is traditionally a place of privacy, and respect for privacy is one of the Sidhe folk's primary concerns. Their realm is a protected, off limits area of nonordinary reality. As we learn from the old tales, one must be invited into it, lured into it, or kidnapped into it. Occasionally someone may stumble into it unawares, but it is a place where humans are generally not appreciated. The folk tradition attests to this need to not disturb the Sidhe or bother them unnecessarily. Furthermore, it does not make sense to steal back the person's energy if the Sidhe needs it. What would prevent them from simply stealing it back again? Restoring a person's vitality is not a game of ping pong with the faery world. Clearly the rescue needs to be finessed.

A rescue journey must be undertaken with the assistance of helping spirits from the Sidhe. Faery doctors have 'friends' among the faeries, and in some historical accounts faery doctors are thought to be 'with the faeries' quite often. Biddy Early, for instance, a famous faery doctor in County Clare in the 19th century, was thought to be with the faeries every night. A nineteenth-century observer on the Aran Islands explained faery doctors this way: "There are many that can do cures because they have something walking with them, what we may call a ghost, from among the faeries."[12] As in core shamanic work, the real healing is done by the spirits. Compared with core soul retrieval work, the shaman faery doctor really has less to do since it is the contacts in the Sidhe that perform the actual rescue and return of the client's vital energy to the shaman who then, in turn, restores it to the client.

Faery doctoring requires extensive commitment on the part of the shaman and client to fill the 'energy gap' created in the Sidhe after the rescue. One account from the 19th century tells how a woman fell sick for no apparent reason, was diagnosed by the faery doctor as having been 'swept' away by the fey folk, and then rescued so that she lived another twenty years. Her husband, however, was unable to keep his livestock from dying. He lost an animal every year for the next ten or twelve years.[13] Eddie Lenihan, an Irish storyteller and collector of faery lore, describes in *Meeting the Other Crowd: The Fairy Stories of Hidden Ireland*, how after a man's son was cured, a storm blew up the Shannon River, and swept the man's three pigs into the water, and they were never seen again.[14] Reimbursing the Sidhe for the returned health and vitality is paramount.

Faery doctors themselves might be inflicted with illness or injury to various degrees of severity after they perform cures. In the older tradition it is assumed that the cures displeased the Sidhe. Biddy Early "used to get a good grueling" when she gave out a cure that irritated them.[15] Other faery doctors complained that they would get a pain in the leg or hand, for example, when they did healing work.[16] My own understanding of this process is that the spirits are not so much displeased as they are eager to remind us that some offering or sacrifice must be made in exchange. If it is not offered, or offered in the right way, then it will be taken. Most faery doctors had means of protection—charms, amulets, herbs—to ward off harm from malicious spirits. This practice seems congruent with basic shamanic work in that shamans only do healing when they know they are filled with power and have their helping spirits with them.

Reimbursing the Sidhe

As part of the exchange or 'deal' in achieving the rescue, the Sidhe often suggest to the faery doctor ways that he or she and the client can make up the loss in the Sidhe by various acts of exchange. The bottom line here is that faery doctoring only works if the shaman and the client are willing to incorporate certain activities into their lives in order to maintain this critical balance between the worlds. Shamans do this already to some extent, but faery doctoring requires additional input. The reimbursements are generally in three areas that folklore tells us are of perennial interest to the Sidhe: strength, beauty, and love. These are the major qualities and features of the Sidhe, these are the fibers that weave the faery world together, and these are the elements for health and wellbeing. In this respect the Sidhe is a proto-world for our own, a model for the conditions that would make human life more fulfilling: strength, beauty, love. In the old folk tales the Sidhe usually abduct someone young because in youth these qualities are fresh and vigorous. Remember one of the most common names for the Sidhe is *Tir na nOg*, or the Land of Youth, not because all the spirits there are young—there are old faeries and there is death among the fay folk—but because the virtues, excitement, and intensity of youth are the fabric of their world.

In shamanic work the client needs to take responsibility for his or her healing; the same is true in faery doctoring. My experience is that the Sidhe ask for activities that will increase health and strength in the client's and shaman's own lives or their environment, create more beauty and joy in their lives, and/or express love and affection for their lives or the environment. The Sidhe recognize that the environment, both natural and human made, is a common ground between them and us. The environment is part of what we share with them.

Activities that would fulfill these conditions could include: blessing the Sidhe at dawn or dusk with a short prayer; singing or reciting poetry or playing music for them on some regular basis; dancing; cleaning up clutter in homes or along the roads; putting out food and drink for them on a regular basis; building a shrine or faery home outdoors; creating a piece of artwork; praying or blessing them whenever passing a faery haunt or a beautiful setting in nature; changing some unhealthy living habit. These activities might be required of both the shaman faery doctor and the client; some might be specified for one or the other.

In addition to activities that reimburse the Otherworld for returned energy, faery doctors need to manifest certain characteristics or virtues that have been traditionally admired by the Sidhe. These include honesty, strength, joy, optimism, cheerfulness, generosity, truthfulness, neatness, respect for privacy, and fair dealing. In other words the faery doctor is meant to represent some of the most esteemed values in our own society. While none of us are paragons of perfection, the faery doctor needs to practice these virtues and witness them in the community. Again, what we see here is the Sidhe being a prototype for human society, or in the current parlance, the Sidhe contains the 'original instructions' given in primal times for how humans are meant to live on the Earth.

Fasting on the Sidhe

The faery doctor, and perhaps the client as well, may have to fast to elicit the Sidhe's cooperation in healing work. Fasting is a traditional activity to enlist the sympathy of the fay folk. 'Fasting on the Sidhe' can be found in the oldest myths and legends in which people fasted on a faery mound or at a stone circle to acquire knowledge or help in their lives or the lives of their people. Historically the Irish used to fast at someone's doorstep as a public protest to call attention to a grievance against the person, and in more modern times the Irish have used fasting as a political protest against English occupation and prison policies.

Fasting calls attention to the importance of a situation. The faery doctor and client might need to fast for a rescue to be taken seriously by the Sidhe. It also affirms that the person fasting knows that it is the spirit that is important here, not simply the body. When we fast we deny the body its food for a period of time in order to acknowledge the spirit's primacy in our wellbeing. Furthermore, when we fast, the body thinks we are dying. And in fact, we will die, if we never eat again. So the ritual of fasting expresses our faith in the survival of the soul and spirit beyond the life of the body. We live more as spirit when we fast and that aligns us with the spirit world, creating greater solidarity with the people of that world. And lastly, fasting is a way of denying oneself the use of resources (food) as a way of saying we desire to correct the imbalance caused by our culture's greed and neurotic consumption of resources.

Running on empty

A client who benefited from faery doctoring is a man in his mid-fifties who described his condition as "running on empty, tired, no energy, listless." His life at the time was filled with professional, family, and personal tasks. I did the rescue work long-distance when he could lie down and be open to the healing. Part of the exchange was for him to write three songs to honor the Sidhe, record them and send them to me so that I could sing them every day for a week. After I completed the journey and before I called him to report about it, he rose from the bed where he was lying, went to look out a window, and thought, "I feel like singing." He later reported that his mood and energy levels "showed definite improvement that is noticeable but not total." Singing the songs regularly made him more aware of "how things uplift me or bring me down." Now when he feels his energy flagging, he turns to the songs for help. Composing songs inspired him to seek lessons from a local singer/song writer. He states that "faery doctoring engaged me with my own resources, and opened an area of creativity I'd let lay dormant a long time."

He was also advised by the Sidhe to organize his environment more carefully and cut back on some of his activities, which he did. He takes time at the end of each work day to organize his files and clean up his desk. He also tries getting to sleep earlier. While these are practical activities that one would expect to help reduce strain, the important point here is that he needed the faery doctoring work to commit himself to these new routines.

The true self is healthy

Another case of faery doctoring is that of a sixty-year-old woman with Lyme disease, which created a swelling in her knee that made it difficult for her to walk. Homeopathic medicine and other alternative methods helped to gradually bring back some strength, but for more than five months she continued to lack energy, was in pain, found it hard to sleep, lost weight, and was unable to reduce the swelling. Other Western and nonwestern remedies "helped somewhat," she said, but did not bring "any major improvement." Antibiotics, she maintains, actually made it worse. Acupressure helped by unblocking *chi* (Chinese for life force), which increased her strength. During a drumming session, she did a shamanic journey I call "Making Love to the Land." Immediately afterwards the swelling was greatly reduced and she was able to sit cross-legged on the floor, something she was not able to do at the beginning of the session. However, the swelling increased again after a few days.

Later I did the rescue journey with her and learned that the follow-up work would include her doing the Making-Love-to-the-Land journey on a regular basis, singing each day outdoors to the spirits of the land, and spending more time at the river. I was asked to offer prayers for her each day at sunset. We continued these practices for several months and she incorporated other spiritual practices on her own, such as meditating, spending more time in nature, continuing her usual shamanic work, and doing yoga. She made sure she had whole-food nutrition. Her response was quite dramatic. Immediately after the initial journeys she felt "a turn around" in her condition. She had more overall energy, less pain, and her knee continued to improve. In the sixth month the swelling disappeared and she felt back to her normal self with good sustained energy. She had now gained back her normal weight and was feeling very strong with no adverse effects from the Lyme disease. She believes that the faery doctoring work brought her into contact with what she calls her "true self, which is always healthy." She continues to sing to the spirits of the four directions and spends time by the river.

Born out of faerie

A third case of faery doctoring involves a newborn child who had difficulty digesting food, was colicky, and had trouble sleeping. A series of doctors tried but failed to find an accurate diagnosis for the complex of troubles. (In traditional Celtic society many newborn ailments are considered to involve faery intrusion and babies are at high risk for being 'taken.') With the parents' consent I journeyed to find that the girl had spent a lot of time in the faery world before being conceived and had left energy there with the faeries. I then asked the parents if they had difficulty conceiving her, and they confirmed that they had tried for over a year. Interestingly, they each got a tattoo in order to attract the child, after which they were successful in getting pregnant. The rescue journey involved my blowing the returned energy into a blanket the baby used and returning it to the parents. The energy then transferred to the child. The child obviously did not have reimbursement tasks, but as the faery doctor I was asked to sing nursery rhymes each day for three weeks. The parents noticed improvement and discovered a medical doctor who more accurately diagnosed the baby's condition as a type of acid reflux. With better treatment the child improved. This doctor led to others who made better diagnoses of the child's conditions. The girl's parents and I firmly believe that finding the right doctors was a result of the faery work. It is not just nonordinary activity that brings healing; sometimes the nonordinary work triggers a necessary event in ordinary reality. Nevertheless, other afflictions continue to disturb the child, including a urinary or kidney condition, which I believe is also faery-related. As of this writing both Western medical and faery doctoring treatments continue.

Other considerations

Faery doctoring involves more than just a 'journey to rescue stolen vitality.' It may require a practitioner to reorient his or her life shamanically to live and work as a faery doctor. Here are some conditions that seem paramount for successful faery doctoring.

Personal contact and entry to the Sidhe

Shamanic practitioners who want to do faery doctoring need to find personal faery entries, or meeting places, to make contact with the Sidhe. Faery work is personal and local. Faery doctors should be engaged with middle-world spirits of the land where they live and use the local faery 'haunts' for this work. I would argue that much shamanic work is personal and local, and it seems odd not to center our practice on the spirits with whom we share, air, water, and other resources. People who live in cities may find it more difficult to do this, but it can be done whether in parks or other landscaped areas or a wilderness or natural area outside the city. At these faery haunts the practitioner can meet the guardians of these entries who might serve as go-betweens assisting in the rescue journeys.

Love-talking

Geancanneach is a Gaelic term meaning 'love-talker.' The many tales about faeries and mortals becoming lovers, or simply falling in love with each other, and the romantic and/or erotic descriptions of the faery realms point to the importance of love in our dealings with the Sidhe. This seems in line with major religious traditions that teach that God is love and that love is the key to human relationships. Love-talking is a practice of praising, blessing, expressing love and affection for the people, animals, places, and objects in one's life. It can be both a faery-doctoring practice and a way of being in the world. From accounts of the daily lives of Scottish Highlanders and Irish peasants in the nineteenth century, we know they were continually humming or crooning or making prayers of praise to God, the saints, nature, their animals, family and friends, the land, the seasons. Keeping songs, poems, and prayers of affection and praise continually on our lips or just on the edge of consciousness might be necessary to be worthy representatives of the Sidhe and to enlist their help in faery doctoring.

Protection

Part of the faery tradition is to have protection against unfriendly or mischievous faeries. Traditional protective items include: a piece of iron, a crucifix, holy water, horse-shoes, bread, salt, four-leaf clovers, St. John's Wort, daisies, rowan, and ash. It's possible that some of these charms are specific to Gaelic culture and are not needed or even available today. Others might be timeless means of protecting oneself from harmful spirits. Modern faery doctors need to journey on this and consult with their faery contacts and spirit teachers as to whether to use traditional power objects like these or to discover their own.

It is important not to grow paranoid about doing faery work. The accounts from nineteenth-century Ireland and Scotland (where we get most of our information about the faery tradition) describe a people in transition, living between the rural life that was beginning to disappear and the modern urban life that was encroaching upon them. They were also part of a Catholic or Protestant worldview that engendered fear and suspicion of anything not orthodox. Rural people also knew that so-called modern, educated people, who seemed to be the wave of the future, did not believe in faeries and considered the faery faith to be a superstition typical of backward people and times long ago. So there were many reasons to be ambivalent about faeries and faery doctoring, and first-person accounts may have reflected this distrust of the Sidhe and the old faery tradition.

We in turn may be exaggerating the need to fear faery mischief based on these accounts, and we must bear in mind that most stories are from people untrained in shamanic practices that dispel much of the general fear of encountering the spirit world. But as in regular shamanic work, there is a need to be filled with power and confident about the assistance from power animals and other spirit allies when dealing with any spirit forces in the universe.

Faery illness as a shamanic calling

Illnesses with faery symptoms may be a form of shamanic calling or a quasi-shamanic initiation. We hear echoes of this in the folk tradition where some, but not all, people who recover from faery illness or abduction become seers and healers in their own right. When a client learns that the spirits are involved in his or her illness and that cooperation with the spirit realm is necessary for recovery, the client may be taking a first step into some type of shamanic life, similar to the initiatory illness often seen in a person's call to become a shaman. Faery doctoring is an opportunity for practitioners to explore shamanism with clients or at least to instruct clients in the need to live, work, and play in harmony with the spirit world.

Faery doctoring and Western medicine

Faery doctors were not averse to working with other healers such as herbalists, bone-setters, clergy, and Western doctors. Faery doctors' healing work involved chants, spells, prayers, power objects (healing stones, sacred water, and talismans) and rituals, similar to the work of the shaman. Some faery doctors were herbalists and bonesetters as well, but if not, they still worked in conjunction with them. Sometimes they complemented the healing work of the local priest who might offer a Mass, say prayers, or perform other liturgical practices for the sick. As Western medicine arrived in rural areas, people began to turn to it, but if it proved ineffective, they would seek out a faery doctor. (Biddy Early, however, was indignant if people went to a medical doctor or Catholic priest first and sometimes refused to treat them.) In other words, faery doctoring can and should complement other healthcare procedures. As I have presented it here, faery doctoring is about relieving certain symptoms by restoring lost vitality and coming into harmony with the spirit world that took away that vitality. In many cases it may be necessary for Western medicine and other healing modalities to contribute to the actual cure of the illness if it is curable.

Conclusion

Faery doctoring in the modern world, at least certainly in America, is still far from being accepted as a serious form of spiritual healing. Even in traditional Celtic countries there has always been a good deal of secrecy and suspicion around it. So there is much to learn, adapt, and reinvent for contemporary people. As Michael Newton has noted, the Gaelic faery tradition "is not a static belief system but a dynamic one. While there are undoubted continuities from the pre-Christian period to recent times, there have also been many times when new ideas have created new patterns and old beliefs have been forgotten, reanalyzed, and amalgamated with others."[17] We are living in one of those times of creation right now. The practices I have discussed here are, in some ways, experimental as I and others learn, practice, and adapt the traditional material, but they feel right, in terms of being true to the folk tradition and in terms of creating a practice suitable for today's world. If we as shamanic practitioners journey on these matters to our spirit teachers and the spirits of the Sidhe, evaluate what we learn, and use our shamanic skills and knowledge carefully, we can certainly develop a modern practice of faery doctoring for healing the body, mind, and spirit of modern people.

References

[1] Harpur P. *Daimonic Reality: Understanding Otherworld Encounters*. New York, NY: Arkana/Penguin Books; 1994; 176.

[2] Thomas K. *Religion and the Decline of Magic*. New York, NY: Charles Scribner's Sons; 1971; 665, 667.

[3] Yeats WB. *Writings on Irish Folklore, Legend, and Myth*. New York, NY: Penguin Books; 1993; 9.

[4] Bourke A. *The Burning of Bridget Cleary*. New York, NY: Viking; 1999; 158.

[5] Newton M. *A Handbook of the Scottish Gaelic World*. Portland, Oregon: Four Courts Press; 2000; 255.

[6] Jolly KL. *Popular Religion in Late Saxon England: Elf Charms in Context*. Chapel Hill, North Carolina: The University of North Carolina Press; 1996; 146.

[7] Carmichael A. *Carmina Gadelica: Hymns & Incantations*. Hudson, New York: Lindisfarne Press; 1992; 29.

[8] Harpur P.; 223.

[9] Evans-Wentz WY. *The Fairy Faith in Celtic Countries.* New York, NY: Citadel Press/Carol Publishing Group; 1966; 46.

[10] O'Crualaoich G. *The Book of the Cailleach: Stories of the Wise-Woman Healer.* Cork: Cork University Press: Cork; 2003; 73.

[11] Ingerman S. *Soul Retrieval: Mending the Fragmented Self.* HarperSanFrancisco; 1991.

[12] Yeats WB.; 222.

[13] O'Crualaoich G.; 212.

[14] Lenihan E. and Green CE. *Meeting the Other Crowd: The Fairy Stories of Hidden Ireland.* New York, NY: Jeremy P. Tarcher/Putnam; 2003; 267.

[15] Lenihan E. *In Search of Biddy Early.* Dublin: Mercier Press; 1987; 27.

[16] Yeats WB.;224.

[17] Newton M.; 213.

About the author

Tom Cowan has been a practitioner, student, and teacher of shamanism for thirty years. He has studied and taught for the Foundation for Shamanic Studies, and has conducted shamanic training in North America, Europe, England, Scotland, and Ireland. He is the author of *Fire in the Head: Shamanism and the Celtic Spirit* and *Yearning for the Wind: Celtic Reflections on Nature and the Soul.* He is on the board of directors of the Society for Shamanic Practitioners and is an editor for *The Journal of Shamanic Practice.* He lives in New York's Hudson River Valley.

Coming Home

XVIII

Shamanism and War-Induced Post-Traumatic Stress Disorder

Edward Tick, PhD

Even though my physical body survived, my soul was horribly mangled. This intangible wound in my core was so severe, it left me depleted of life force. My normal range of sensory experience was so grossly impaired that I could not taste food and my interface with life consisted of raging anger and an adrenaline rush. I felt as if I was bleeding out of an invisible wound and was aware that my soul had ruptured and I was slowly dying inside. I felt like a zombie, the living dead, a lost soul.

This is the way Sam Nielson, a combat veteran of the 1993 Somalia incursion known as Black Hawk Down, described his experience of post-traumatic stress disorder (PTSD).

The American Psychiatric Association first entered PTSD into the list of diagnostic categories in 1980. In the current edition of the *Diagnostic and Statistical Manual of Mental Disorders* (DSM-IV) a cluster of symptoms of PTSD include sexuality and employment difficulties; substance abuse; threats to one's own or others' lives; intrusive thoughts and memories; alienation and mistrust; dissociative states; memory loss; sleep disorders such as recurrent nightmares; psychic numbness; depression; startle response; flashbacks; and rage. These symptoms occur together and are experienced as out of the sufferer's control.

Doctors often misdiagnose post-traumatic stress as one or two of its components, usually depression or substance abuse. This can occur when the healthcare practitioner does not recognize the holistic nature of the disorder. Such misdiagnosis leaves the patient feeling misconstrued and disappointed, and may discourage cooperation in a healing regimen. Several groups of trauma survivors, including Vietnam War veterans, Holocaust survivors, and women survivors of sexual assault, lobbied for many years to achieve public and professional recognition of the unique set of symptoms they suffered resulting from prolonged and severe threat, violence, and abuse. They knew something was different about their symptoms long before it was officially recognized.

Post-traumatic Stress Disorder

Swiss physicians in 1648 diagnosed what we now call PTSD as 'nostalgia.' German and French doctors called it 'homesickness,' and Spanish doctors called it 'to be broken.' During the American Civil War, the same cluster of symptoms was known as 'soldier's heart,' 'irritable heart,' or 'nostalgia.' More famously, during World War I it was called 'shell shock,' and during World War II 'combat fatigue.'[1] During the twentieth century's wars of mass slaughter, doctors treated the disorder as an acute breakdown, limited in time and scope, due to character flaws, especially cowardice. The treatment of choice was to get the afflicted combatant off the front lines and out of immediate danger, give him three square meals a day and a few days of bed rest, and then return him to his unit as quickly as possible. In this way they sought to reduce the loss of large numbers of shocked and terrified troops while keeping the front lines continuously supplied.

Military psychiatry during the mass warfare of the modern era was not able to concern itself with chronic debilitation from combat trauma. Its strategies for addressing combat shock did little to heal the afflicted psyches of broken soldiers. In addition, the masculine myth that during combat only the weak or cowardly break down was maintained and reinforced. During World War I, the British executed 306 soldiers who broke down during combat and refused to return to the front lines. Relatives of Private Harry Farr sued for and finally received his pardon due to shellshock in 2006, ninety years after his execution.[2] In a famous incident during the invasion of Sicily in World War II, Gen. George Patton slapped, kicked, threatened, and berated two American GIs who had been evacuated to hospitals with shellshock.[3]

We have inherited basic assumptions about manhood and service including the notion that men and now women too, can and should be able to 'take it,' by which we mean, tolerate the intensity of fear, rage, loss, pain, and suffering of war. Veterans, their healthcare practitioners, and the public may assume cowardice, weakness, or other negative character traits to be root causes of PTSD. Such judgments may further traumatize or alienate someone already shaken to their foundations. One prevailing belief is that the experience of war is not different in kind but only in intensity from civilian experiences. Many veterans report that in psychotherapy their counselors discouraged them from discussing war experiences and allowed them only to examine their childhood experiences. As Sam Nielson, reported to me:

> I was frustrated with both individual and group therapies because neither the counselor nor the doctor wanted to let me tell, or even to hear my story. I saw this happen to other friends and they shared my sentiments about therapy as well. We were all enraged that people didn't care. They wanted us to talk about "where you are now," or "how you feel today," not how we felt when we were killing people or seeing our friends killed. This was absurd. I wanted to get the shit off my chest and see if I could comprehend what I lived through, and go back and purge my knotted up feelings that I could not express at the moment when men are aiming their guns at each other. Whatever these professionals were doing, it was not helping; it only made things worse.

Steering veterans away from discussing war experiences in therapy may be due to the belief that significant life-shaping experiences only occur during childhood. Thus, healthcare practitioners assume that new experience will not alter a warrior's personality. James Hillman has called this 'the developmental fallacy.' [4] It may also be due to our classification of PTSD as an anxiety disorder because a dominant strategy is to teach the afflicted to steer away from stress triggers so not to awaken symptoms. These therapeutic issues can unwittingly deny the impact of war trauma and reinforce societal silence about war's conditions and aftermath. It keeps the war, as one combat vet said, "locked in my head."

Trauma-and-recovery therapists understand that experiences of significant intensity, threat, and strangeness can totally throw a person off his or her trajectory. Yet some therapists assume that they can generalize from the treatment of one type of trauma to all forms of trauma. They may equate, for example, rape victims, car accident survivors, and war veterans. Focusing on the similarity of patients' symptoms, they may not recognize the special conditions experienced by those who became sanctioned killers during combat.

Nielson insists,

> Returning veterans are not exactly 'primed' to engage in either conventional or new-age services… At best, they may 'go through the motions.' This is especially true for killers. Therapists do not distinguish

well enough between veterans who killed and 'office veterans' who were not engaged in actual face-to-face killing.

Survivors of war know that there is a vast continuum of exposure to and participation in violence. It proceeds from civilians who have never experienced war to civilian survivors, and from non-combatant veterans stationed stateside to those behind the lines, to personnel supporting or exposed to combat and its losses, and finally to those who actually did the fighting and killing. Veterans spontaneously organize themselves and the world according to how deep in the danger and killing they were. They reserve greatest honor, respect, and even fear for those on the ground in the gravest danger. They differentiate people into those who 'get it' and those who don't. To 'get it' means to see through the eyes and feel with the heart of one who has been in the kill-or-be-killed situation, who has experienced all of life focused on a razorblade moment and been changed by it forever.

Another consequence of the modern interpretation of post-traumatic stress may result from the goal and practices of transitioning the veteran from combatant back to a stable and participating community member. This noble ideal fails to recognize several important dimensions of the war experience. It equates serving in wartime with being a warrior; however, as we shall see, being a warrior entails far more than experiencing and surviving combat. It also equates the goals of homecoming and return with successful adaptation to life as defined by civilians in mainstream society. Warriorhood, however, is a different and unique identity. It interprets PTSD according to its present classification as a stress and anxiety disorder, meaning we reduce the overwhelming and complex experience of war to a category of severe stress. It means we measure veterans' functioning against the civilian norm and classify their degree of disability. This fails to recognize that a veteran's transformation of character due to wartime trauma is profound and while it may change, it will never go away.

Our Western interpretation does not recognize, as traditional societies did, that after profound non-normative life experiences, the survivor becomes something other than what he or she was before. Summarizing his frustration with these conditions as he tried to find help recovering from surviving Black Hawk Down, Nielson says:

> I was past the point of frustration with the VA, with their 'meds,' with their detached, obfuscating denial of the true problem that combat veterans have to deal with. That problem is veterans have had their hearts and souls torn apart from engaging in warfare under a set of false

pretenses. I know this is, was, my particular problem. I truly believe this is what lies at the core of all American veterans' issues.

War and warriorhood from a shamanic perspective

Ideas about warriorhood, wounding, and recovery vary widely. According to the shamanic perspective the soul is a living experiential reality. Our souls are part of nature, other human and nonhuman beings, and the dead. All creatures, natural beings, and processes—animals, plants, stones, clothing, colors, and the weather—have spirits with which we can communicate. These spirits are sources of power. As the soul can become damaged, wounded, skewed, or even lost, healing of both physical and psychological disorders must fundamentally and ultimately occur in the soul.

While the role of warrior is universal, the values, practices, rituals, myths and uses of warriorhood have varied greatly between cultures and eras. Jungian psychology posits the existence of archetypes in the human psyche revealed in recurring patterns of story, thought, and behavior. War is an archetypal experience, the expression of cosmic strife in the human dimension. The warrior is an archetype of both psyche and society. The media has given us countless images of decorated and painted fighters whipping themselves into frenzy and galloping off on the 'warpath,' or more accurately on the 'warrior's path.' In traditional cultures boys and men emulated the warrior's path through most of their life cycle. This path gave males a roadmap through life that included preparation, testing, proving, status, companionship, purpose, service, challenge, and honor. Societies that developed the warrior's path as a primary form of life journey were rooted in shamanism.

Experiences of the spirit world guided and supported every aspect of a warrior's life including preparation for war, initiation through combat, and the return, healing, and reintegration into the culture. The uses of shamanism in warfare were countless. In combat, a warrior might experience possession by animal spirits that he had already had met in vision quests and dreams. They might appear as animal models, allies or helpers, as personal or tribal ancestors, ghosts, culture heroes or divinities. Sitting Bull, whose name came from a hunting encounter his father had with a sacred talking buffalo that stood his ground, received this name after his first battle coup. In his foxhole, the night before the Battle of the Bulge, an American veteran by the name of Merl Sands dreamed of a Native American warrior who would protect him and his company. His unit came through the pitched battle with inexplicably few losses.

The essence of shamanic practice is possession by animals or spirits. In combat, we may regress to and become possessed by our animal nature at its most primitive, awakened by the intensity, altered state, and life-threatening conditions of the battlefield. The word berserk comes from the Norse word for bearskin shirt, a shirt worn by warriors of the pagan northern European tradition. A warrior who wore a bearskin shirt literally went berserk during combat and became possessed, "a wild beast-warrior, irresistible and invulnerable."[5] These warriors became "frantic as dogs or wolves… bit their shields… slew men…but neither fire nor iron could hurt them."[6] Warriors from all times and places attest to their experiences during combat of losing their civilizing inhibitions and becoming animals. Among the Sioux, a man about to attack another was likely to give one or two 'brave grunts,' or growls, like a wounded bear about to charge. Veterans commonly describe themselves as becoming beasts.[7] Jonathan Shay believes that berserk "is the most precise term available to describe" this particular kind of behavior.[8] It includes beastliness, god-likeness, madness, fearlessness, the loss of mercy and other feelings, the hunger for vengeance, ecstasy, a sense of immortality, recklessness, and insensitivity to pain.[9] Ron, a Vietnam combat veteran, described his experience of hand-to-hand combat as "a cosmic battle between comic-book superheroes." Some veterans may not know the specialized meaning of berserk, which is used to describe their mental condition during combat. Sam Nielson said, "I fired several therapists, as I knew they could not handle what I wanted to engage internally—my beast, my berserker, the demon in my shadows that was me."

Possession during battle is not achieved by choice in a contained sacred ritual, but in battle under the most extreme and life-threatening conditions. Thus, Mircea Eliade considers this "a magico-religious experience that extends beyond the sphere of shamanism."[10] Yet we can conceive of this battlefield experience as a form of spontaneous shamanic possession. This involves significant characteristics: sensory bombardment, extreme threat, emotional and physical ordeal. It also includes an intensification of experience; descent into the Underworld; living through a death and rebirth; penetration by spirits and powers beyond the human; mastering conditions that seem impossible; and entering into a permanent relationship with spirits of the living and the dead. Even the taking of life in battle had shamanic dimensions. Traditional cultures believed that "the qualities of a man killed entered into the slayer"[11] and a warrior became responsible for the soul of the enemy he slew. Thus, through proper ritual, a slain warrior could become a helping ally providing power from the spirit world.

Testimonies from ancient and modern fighters attest that those who were possessed truly became as animals or beasts, the most savage and effective warriors during combat. Those who experienced this were transformed forever. Once they had achieved the transformation, they could become animals as instinctual and spiritual powers flooded them during battle. In contrast, warriors who did not become beasts or animals may have retained more rationality or civilizing constraints, or may not have achieved alliance with helping spirits. These warriors were sometimes the weakest and most vulnerable. Thus, combat produces a life-transforming possession that is a necessary survival mechanism during battle but remains with the veteran and often surfaces in troubling ways in later civilian life.

As shamanism supported the warrior's preparation for and experience of battle, it also supported his return. Just as the soul can be helped in its alliances with spirits, it can also be harmed, damaged, or lost because of the taking of a life. Shamanic cultures went to great lengths to provide communal spiritually based rituals for bringing their warriors home and helping them to heal. These cultures recognized that their warriors had become instruments of death and destruction and needed purification of death's imprint before returning to ordinary life. Such cleansing protected everyone: warriors, their loved ones, and the entire tribe. Shamans guided and presided over 'warrior medicine.' Among his many offices and honors, for example, Sitting Bull served as Medicine Chief of the Hunkpapa Warrior Society, responsible for the spiritual lives and wellbeing of the society's warriors. He considered this the most important of all the offices he held.

The Tohono O'odham (called Papago in the older sources) provide a vivid example of warriors' return ceremonies. After their first experiences of taking a life, warriors underwent a sixteen-day ceremony during which they were isolated from their tribe, attended only by experienced warriors, and could not have sex, or even feed themselves. The ritual opened with an interview with an elder who repeatedly asked each new Enemy Slayer: "Did you not want this experience? Then you must endure its many hardships." The ritual only proceeded when each new warrior answered, "Yes!" This and other traditional cultures recognized that isolation, numbness, and confusion are normal responses to having killed. Steven Silver summarizes the benefits of responding to PTSD in this way. "The ritual," he writes, "explicitly embraces and approves the killer's psychic numbing and prescribes a way for dealing with it. The fear of intimacy… that is common in battle survivors… is accepted and even enforced in tribal warfare as an appropriate response to the experience of inflicting death in battle… Numbing is externalized and formalized in a series of taboos; it is prescribed as a chosen response."[12] This ceremony demonstrates that post-traumatic stress is a communal condition rather than an individual pathology.

Warrior medicine included storytelling of war experiences through oratory, song, dance, mime, and other artistry. The seeking of visions and participation in rituals, meant to achieve spiritual help for extraordinary conditions, also occurred. It included working with the warrior's protective spirits as well as the spirits of those slain, initiation as warriors into the social class of warriors, advancement up the ranks of that class, and service to other members and the tribe. In addition, it included restitution in the community as the tribe accepted his stories as part of their sacred lore, honored him for participation, and transferred responsibility from the individual back to the social group who benefited from his service.

Shamanism in warfare and its healing

By taking up the practices of shamanism that warriors have used throughout the ages, the battle-fled soul can begin to return. As a combat infantryman during World War II, the Canadian author Farley Mowat survived the brutal march of combat from the invasion of Italy through the capture of Germany. Immediately after "the mad, nightmare creation… the sick and corroding fear… the senseless slaughter," his sanity-saving recourse was to retreat into the deep arctic "where the echoes of war had never been heard… with the picture of the deer held firmly in my mind as a spiritual talisman."[13]

Rod McKay and Conner Salk, both Vietnam combat veterans, adopted Native American spirituality long before engaging in psychotherapy, in order to restore connection to nature and spirit as well as to bring some organization and integrity to their war-shattered personalities. Sam Nielson reports years of failed therapy, overdosing and over-reliance on medications to control symptoms, crippling depression and alienation. Finally "my first experience where I truly felt the presence of the great originating Mystery, our Creator, was during my first sweat lodge. Only during and after that lodge did I rediscover that I had a reason to live. I could feel a small pulse inside me, even if I really did not know its exact purpose. I declared my intention to forge a new path and turn the steering-wheel of my life over to Great Spirit, or God."

Understanding and utilizing the shamanic path can reconnect the traumatized soul with nature, spirit, and divinity; reveal, interpret and affirm combat experiences that are otherwise inexplicable and remain hidden; and offer a time-honored roadmap for the soul's return from war. Nielson continues:

I found myself participating in Native American sweat-lodge ceremonies. I moved beyond religion and churches into a direct relationship with our Creator, Great Spirit, and True Source. I explored the realm of shamanism, looking into the teachings of several indigenous shamans from different cultures where there was no difference or separation in any aspect of one's life. The ceremonies, rituals, and medicines they used, which came from plants that occurred naturally in nature, were all a way of life where everything was connected and made up a harmonious 'whole life' that was balanced. This made sense to me. I understood it somehow. It was here, in the realm of traditional shamanism, that I made the connection with my own soul. It occurred as I journeyed down the path of two traditions: Native American traditional medicine and Peruvian shamanism.

The world is exploding around you. Time does not exist. Your friends and adversaries are straining beyond strength and endurance to kill or be killed. Your heart and senses are on overload. All rationality has evaporated. You exist on adrenalin, training, and instinct. This is the combat experience and it occurs in an altered state. Even in today's secular and mass-army warfare, soldiers may experience shamanic occurrences during this altered state. Often veterans will only speak of them when they are confident that their healer is familiar with such experiences and the spiritual traditions that host them.

In modern warfare, spirit animals may be discovered and used. One combat infantryman in Vietnam found a canine-like skull in the jungle. Alone in the green darkness, he extracted several teeth from its lower jaw and added them to the protective necklace he wore that included a crucifix and peace symbol. He thought of the teeth as wolf's teeth and reported that during combat "I called the energy of the animal to be with me." He became a fierce and effective warrior, stood up in the middle of an ambush screaming, "Nobody lives forever," and led his comrades through a blizzard of fire to safety. By donning the animal's parts, calling upon its spirit, declaring his vision of life's brevity, and acting fearlessly, he replicated the traditional warrior's shamanic initiation.

Warriors encounter the spirits of slain enemies and civilians during and after warfare, which helps them to explain and relieve some of the most troubling symptoms. Bill Cargill, a combat infantryman in Vietnam, killed a Viet Cong soldier attacking him during a nighttime firefight. When dawn broke, he discovered that the body, just yards from his foxhole, was a teenaged boy. From that moment on, Bill had nightmares of the boy, seeing him in many guises. Only after returning to Vietnam with me for healing could Bill affirm the shamanic dimensions of his experience. His revisit to the sacred ground of combat began to transform the ways he carried his war experience, and from then on, he did not just dream about but also saw the souls of the dead. As he said, "What really bothered me most were not the flashbacks of war or its horrors that kept coming to my mind in dreams, but the fact that I could see the legions of fallen soldiers, both American and Vietnamese. They were walking across those vast rice paddies, all with their arms extended as if asking for help, help to get home. I could not take my eyes off the fields."

Bill visited his battle site and Viet Cong cemeteries, praying for the boy. He took a stone from the site to carry as a sacred amulet in memory of the boy. Then we drove to Nui Ba Den, near the Cambodian border and he said, "The idea and concept of warrior spirituality began, for me, with that ride to Lady Black Mountain on that sunny day in May, 2001." He explained his spiritual transformation and healing through the practice of warrior medicine in the Vietnamese tradition:

> As Doc and I ascended the mountain, we were taken with the beauty of the scenery and thoughts of the war. When we reached the path that led to a Buddhist temple, we took off our shoes and Doc went inside while I turned around and walked back to a stone wall from where I could see the vast rice fields. I was mesmerized by the beauty and sad at the thought of war's destruction of such a beautiful land and people. Something had pulled me back to that wall, and as I stared into the land and sky, a boy appeared before me, a small boy about fourteen years old. His arms were extended as if asking for help, his palms were up and a smile was on his face. He was asking special prayers be said for him so that his soul could rest. Doc came up behind me and asked what I was doing. I tried to explain to him that I was talking to a young warrior I had killed many years ago. The boy and I were talking through our souls. That was the only way I could explain it. Our souls touched and we understood one another. Doc hurried to get a Buddhist priest who was nearby and asked for a confirmation of spirits around us. After telling Doc that indeed there were spirits there the priest began special prayers for the boy. We joined him in prayer, lit joss sticks to help carry our prayers to heaven, and I found new peace in my life.

Bill accepted the traditional Vietnamese belief that when a person dies by violence and lacks a proper ceremonial burial, his soul becomes lost. He affirmed that killers have an intimate and permanent connection with and responsibility for those they killed and came to believe that his nightmares and day visions were not idiosyncratic pathological symptoms, but rather souls trying to reach him. As in shamanic warrior traditions, Bill now embraces the boy-warrior as his spiritual ally and helper. And from the time of his vision and ceremony to the present, his nightmares and ghostly visions ceased and joy entered his heart; he felt the boy's spirit was at rest, and his own spirit was now as strong as two people's and at peace.

Dr. Jim Foster was a radio operator on reconnaissance teams in the jungles of Vietnam. Inexplicably, and to his utter shock and despair, several times he was the only survivor that returned from the mission. The concepts of warriorhood from shamanism aided him in understanding these disturbing and transformational combat experiences. He reported that as a young draftee, barely twenty years of age, he did not want to serve in the military. "A civil war in a strange country in Southeast Asia ... what was that all about and why me? I lost innocence on the front lines within two weeks in the country. Moreover, when the guns began to fire, something strange happened. I never knew what it was until I got it back. My soul was estranged, separated from my body and mind. Fear had penetrated my DNA in 1968 creating a barrier against my very own soul." He worked hard for his healing, including traveling back to Vietnam:

> For the past ten years, I diligently worked on healing my emotional wounds from war—from many counseling sessions, to writing books, even traveling twice back to the land of my nightmares. Regardless of my efforts, there always seemed to be something missing—AWOL (absent without leave)—from my healing. I had read many self-help books on the subject, but none more powerful than *War and the Soul*.[14] The title scared me ... could this be the missing link? I signed up for a spiritual pilgrimage with the author for a soul-retrieval ritual and ceremony.

In February of 2006, Jim and I traveled together to Greece to study the ancient citizen-warrior tradition, explore its spiritual components, and to participate in shamanic healing ceremonies. These included prayer and meditation in a warrior's cemetery outside the ancient walls of Athens, entering into a universal fear and grief for the losses from all wars, and calling the warriors of all times and places to support and witness his transformation. Jim declared that the visit to this cemetery was more demanding and grief-wracked than his visit to The Wall in Washington D.C. From the cemetery, we proceeded to the ancient city gate and stood on the spot where Pericles delivered his famous Funeral Oration of 431 BCE. In the presence of companion travelers, Greek citizens, and the felt presence of ancient spirits, we recited parts of the speech that affirm the eternal life-preserving values and duties of warriors. After the recitations to Dr. Foster, he then gave his own oration:

> I was reunited with my soul once lost in battle. A shamanic practitioner called in the spirits and my human barriers broke down. I was neutralized to become the 'hollow bone.' I was then open to receive my soul lost for nearly thirty-eight years. Poems, speeches, prayers, and ritual proceedings by my fellow pilgrims helped me to find what was absent from my process.

Later, he participated in the ancient healing practice, also with roots in shamanism, of Asklepian dream incubation. During this ritual, a supplicant fasts and prays for a healing dream. He is then 'incubated.' With ritual and community support, he separates from the ordinary world and enters a sacred dream chamber where he sleeps as his soul calls for a healing dream.[15] That incubation marked the night that his nightmares of combat permanently ended:

> I feel like a kid again. Like the kid I was before having to go to war. My intuition is stronger and I appreciate and love myself again, something I can hardly remember feeling before. My emotional mind seems to be free as a bird in the sky. Furthermore, I am no longer a disgruntled Vietnam Veteran, but rather a proud warrior united with the warrior spirit of all times and places, whose service was in Vietnam.

Today Bill Cargill, Jim Foster, and Sam Nielson consider themselves returned warriors, not traumatized or disabled veterans. Through their shamanic study and practice, they have developed spiritual warrior identities of honor, dignity, and purpose. Sam eloquently summarizes his warrior identity: "My ultimate purpose is to serve humanity as an instrument for our Creator. The duty inherently contained within this is staying connected to the will of our Creator, ensuring that my ego or other self-serving interests do not interfere." Bill affirms the necessity of a shamanic healing path: "My experiences on Lady Black Mountain, combined with many more, have reinforced the warrior spirit in me. If it were not for spirituality I could not heal because the wounds of war are in the soul much more than in the body."

Conclusions

The soul is our center, our true self, the experiential source of our inner life. War's purpose is to defeat another people, tribe, or nation defined as an enemy. The soul that participates in warfare, whether as combatant or civilian, perpetrator or victim, is inevitably wounded, disordered, or distorted. The soul of both survivors and those killed are lost in war. Before war, our veterans and survivors were ordinary men and women developing along conventional trajectories defined by the people, places, times, and values in which they grew up. War tore them open. War made them raw. War reduced them to the primitive and immersed them in primordial and instinctual realms. War exposed naked soul in naked existence blasted from within and without by energies of cosmic dimension. This exposure plunged them into an altered state of consciousness, threw them headlong into the spirit world, in which they had spontaneous shamanic experiences.

If we talk with veterans about how to treat, fix, or control their PTSD symptoms or if we apply conventional standards of physical or mental health, they may judge us as 'people who don't get it.' They may refuse our guidance on the healing path, rebel against, or quit the healing relationship or regimen we offer. Veterans have died to their civilian identities and been reborn as something else. When we strain to return them to the conventional, they feel pathologized and we reinforce their alienation. However, we can demonstrate that we understand and can facilitate their transformation to warriors. Rather than couple broken veterans with counselors, we can work together as wounded warriors with shamans. In these roles, we can speak with them about what happened to their souls, about the moral, spiritual, and shamanic dimensions of their experiences.

We can discuss the things they witnessed that no one should ever see and the things they did that no one should ever do. We can share the decisions they made. We can contemplate the hair-trigger of time and fate in which they dwelled. We can exhume the images of themselves that war fostered and they cannot accept or forgive. We can help pull them out of the moral quicksand that threatens to suffocate them. We can talk with them about the eternal trials and wounds of the soul. We can search with them for those unexpected visitations of spirit that occur only when we are broken. We can enter into the dark, Otherworld reality in which they dwell, and walk with them. We can seek spiritual aid through guidance, stories, and rituals modeled on ancient warrior traditions. We can create reconciliation to redress the wounds against life that oppress the veteran. Then they may open the door to the Underworld and we may become their traveling companions. Then the spirits that were loosed during war, whether of the survivor or the slain, may find peace, meaning, and lifelong alliance. When the veteran makes the journey home, the healer will be transformed.

References

I gratefully acknowledge and salute the veterans who shared their experiences reported herein. Their stories are used with permission of veterans who wish to offer public testimony to his and others' shamanic combat and healing experiences.

[1] Tick E. *War and the Soul.* Wheaton, IL: Quest Books; 2005; 97-103; Gabriel R. *No More Heroes: Madness and Psychiatry in War.* New York, NY: Hill and Wang; 1987; 16, 43-44.

[2] "Britain: Soldier executed in 1916 pardoned." *New York Times* Aug. 16, 2006; A7.

[3] National Institute of Mental Health, 2002, at Statistics, Mental Illness Research Association. www.miraresearch.org/understanding/statistics.htm.

[4] Gabriel; 72 – 77.

[5] Eliade M. *Rites and Symbols of Initiation: The Mysteries of Death and Rebirth.* Trans. Task WR, Woodstock, CT: Spring Publications; 1995; 81-83.

[6] *Ynglinga Saga.* In: Ellis Davidson HR, *Gods and Myths of Northern Europe.* New York: Penguin; 1979; 66.

[7] Vestal S. *Sitting Bull: Champion of the Plains.* Norman & London: Univ. of Oklahoma Press; 1989; 44.

[8] Shay J. *Achilles in Vietnam: Combat Trauma and the Undoing of Character.* New York: Atheneum; 1994.

[9] Shay; 78-99, listed 82.

[10] Eliade M. *Shamanism: Archaic Techniques of Ecstasy.* Princeton: Princeton Univ. Press/ Bollingen Foundation; 1972; 104.

[11] Vestal; 86.

[12] Marmon Silko L. *Ceremony.* New York: Viking Penguin; 1987.

[13] Mowat F. *People of the Deer.* New York: Pyramid; 1976; 16-17.

[14] Full case reported in Tick, *War and the Soul.* 256-59.

[15] Tick E. *The Practice of Dream Healing: Bringing Ancient Greek Mysteries into Modern Medicine.* Wheaton, IL: Quest Books; 2001.

About the author

Dr. Edward Tick, author of the groundbreaking book *War and the Soul* and co-founder of Soldier's Heart, is a practicing psychotherapist specializing in veterans with PTSD. He received his master's degree in psychology from Goddard College, Vermont, and his doctorate in communication from Rensselaer Polytechnic Institute, Troy, NY. He continues his pioneering work with Post-traumatic Stress Disorder (PTSD) with the military, veterans and other trauma survivors with innovative yet time-honored methods. He has extensively studied classical Greek, Native American and Vietnamese Buddhist traditions and successfully integrates their methods into modern clinical work. He is the U.S. Army's chaplaincy trainer in PTSD for 2012. He is also the author of *The Golden Tortoise: Journeys in Viet Nam; Sacred Mountain: Encounters of the Vietnam Beast*; and *The Practice of Dream Healing: Bringing Ancient Greek Mysteries Into Modern Medicine.*

XIX
Conclusion

Cecile Carson, MD

This book has been an attempt to not only enlarge our approach to patient care, but also to examine how we tend to view current allopathic medicine: as a battle, as doing violence against disease. In these pages, the seamless integration of shamanism into medical clinics, surgical suites, psychotherapy offices, in-patient hospice programs and government veteran health services is a natural consequence of a spiritual stance toward life, of lenses through which we can look at our work in the world with eyes and arms that can hold both sacred and profane dimensions without having to choose.

Healing as re-ordering

Over the years, the most meaningful definition of healing I have found is that of 're-ordering.' At the physical level, re-ordering can be understood as an adaptation to the challenges illness may have wrought in the body. At the emotional level it can be seen as a shift in relationship to self and others, of navigating grief and anger, and of the graceful reckoning with the changes of one's roles in life that a health crisis brings. At the soul level, re-ordering involves the disruption of the ego and personality enough to open to the mystery of falling ill, the descent into the unknown, the discovery of the bare bones of who we are, and the embracing of our old friend Death. In those dark nights of the soul, if we are lucky, we truly discover that we are never alone.

I have found that defining healing as re-ordering produces an honesty and a re-framing of the outcome of healthcare for patients: we are never the same after that descent and return, and it unburdens us to not have to pretend otherwise. In my primary care and counseling work with patients facing life-threatening illness over the past three decades, countless numbers have told me, often in a conspiratorial whisper, "I can't believe I'm telling you this, but cancer (or HIV) is the best thing that's ever happened to me. I know who in my life is really there for me, my priorities are clearer, and life is truly precious."

The final piece of re-ordering, then, is moving forward transformed and more fully present to our lives, finding that illness has not come as an enemy but an ally. If this third level of healing is bypassed, and we do not see or take in the soul lesson that illness brings, the spirits bring it to our door again and again. In shamanism, we recognize that we are eternal spirits embodied in historical time[1] and that the spirits are less interested in what happens to our physical bodies than what happens to the progress of our soul.

Much of our present behavior as clinicians is fear-driven; when we cannot face the inevitability of our own death, our response to our patients' profound or puzzling illnesses is often over-utilization of medical technologies and emotional withdrawal from them at a time they need our presence and 'holding' the most. In death-phobic Western society, the good news of shamanism is that even as we lose our physical bodies at the end of this life as we know it, there is an aliveness and sentience that continues as we move into the role of Ancestors. Presently in the U.S. we spend 40% of Medicare dollars on the last few months of patients' lives,[2] struggling to keep death at bay. Shamanism, on the other hand, gives us the direct experience that death is not a failure of medical care but rather a natural stage in the completion of life and an important next step in our soul's progress.

We also see in these pages that working shamanically as clinicians is not just a set of methods, but a way of viewing life. In allopathic medicine we use the term 'attending' as a noun to describe the clinician responsible for a patient's care, but as we embrace a transpersonal dimension, 'attending' expands from noun to verb and we find a progression:

"When you *help*, you see life as weak; when you *fix*, you see life as broken. When you *serve*, you see life as whole. From the perspective of service, we are all connected: all suffering is like my suffering, and all joy is like my joy."[3]

Through this progression we find the tempering of 'standard of care' with "how is love best served?" to bring shamanism into a living, breathing presence in our service to patients, rather than a methodology alone.

Healing as community

Being in service to others also includes the importance of community for both patients and healers, and the power of the community to receive and embrace individuals in their brokenness and to share the responsibility of re-ordering as a collective, as Tick's illumination of the healing process for veterans so deeply illustrates. I believe those of us who face life-threatening and soul-threatening illness need a community to provide a framework in support of what it means to 'come home' raw and transformed, and to be properly 're-named' and 're-membered.'

In these chapters are several templates for considering a community approach to shamanic work, such as Rysdyk's model of reverent participatory relationship and Farey's work with the spirit of a community health center. The illness in our healthcare system can also be addressed communally by sharing and teaching combined 'mastery' + 'mystery' models of healing, by creating healing stories of who we are and what we're about that Roberge elucidates, through the dreams we can have of what is possible, through the journeys we can make to the helping spirits for guidance. We need large doses of Davis' opportunism, Proskauer's courage to leap and be transformed, and Silverberg's seeing the shamanic in ordinary encounters as we take on our work of integrating shamanism into contemporary healthcare.

Many shamanic healers work in isolation as they stretch the boundaries of what is possible in patient care, uncertain of how they may be received by others. This book can hopefully serve as a form of community to help find support, words, and frameworks to connect us to each other and to remind us that we are not alone in our endeavors. The twenty authors in these pages give only partial voice to the hundreds more who are also doing the work.

The greater Circle

The spirits are guiding us, transforming and adapting shamanism to a variety of cultures and healers and contexts. We know there are many roads up the proverbial spiritual mountain; shamanism is but one, though its methodologies and sacred underpinnings provide a means of spiritual engagement that is extremely accessible. Remembering the greater Circle to which we all belong is the important key that Nasrudin is searching for. Our interconnectedness in this great Circle is what brings the joy to the work, regardless of the outcome in ordinary reality.

Hillman says, "The model we hold in our minds creates the case before us."[4] What will each of us carry in our minds to make our work 'spirited medicine?'

References

[1] Meade M. "Initiation and the Soul," in *The Sacred and the Profane* CD, Mosaic Foundation, WA: Voices Multicultural.

[2] Riley G. a HCFA actuary, with Lubitz J. conducted the analysis and published it in *New England Journal of Medicine* 1993.

[3] Remen R. "In the Service of Life." *Noetic Sciences Review*, Spring, 1996.

[4] Hillman J. *Re-Visioning Psychology.* New York: Harper Collins; 1975.